HISTORY, MYSTERY and HAUNTINGS of SOUTHERN ILLINOIS

EXPANDED, UPDATED & REVISED

CONTAINING ALL 3 PREVIOUS VOLUMES

NOW IN 1 BOOK!

Bruce L. Cline

along with Lisa Cline, Kale Meggs & Tracey Todd Bragg

Published by
IllinoisHistory.com
PO Box 1142
Marion IL 62959

Front Cover
Goddard Chapel in Marion's Rosehill Cemetery during filming for the independent film *Dig Two Graves* in January 2013. Photograph by Jon Musgrave.

Back Cover
Abandoned house near Harco. Photograph by Bruce Cline

Cover Design
Jon Musgrave

Library of Congress Control Number:

International Standard Book Number (ISBN)
paperback: 978-0-9891781-1-2

Printed in the United States of America
2nd Edition

PRAISE for *HISTORY, MYSTERY and HAUNTINGS of SOUTHERN ILLINOIS*

"Bruce Cline is one of the brightest documentarians of all three facets - history, mystery and hauntings in the Southern Illinois area - to emerge in decades. His books are succinctly yet brilliantly chronicled, and give overviews of little-known and/or long-lost anecdotal tales, many of which he has discovered to be fact and not just legend or lore. With research capabilities as a strong point, Cline also is immersed in the "creepy" that accompanies such tales, being a paranormal investigator. For an incredible read of our beloved state of Illinois and the "forgotten" portion of it "Little Egypt," lend your time to this book... you won't be disappointed."

—Angela Mason, author of *Death Rides the Sky: The Story of the 1925 Tri-State Tornado*

"Bruce Cline is intimately familiar with the history and folklore of Southern Illinois. He has spent years exploring every nook and cranny of his beloved Little Egypt, and you can expect to learn a lot about the region when you pick up one of his books. Whether you are a veteran legend tripper or just getting into ghost stories for the first time, History, Mystery, and Hauntings of Southern Illinois will not disappoint."

— Michael Kleen, folklorist and author of *Haunting Illinois: A Tourist's Guide to the Weird & Wild Places of The Prairie State*

"I never thought Southern Illinois and the Bermuda Triangle would have something in common. Bruce Cline changed my mind about that. Strange lights at night, people that disappear, never to be seen again and mysterious stories... but still keep you from going out to sea at night... or in our case, the woods... I like to read at night, just before going to bed, but with this book... I'll make time in the light of day, to have the hell scared out of me."

— Scott Doody, author of *Herrin Massacre*

Table of Contents

Acknowledgments

The Little Egypt Ghost Society team of paranormal professionals who made this book possible are Bruce Cline – Founder and Director, Kale Meggs – Investigator and Historical Researcher, Tracey Bragg – Investigator and Historical Researcher.

We wish to thank the following individuals for their time and support in making this book successful: Sandy Vinyard – former concessionaire of the Rose Hotel, Scott Thorne – Ghost historian and owner of Castle Perilous Games, Carl and Kelly Rexroad - owners of The Bookworm Bookstore, Josie Brooks – owner of The Book Emporium, Jack and Angela Howser – owners and publishers of *Disclosure*, and Michael Kleen for the map.

Special thanks to my parents Lyle Cline, Emeritus and Nancy Cline, Emerita, Southern Illinois University Department of Mining and Mineral Resources Engineering for proofreading our book.

Here are the original three books in the History, Mystery and Hauntings of Southern Illinois series. They are now out of print and considered to be rare and  collectable. If you are the proud owner of any of them, congratulations and thank you for your support. If not, don't fret. This second edition of History, Mystery and Hauntings of Southern Illinois contains all of the stories from the original three with the addition of more stories, more photographs, updates and actual directions to most of the locations.

Map

LITTLE EGYPT

Counties

Foreword

As the earliest part of the state to be settled by Europeans, Southern Illinois is steeped in history. From the French settlements at Cahokia, Fort de Chartres, Fort Massac, and Kaskaskia, to the convulsions of the American Civil War, to the present day, the region popularly known as "Little Egypt" has been filled with legends, folklore, and ghost stories. For those interested in ghost lore, Southern Illinois offers some of the oldest ghost stories in the state.

And why should it not? Anywhere a majestic lodge like the Rose Hotel can stand for nearly two centuries is bound to be haunted by some specters of the past. These strange tales go all the way back to 1719 when the French brought slaves from Santo Domingo to the Mississippi River. Some of these slaves, they feared, possessed supernatural powers, and at least one paid for it with his life.

As far as the folklore of Southern Illinois is concerned, two books stand out: *Legends & Lore of Southern Illinois* by John W. Allen and *Tales and Songs of Southern Illinois* by Charles Neely. One was published in the 1930s and the other in the 1960s. Not much has been written on the subject since then, and so when Bruce approached me about publishing his book on the legends and lore of Southern Illinois, I was very excited.

Some of the stories in this book are old favorites, but many are brand new. Bruce has not only read about these places, in many cases he has been there partaking in the story itself. That is a rare quality. I have no doubt that readers will find many surprises contained within the pages of this book.

Michael Kleen
Rock River Valley

Preface

The choice of what stories to include and what stories to leave out of this book was a difficult one. Decorum and good taste excluded some stories (such as one involving an investigation in which a client may have been having an affair with an attractive "ghost.") Some stories were not used due to what we call the "fruitcake factor." This involves individuals who watch one too many episodes of paranormal TV shows such as *Ghost Hunters* or *Ghost Adventures*, letting their minds run wild with every imaginable type of haunting. Some stories we encountered were works of fiction. We only release stories that we have personally investigated or those that have been told to us as being true.

Other stories that did not make the cut were those dealing with demonic possession. In our experience and through much research, we have determined that demonic obsession is far more prevalent than demonic possession. Client confidentiality, however, was the most common reason that we were unable to disclose publicly some of our paranormal investigations. We decided to keep secret (although all locations are in the Little Egypt Ghost Society archives) some locations to prevent misguided and malicious visits from a certain segment of amateur "ghost hunters." We hope you enjoy this third volume of our series on the history, mystery and hauntings of Southern Illinois.

Happy Hauntings,
Bruce Cline, Director
Little Egypt Ghost Society

Introduction

My interest in ghosts and the paranormal started at an early age. When I was about eight or nine years old I had my first ghostly encounter. My brother and I were spending the night at our grandparent's house in Marion, Illinois. After a fun day of play in the garden and woodshed, we retired for the night. Of the three bedrooms in the house, we were to sleep in the middle bedroom. At some point during the night, I woke up and noticed a dark shadow on the wall opposite the window. It was a shadow of a large dog or wolf-like creature. There were no pets in the house to make such a shadow. I was so scared that I pulled the covers over my head and did not sleep the rest of the night.

A couple of years later, in 1966, a new TV show came out that was called *Dark Shadows*. The show was about a 175-year old vampire named Barnabas Collins. I rushed home from school every day to watch it. I was fascinated with the idea of vampires and the paranormal. Instead of experiencing fear, I became curious and started studying all things paranormal as well as folklore and history. This led me to start a club that I called the Gaslight Ghoul Club. Members of this club would spend many late night hours around campfires or in my tree house telling spooky stories.

Eventually, college, careers and raising a family took up much of my time. It was not until 2007 that I started the Little Egypt Ghost Society. We were interested in ghost hunting, but we were also interested in history and mysteries. The way we approach the paranormal is to research history. Once you know the history of a person, location or thing, there may be some mystery associated with the historical events. We found that many times, there is a haunting associated with the mysteries that history has to offer.

Once we became established as credible paranormal investigators and historians, we started receiving many calls from individuals and businesses seeking our help with what they considered paranormal activity. Our group is made up of skeptics—optimistic skeptics to be exact. We use research as well as "ghost hunting" equipment to document and try to arrive at a logical explanation for reported paranormal activity. Only after we have ruled out all naturally occurring and logical explanations do we consider that the events may have a paranormal explanation.

The stories that you will read in this book came from our case files, local history, and folklore. Like most people, the members of the Little Egypt Ghost Society enjoy a good spooky story. While we won't vouch for the truth of every story presented, we will state that they all have been told to us as being the truth. We hope that you enjoy the stories presented in this book as well as the history, mystery and hauntings that are to be found in Southern Illinois.

This is the final volume of our trilogy about the history, mystery, and hauntings that make Southern Illinois unique. With new stories, amazing tales and haunting events, the lore of the area comes to life in the pages of this book.

Legends & Lore of Southern Illinois (1963) and *It Happened in Southern Illinois* (1968) published by John W. Allen were the first books devoted to the history, mystery, and hauntings of Southern Illinois. The rich history of the area lends volumes of material begging to be told. Since that time, very little has been written about the history, mystery, and hauntings unique to the southern part of Illinois known as Little Egypt. The members of the Little Egypt Ghost Society decided to fill that void by collecting and publishing the stories of the region that have never been heard or were long forgotten.

What started out as brief accounts of interesting history, mysteries, and hauntings encountered by members of the Little Egypt Ghost Society led to the creation of our first book, *History, Mystery and Hauntings of Southern Illinois*, which was published in 2011. The overwhelming success of that book had our fans clamoring for more.

The following year we released our second book in the series, *More History, Mystery and Hauntings of Southern Illinois*, which was published in 2012. The third book in our Southern Illinois trilogy, *Even More History, Mystery and Hauntings of Southern Illinois* followed in 2013.

For this 2nd Edition of *History, Mystery and Hauntings of Southern Illinois* I decided to compile all three of our books into one volume with additional stories, updates and other useful information.

We sincerely hope that you find all of our books to be exciting, informative and fun to read.

Bruce Cline, Director
Little Egypt Ghost Society
Summer 2014

Gaslight Ghoul Club

2012 marked the 45th anniversary of Southern Illinois oldest paranormal group. In 1967, I formed the Gaslight Ghoul Club. The club was started after my friends and I became fans of the TV show *Dark Shadows* starring vampire Barnabas Collins. Membership was by invitation only.

This distinguished club had its headquarters in my backyard tree house that was located on South Main Street in Harrisburg. The tree house was built by my dad and grandpa. It was painted Chinese Dragon Red and had chicken wire covering the windows. There was a trap door in the floor through which we could pull up the ladder to prevent cowans and eavesdroppers from gaining access to our hideout.

Many an adventure started in the tree house. Gaslight Ghoul Club members would meet there to share ghost stories and discuss ways to turn into vampires, werewolves, ghosts, and other scary creatures. Many times we would sneak out after dark and go "werewolfing" at Sunset Mausoleum in Sunset Lawn Cemetery. Other nights would find us at the old abandoned slaughter house near Brick Hill. Fun filled afternoons were to be had at the Humm Salvage Yard next to the railroad tracks. We would play in the wrecked cars and trucks and gawk into the ones that still had blood and tissue left over from fatal car crashes.

The Gaslight Ghoul Club was even in the movie business for a while. Mom and dad gave me an 8mm movie camera for my birthday. We got the club members together and made a great movie called *The Daytime Vampire*. I had to call it that because I didn't have any way to film after dark. All the scenes were shot in full daylight. We even had a time lapse scene in which I drove a wooden stake through my brother's heart (he was the vampire) and he dissolved into a skeleton.

The Gaslight Ghoul Club was responsible for collecting and preserving many tales of ghostly lore. From time to time we open the secret vaults of the Gaslight Ghoul Club to share the eerie tales with our friends. Today, the Gaslight Ghoul Club continues as the Little Egypt Ghost Society based in Carbondale.

Why are we called the Little Egypt Ghost Society?

Southern Illinois is known as "Little Egypt" due to a strange coincidence on one occasion between the southern tip of Illinois and ancient Egypt. If you will turn to the Bible you will find a story about a great famine. The patriarch Jacob upon hearing there was corn in Egypt; he said to his sons, "Why, look ye on one another. Behold, I have heard there is corn in Egypt; go you down there, etc." Further reading from the Bible will reveal that when the famine was over all the earth the storehouses or granaries of Egypt were opened and all the other countries came to Egypt to buy corn.

The wickedly cold winter of 1830-1831, known as the "Deep Snow," was the longest and most severe ever recorded in Illinois. These frigid conditions resulted in little or no corn being planted in the state of Illinois in 1831, north of Jefferson County, until the month of June. To add to this disaster, there was a heavy, killing frost on the night of September 10, 1831, which destroyed many of the late crops in Illinois. In fact, all corn crops north of the 38th latitude were ruined completely. The year 1832  was known as the great "Corn Famine" in Illinois. The entire state north of the 38th latitude had no corn and had to bring it in from other locations.

The counties in the southern tip of Illinois starting at Jefferson County and the ones adjoining it all had plenty of corn. The farmers of Southern Illinois began shipping their corn to the counties to the north. The people of the time, remembering the Bible story of the 10 sons of Jacob going down to Egypt for corn, began telling others that they "have heard there is corn in Egypt, and have come to buy for ourselves." This is the origin of Southern Illinois being called "Little Egypt." Today all of Southern Illinois is very proud of its heritage and the endearing nickname of Little Egypt.

When we formed our ghost hunting and paranormal investigation team in 2007, we wanted a name that would reflect the unique character of Southern Illinois. After much research and thought, we chose to call ourselves the Little Egypt Ghost Society.

How to Get Started as a Ghost Hunter

While not all cemeteries are haunted, some of the older cemeteries can be good places to ghost hunt. Not all of the dead that are in cemeteries are at rest. Some spirits remain on Earth due to unfinished business, a special attachment of the dead to the living or an attachment of the living to the dead. Others were so evil in their lifetime that they fear final judgment and choose to remain on Earth.

Here are some tips to help make your visit to a cemetery more interesting.

In some of the older, abandoned cemeteries the gravestones may be small, embedded in the ground or overgrown by weeds. Be sure to check for burials outside of the main boundary of a cemetery. In some instances if a person was a suicide or criminal, they were not buried in the main cemetery. Such burials can be a source of paranormal activity.

Graves can be located on both sides of a fence. If a cemetery has been neglected, the dead who are buried there may be resentful and will show it in ways that you may be able to detect with EMF meters, digital cameras and digital voice recorders.

Relocated cemeteries like we have in Williamson County when Crab Orchard Lake was made in the 1930s are great places to locate paranormal activity.

Some of the new cemeteries were built on former sites of historic burials or even Indian burial grounds.

Military cemeteries like Mound City National Cemetery in Mound City, Ilinois, have known hauntings. Check the area immediately outside the main gates for any "hot spots."

If a grave site is known to be haunted, sometime the gravestone will give clues to how the person lived and or died.

If you take photographs in a cemetery, download the images before leaving if possible. On more than one occasion I have had my camera images mysteriously deleted when I exited the area and returned to my home.

Spiritualism was very popular in Victorian times. Many people thought that the dead could and would return to visit family members and acquaintances after death. Look for burials dated in the mid to late 1800s and you may be rewarded with an apparition.

Be sure to pay special attention to mass graves, unmarked or lost graves. Many spirits will remain near graves where the gravestone is missing in hopes that someone will remember them. Other good areas to check are grave sites of people who died tragic deaths, neglected graves and anything else that seems out of place.

To find unmarked or lost graves, look for a discolored area of the ground that may be sunken in. Many old burials used wooden coffins that rotted and collapsed making depressions in the ground. In the fall, leaves will fill in these depressions making it easier to spot the lost graves. This is very true on the north side of Oakland Cemetery in Carbondale. This is the location of many unmarked graves of railroad tramps and hobos that were thrown off the train that passed through the cemetery in the late 1800s. Many coffin shaped depressions can be seen there.

Limestone markers and metal fences can store energy. Be sure to check these areas with an EMF meter for unusual readings in the 2 to 7 milligauss range.

Some of the older cemeteries had receiving vaults where dead bodies were stored until frozen ground thawed enough for the grave to be dug in winter months. These receiving vaults can be excellent sources of paranormal EMF fields and EVPs.

When checking the cemetery, notice how the gravestones are aligned. Most will be facing in an east/west orientation. Occasionally, you will find a gravestone that is oriented to the north/south. Pay special attention to these strangely-aligned gravestones.

The best time to ghost hunt in cemeteries is after dark. The reason is that there are fewer things to distract you visually or by hearing. The quietness of nighttime makes it easier to get good EVPs. Also, at night you will be better able to detect temperature differences that may indicate "cold" or "hot" spots that are sometimes indicators or paranormal activity.

Be sure to notice any unusual smells, such as lilacs or roses where no flowers are present. We have detected the mysterious aroma of roses in Salem Cemetery in Carrier Mills and lilacs in a relocated cemetery near Crab Orchard Lake and Carterville. Michael Farmer reports that he and his wife have caught several different aromas in cemeteries to include tobacco, liquor, peppermint, gunpowder (particularly in Civil Way cemeteries), and a few strange ones such as urine, vomit, pickles, maple syrup, and coffee. There are also foul odors that have a musky base to them. Sometimes the foul odors can be overwhelming.

In the late 1800s and early 1900s, some gravestones were made out of zinc. They look like bluish gray stone, but are actually metal. These gravestones have removable plates where some people used to store various items in secret. Oakland Cemetery in Carbondale has one zinc gravestone. Many people who believed in Spiritualism had zinc gravestones.

Ghost hunting equipment and how to use it

Readers of my first two books, *History, Mystery and Hauntings of Southern Illinois* and *More History, Mystery and Hauntings of Southern Illinois*, have often asked me about the ghost hunting equipment that we use on our paranormal investigations. Common questions are, "What is a **PX Device**?" "What is the difference between **EMF** and **EVP**?" "What is the **GHOST METER**?" "What does **IR** mean, and how does a person use all of this seemingly complicated equipment?"

During our many years of ghost hunting and paranormal investigations we have acquired a vast "arsenal" of equipment. Some items were fairly expensive and others were very affordable. After extensive field testing, we were able to determine what equipment works best in what situations. We very quickly discovered that not all paranormal investigation equipment is all that it is cracked up to be. Unlike what you see on the ghost hunting TV shows, you don't need several cases of high priced equipment in order to conduct a successful ghost hunt or paranormal investigation. All you really need for a successful investigation is an open mind, basic research, a digital camera and digital voice recorder.

EMF METER – We use three different models. They range from the very inexpensive **GHOST METER** to the moderate price **K2 (K-II) EMF METER** to the relatively expensive **MEL-8704 METER.** **EMF** is short for electromagnetic field and can be naturally occurring, man-made, or paranormal. Paranormal activity will usually register in the range of 2.0 to 7.0 milligauss. An **EMF** detector locates and tracks energy sources, and picks up on fluctuations in electromagnetic fields in the surrounding environment. Because spirits are comprised of energy, it is believed that when an anomaly is present, it disrupts this electromagnetic field. We use **EMF METERS** to rule out man-made sources before determining anything paranormal.

The **GHOST METER** measures EMF. It has three indicators of EMF activity, analog meter scale, flashing lights, and an audible tone. This device measures EMF on two scales: 0-5 and 0-50 milligauss. This meter has been calibrated to ignore the extremely subtle EMF emissions surrounding the human body, yet is sensitive enough to detect the small, distinct, erratic EMF energy frequently found at haunted locations. Some ghost hunters use this meter as a communication device by asking spirits to make the light and audible tone react in response to questions.

The **K2 (K-II) EMF METER** does not measure EMF, it only gives an indication of EMF in five ranges using five colored LEDs. Some ghost hunters use this meter as a communication device by asking spirits to make the LEDs light up in response to questions.

MEL-8704 METER measures EMF and temperature. This meter has a dual display that displays EMF and temperature simultaneously. It has an EMF "Burst Mode" feature for tracking dynamic EMF movement. Paranormal activity will usually register in the range of 2.0 to 7.0 milliGauss. When you experience a cold spot in a haunted house, it is because whatever spirits are present need to absorb the energy around them in order to manifest (either physically or audibly). A 10 degree drop in your base temperature reading could indicate paranormal activity.

COMPASS - A regular compass can be used to find ghosts. When a ghost is near, the compass arrow spins around and can't find north.

DIGITAL CAMERA - We have found digital cameras are excellent for documenting the location of paranormal investigations. Not only do they allow you to instantly see the photo, they are also able to capture photos in a limited **infrared (IR)** range of light. Digital cameras can pick up a range of light well beyond that of the human eye. You can test your digital camera's sensitivity to **infrared (IR)** by aiming a remote at your camera and holding down a button while clicking a picture. You should be able to see the **IR** light in your viewfinder. You will not be able to see the **IR** light with your naked eyes.

DIGITAL VOICE RECORDER – These are used not only for recording **EVP (Electronic Voice Phenomena)** but also for documenting your investigation. EVPs are heard when an intelligent being is attempting to communicate with us. This can come through as a voice, taps, or other audible disturbances. This is particularly notable when heard as a response to a question or a request for signs of one's presence. **Digital voice recorders** are capable of recording sounds well beyond the range of normal human hearing. When the recording is played back, many times you will hear voices and sounds that you could not hear with your unaided ear. These mystery voices and sounds are **EVPs**.

NIGHT VISION CAMCORDER – We use Sony Night Shot camcorders (currently not available). These camcorders allow us to film in complete darkness. Adding an external **Infrared (IR)** light greatly improves the distance of the internal "Night Shot" system.

PX DEVICE- is a paranormal field experimental device. It works by measuring changes in the "environmental" energy fields around it. It modulates the energy changes into audible speech using a synthesizer chip, an extensive English word dictionary, and a function that phonetically sounds out words. It has 7 modes that include:

1: Dictionary Mode - the **PX** has 2048 internal words that are used in this mode.

2: Phonetic Mode - the **PX** will use phonemes to speak.

3. Reverse Phonetic Mode - The **PX** will reverse the phonetic output in effect it talks backwards.

4. Touch Mode - this mode is used to detect if the device is being touched.

5. Voice Change Mode - this mode is the same as #1 dictionary mode except the voice can be altered detected inputs.

6. Repeat Mode - in this mode the **PX** will repeat the last words spoke from last said to first up to 400 words.

7. Energy Mode - this mode allows the user to set the sensitivity of the device with one of 3 preset levels.

We have had several experiences where the **PX DEVICE** generates words that are not in its programmed vocabulary. Many times, the words generated by this device make sense in context of the situation that we have encountered.

TEMPERATURE MEASUREMENT DEVICES – come in two types, **infrared (IR) thermometers (pyrometer)** and **ambient air thermometers.** The **IR thermometer** will only measure the temperature of a solid surface that the IR beam is aimed at (up to a distance of about 10 feet). Ambient air thermometers will measure the temperature of the air. When you experience a cold spot in a haunted house, it is because whatever spirits are present need to absorb the energy around them in order to manifest (either physically or audibly). A 10 degree drop in your base temperature reading could indicate paranormal activity. Don't make the mistake that many novice (and some "experienced") ghost hunters do of thinking that IR thermometers register the temperature of a room or other location.

Alexander County

A.B. Safford Memorial Library Haunting

Cairo

The A. B. Safford Memorial Library in Cairo, Illinois is haunted by ghost known as "Toby." This specter is known to haunt the second floor of the library.

Various staff members and patrons have reported the sounds of footsteps after dark. It is believed that Toby is responsible for creaking sounds that come from an antique rocking chair even though no one is sitting in it and the chair is not in motion. On more than one occasion, librarians have been spooked when lights have mysteriously switched off and back on. One night a "ghost light" was seen emerging from behind a desk that traveled down the hall before vanishing into a stack of books.

The A. B. Safford Memorial Library is located at 1609 Washington Avenue in Cairo, Illinois.

—•—•—•—

Masonic Lodge Ghost

Cairo

Many paranormal occurrences have been reported in the Cairo Masonic Lodge No. 237, A.F.&A.M. Lodge members say that the building is haunted by one of its Past Masters by the name of Harry August Eichoff. Harry was born on February 15, 1864 and died in Cairo, Illinois on May 30, 1937. His funeral service was conducted on the second floor

of the Masonic Lodge.

Most of the paranormal activity occurs on the second and third floors. Some of the strange things reported are the sounds of heavy footsteps, cold spots, the feeling that someone is watching you from behind, doors that were shut only to be found open later. Three lights next to the altar will turn on after being turned off, locker doors that will open without explanation and cameras that fail to take photos.

The Little Egypt Ghost Society was invited by members of the lodge to conduct a paranormal investigation of the lodge. Shortly after our investigations team arrived at the lodge to interview some of the lodge members, we discovered that the new batteries that we had just put in one of our digital cameras and two of the digital voice recorders were dead!

After interviewing the members, we were taken on a tour of the lodge. We all took numerous, interesting photos. After leaving each area, I reviewed my digital photos to make sure they turned out OK. Upon going to a new area of the lodge, I discovered that my previous photos were missing! I returned to re-photograph the area, and much to my dismay... the photos were mysteriously erased again!

I took some more photos and reviewed them to make sure they were all there. When we finally left the lodge, we all met in the parking lot to discuss what we had found. When I checked my digital cameras to show off the great shots I captured, I discovered that all of my photos had been erased again!

It seemed like the spirits at the Masonic Lodge did not want us to leave with any photos on our cameras. 'My theory is that since I am a Master Mason and swore a "blood oath" not to reveal secrets of the Masonic Lodge, the spirit of Harry would not let me break my oath by revealing any "secrets" with my camera.

The Cairo Masonic Lodge is located at 900 Poplar Street in Cairo, Illinois.

Courthouse Caper

Thebes

In the early 1800s, when Illinois was still a young state, there was great debate about where the county seat of Alexander County should be. Would it be Cairo or Thebes? According to an old story told by Abraham Lincoln, it happened in this fashion. He stated that Thebes was already the county seat, but Cairo was growing rapidly and thought that the county seat should be moved to Cairo. Tempers were flaring and the Thebans said that Cairo was no more than a daub of mud on the tail of the state. That statement did not set well with the fine citizens of Cairo.

Just before the election was held to decide the location of the county seat, a Cairo man came up with an inspired scheme. He fetched a green animal hide and stuffed a large boulder inside. He tied this bundle behind his mule and dragged it around the countryside. The next day he made sure that the townsfolk of Thebes made notice of the strange marks on the ground. He suggested that the marks were made by some species of large serpent. Rumors were spread that dogs, cats and small farm animals were missing.

Greatly alarmed, the citizens of Thebes took up arms and went in search of the great serpent that was supposedly decimating the small animals of the farms. So frenzied were the Thebans in their search for the mystery serpent, that many of them did not make it back to town in time to cast their votes for the county seat. Cairo won the vote hands down.

The Thebes Courthouse is located at Oak and 5th Streets in Thebes, Illinois.

— ● — ● — ● —

Calhoun County

'Mesopotamia' of the West

Hardin

The Republican newspaper in Hardin, Illinois, published the following story in their July 28, 1904 edition:

From 1815 up to 1820, the St. Charles settlers, who had rapidly increased under the daring Boon, began to extend their settlements as far as Lower Dardenne, Barique and Cuivre creeks, on the Mississippi. It appears that this increase was due to the inalienable right and natural tendency of woman to follow the fortunes and share the vicissitudes and bonnet and ribbon money of men. With a weakness as common to man then as it is today, be left his lethargy and fishing tackle in the shade and emerged as a hod carrier and master mason. The rest was the erection of several good forts inside which the women and children could repair for safety. This done they found frequent opportunities of visiting "Mesopotamia" of the west — the hallowed precincts of what is now the county of Calhoun. The chief allurements to it were the vast numbers of wild turkey and deer, the presence of honey and, we suppose, the absence of women.

On one occasion a lot of "harum-scarum" young men, against the advice of the older ones, crossed from Cap au Gris, Missouri, to take in a lot of wild turkeys, whose cries they distinctly heard. As they passed into the woods, the turkeys receded until all had passed some distance into the forest. It was but a short time until the forest echoed the tramp of their re-turning steps. They came hastily, too, for not far in their rear was a lot of savages anxious for their scalps. Plunging into the river they hardly succeeded in escaping with their lives. One poor fellow, whose name is now forgotten, was hedged in from his companions and driven to the top of the bluff. Being as daring as he was desperate, he actually forced his horse down the declivity, and plunging into the river, followed by a shower of arrows, he reached the Missouri shore in safety. It is needless to say that the turkey cries proceeded from the Indians. On another occasion, a party of Indians who were on a raid of murder and robbery attacked the few settlers and trappers then in the Point. The settlers seemed to have been ready for them, for they were organized and gave them a hot chase and had the pleasure of reaching Cap au Gris ferry landing in time to see the Indians safely landed with their spoils on the Missouri shore. One Indian brave was so delighted with their discomfiture that stepping forward to the bank, he stooped down to a very undignified position and signaled his contempt for the party. Captain Adderton, who told this to the writer, thought it was Capt. Nixon who took up his rifle with an oath, and firing at the savage, dropped him dead in his tracks. The incident is well remembered yet among the few and the place is known as "The Long Shot."

Clark County

Martinsville Cyclone

Martinsville

The following story comes from the November 15, 1912 edition of the *Marshall Herald*:

The most destructive storm in the history of Clark County passed over Martinsville last night, leaving death and destruction in its path. The dead is Mrs. George Baker, while her husband is at the point of death from injury and exposure. The loss of property includes the buildings at the fairgrounds, several homes, a large number of barns livestock, crops in the field and woods and orchards.

The cyclone which devastated Martinsville was between 9:15 and 9:20 Tuesday evening. It passed quickly and in a few moments only the wreckage told that a storm of such violence had passed. The storm first struck in the vicinity of the fairgrounds tearing down all the stalls, amphitheater, and other buildings and scattered the timbers for more than a mile.

Across the street from the south side of the fairgrounds, it struck the residence of Joseph Byram. This house was blown from its foundation and the house and contents completely destroyed. Northwest from the fairgrounds, it struck the home of William Berkley moving it twenty feet from its foundation, completely wrecking the home. The room in which Mr. and Mrs. Berkley were sleeping escaped the falling timbers and the family suffered no injury.

One quarter of a mile from the Berkley home, it struck the home of Mr. and Mrs. George Baker. Here the storm seemed to of been at its height and to have vented its full furry. The Baker home was utterly destroyed. Mrs. Baker was thrown more than 50 feet from the house and was probably instantly killed by falling timbers and by the fall. Mr. Baker was also hurt in the debris of the falling house. He was badly injured but struggled to his feet and tried to get to a neighbors in search of aid.

After going a short distance he became unconscious and the searching parties found him lying in a nearby field. He was immediately cared for but owing to his age, it is thought that the hurt, shock and exposure will prove fatal. Mr. Baker is seventy-five years of age and his wife was seventy-three. Having taken its awful toll of human life, the storm passed on to other scenes of destruction. Across the lot from the Baker home, the house of William Sloan was demolished. The freak of the storm at this place was the tearing away of the roof on the north side of the house and leaving the porch and the south side of the roof uninjured.

The barns belonging to Frank Berger, William Brosman and Thomas Husted were completely wrecked. Much livestock and many chickens were killed. Most of these farmers had hay stored in their barns and this was a total loss. The cyclone came from the southwest and traveled to the northwest and the path of the storm was from a quarter to a half mile wide and about two miles long. Corn standing in the field was shucked as clean as if done by human hands. The house in which Frank McCormick was staying was completely destroyed as was the barn on the premises but Mr. McCormick and his horses escaped without injury.

In the Taggart woods, the storm cut a path 200 feet wide, laying low the timber as neatly as if it had been done with an ax. Another freak of the storm was in picking a pump out of a well at the fairgrounds and laying it out straight and uninjured in front *of the well. The pump taken from the well was 20 feet long. Telegraph and telephone wires suffered greatly and there is only indirect wire connection with Martinsville today. Fresh reports of damage are coming in today and the total will reach many thousands of dollars.*

Fortunately the storm missed the business portion and the more closely settled residence portion of the city or the damage and loss of life would be greater. This is said to of been the most violent storm this county has ever known. From the path of the storm one would judge that it was not so much in the shape of a twisting cyclone as a straight one.

Clinton County

Lost Treasure

Carlyle

Carlyle is the site of John Hill's Fort. This fort was built in 1812 to protect the settlers from savage Indian attacks. However, the fort was unable to protect a man by the name of Young. He was killed by an Indian raiding party near the fort.

After his brutal murder, he was buried in an unmarked grave. Word soon got out that the man's mother claimed to have sewed $5,000 inside the lining of her dead son's coat. Many people tried unsuccessfully to locate the hidden grave. Today, Carlyle is pockmarked by many shallow diggings where treasure hunters have tried in vain to locate the $5,000 that was buried so long ago.

Witchcraft in the Woods: History or Myth?

By Tracey Todd Bragg
Trenton

Rhoda Penn Calbreath was born on December 6, 1826, some 134 years after the Salem Witch Trials. Yet, prior to her death in 1876, she found herself face to face with the eyes of a witch, in the form of her daughter Hester.

Rhoda lived near Lebanon, Illinois with her husband, John Hamilton Calbreath. After her death in 1876, she was interred in a remote cemetery located in a wooded area near Trenton. Local legend has led to Rhoda's grave being a popular destination for thrill-seeking teenagers. Reports have said that attempts to photograph her grave site are futile; the pictures are blurry. This is an interesting story, except there is a quite clear picture of her gravestone on the internet. Is this to say that spirit activity hasn't led to unclear pictures in the past?

As any paranormal researcher will tell you, activity peaks and subsides, and we often photograph the same area multiple times for review. All the pictures being blurry would only make us believe it was a camera malfunction or other disruption. One picture being clear while another is not is more, rather than less, indicative of possible activity. Another tale says that if you kneel on Rhoda's grave, your knees would bleed. This is a little vague for a report, giving that since it is a popular gathering site for teens it could lead one to believe broken beer bottles could be the culprit.

One account is more difficult to rebuke. After hearing the stories and legends, a group of students from the local college decided to spend the night at Rhoda's grave. Armed with equipment and ready for activity from beyond, the group captured an amazing EVP with their digital voice recorder. The ghostly voice spoke out from the grave "Mommy, please don't kill me." Obviously the voice of a child, begging for mercy from the person she most trusted: her mother.

What is the cause of all this turmoil at the final resting place of this woman? As the story goes, Rhoda was the mother of a young girl named Hester. While walking in the woods near their home, Rhoda came upon her daughter alone in a clearing. Her heart was broken to discover her child practicing the evils of witchcraft. The tale is told that unable to accept such wickedness even from her own daughter, she killed Hester in the woods, ending the child's life and beginning a mystery that haunts Southern Illinois to this day.

Interestingly enough, through research of census records, there is no indication that Rhoda and John had a daughter named Hester. Documents indicate they had four daughters: Sarah, Caroline, Josephine and Theodosia; but no Hester. Seemingly, this would debunk the whole story except for facts that anyone who researches old records knows:

records are not always complete. Births and deaths occurred without being documented. Records were lost. Registers burned in courthouse fires. And some simply never submitted the information.

It was also common in those days for children to be called by different names than their given ones. Any of the four daughters could have been known by Hester, a loving family nickname passed down. The name could have also changed after years and years of retelling. A lack of documentation does not in itself debunk a legend. There was often a real story, a quite true story, which led to the myth. A story, somewhere in time, led to the haunting.

Edwards County

Old Bone Gap

Bone Gap

Was it a misunderstanding of an old French name or something else that gave us the community of Bone Gap. This stretch of prairie in the Wabash Valley had been known to French voyageurs and trappers for more than a century by the time a group of pioneers from Virginia settled this area in the 1830s. At the time the Piankashaw tribe still occupied the area and had an encampment in a gap or opening of a small group of trees about a quarter mile east of the current community limits.

The French had given the area the name Bon Pas, which translated literally means "good step," or more likely, "good passage." However, the Appalachian settlers who emigrated with Illinois became notorious for garbling foreign words with their accent. As early as 1837, John Mason Peck described the community as Bon Pas Settlement, "near the southeast corner of Edwards County, between the Bon Pas creek and Little Wabash river. It is a timbered tract, good land, and contains about sixty families." Another Bon Pas, downriver in the northeastern portion of White County he spelled "Bumpau" which is how locals still pronounced the name.

So how did the name become Bone Gap? Remember those Piankashaw? When they headed west for the lands beyond the Mississippi they left their trash – a large mound of bones where they had made camp in the gap in the trees.

It was supposedly then that the "bon" or "bum" became a bone and the pass became a gap.

— • — • — • —

Effingham County

Ramsey Cemetery

Effingham

Ramsey Cemetery came about in 1851 with the burial of Alexander Ramsey, 29. Also known as Casbar, Casbah, and Kasbar, the cemetery has been a popular teenage hangout for many years, although no one's sure how it came to be called Casbah. It's thought the nickname came from the rock song "Rock the Casbah" by The Clash. The cemetery has been the location of many weekend parties, as well as a lover's lane.

Locals think it's haunted. A very lonely and creepy narrow road leads there lined by large trees looming above as you drive by rolling hills and a winding creek. One of the trees even has an eerie Halloween mask of a skull with long dark hair hanging from a limb. Several caves said to be haunted line the creek. Some say a werewolf and a man cloaked in black with red glowing eyes lurk in the darkness.

Many locals admit to partying there and tell of mysterious figures on horseback and cloaked devil worshipers. In 1961 a man blocked the entrance with his car. Distraught as he caught his wife cheating he went into the chapel and shot himself in the head. Other versions say the young man hung himself. Due to vandalism, the chapel was torn down.

Some visitors to the cemetery leave pennies on top of tombstones. When they return later, the pennies have all been flipped to the reverse side of the one it was originally placed. At various times a cloaked figure with glowing red eyes is seen among the gravestones. Many strange sounds and lights have been reported by late night visitors.

Ramsey Cemetery is located in Douglas township about 6.5 miles north west of Effingham, Illinois.

Fayette County

Colonel Greathouse

Vandalia

During a visit to the Old State Cemetery in Vandalia, I decided to use my PX ITC experimental device. I was getting no results until I was at the grave of Colonel Lucien Philip Greathouse. As soon as I stepped foot on his grave, the PX device said "MARTYR and COUNTRY."

Col. Greathouse commanded Company C of the 48th Illinois Infantry. At the battle of Peach Tree Creek on July 22, 1864, rebels used a large brick house owned by Troupe Hurtt as a stronghold. At this time, Lucien, now a Colonel and commander of the 48th, was ordered to seize the house and destroy the rebel occupants. Riding a large claybank horse, and with saber in hand, Col. Greathouse led the charge. With the rebels in pursuit of the broken Union line, one of them yelled, "Surrender, can't you see you are beaten?"

Col. Greathouse replied, "Beat hell, we've just come into the fight!" At that moment a Minié ball struck him in the chest and he was immediately killed. His age at the time of his death was 22 years, 1 month and 15 days.

The body of the colonel was returned to Vandalia and buried in Old State Cemetery. A 16-foot granite monument was placed on his grave detailing the battle in which he had participated. It also contained the following inscription:

> *His Example was Worth a Thousand Men, Gen. W. T. Sherman. The Bravest man in the Army of the Tennessee, Gen. J. A. Logan. He led the command in forty hard fought battles and was killed with the flag of his regiment and country in his hands standing upon the breast works of the enemy before the city of Atlanta, GA in the memorable fight of July 22, 1864. May his God and his Country deal justly by him. LUCIEN GREATHOUSE, COLONEL U. S. ARMY. BORN CARLNSVILLE, ILINOIS 7TH DAY OF JUNE 1842 A.D. AND WAS KILLED AT THE HEAD OF HIS REGIMENT BEFORE ATLANTA, GEORGIA 22ND JULY 1864 A.D. WE CANNOT WIN HIM BACK.*

Recently, a marble stone containing the same inscriptions was placed at the foot of the grave. This new marble stone contains a mystery. Col. Greathouse was in the U.S. Army at the time of his death, why then, is the stone engraved with the insignia of a U.S. Naval officer and two stars of a general?

The cemetery itself dates to June 12, 1823, when the Illinois General Assembly, then meeting in Vandalia as fairly new state capital, voted to establish a burial ground of 1.5 acres at the south end of Third Street. One-third of the cemetery was to be reserved for lawmakers and other state officials should they die while in the capital on official business, particularly as the legislature met in the winter time and the young state had no good system of roads. According to the records, four legislators and one judge were laid to rest there.

Franklin County

The Water Witch and Ghost of Mr. Joab

The Diggins (Barren Township)

Franklin County was extremely dry one summer in the mid-1800s. It was so dry that the residents of Barren Township decided to bring in a water witch to find water for the thirsty community. Every place that was indicated as having water only produced dry wells. After many attempts at finding water with negative results, the water witch said, "Well, we will just have to call this place 'The Diggins!'"

From that point on, this small section in the southeast corner of Barren Township became known as "The Diggins." Ironically, this area is now just east of the Rend Lake Conservancy District office and water treatment plant.

There used to be a log cabin on Joab's Hill on the east side of "The Diggins" supposedly haunted by the ghost of Mr. Joab. Many of the older folk around the area would tell their kids late night stories about it.

— ● — ● — ● —

Townmount Prairie – Indian Battle of 1802

By Kale Meggs

Townmount Prairie

"Don't be Caught Dead Without a Beaver Skin Hat"

A historical maker near Town Mount Prairie Baptist Church might not exist if not the strange fact that no 17th Century European would be caught dead without a beaver skin hat. From the mid-16th Century until the 19th Century, fashionable Europeans used so many beaver skins that beavers were nearly extinct there, causing a huge market in the New World for the furs.

Photo by Crissy Wilkins

The Dutch began trading guns for beaver furs. They became wealthy by giving the Iroquois weapons to use on neighboring tribes who weren't armed so well. This, in turn, allowed the Iroquois to monopolize the beaver trade. One of these tribes was the Shawnee, who were large but spread out. Some of the Shawnee migrated to Southern Illinois when they fled the armed Iroquois. During that same time, the twelve tribes who made up the Illinois Confederacy of Indians slowly dwindled in population down to five: the Kaskaskia, Peoria, Tamaroa, Cahokia, and Michigamea. The Illini tribes and the Shawnee slowly became enemies.

Kaskaskians, fine with their new Shawnee neighbors at first, became upset about the competition at a French trading post near the confluence of the Missouri and Mississippi Rivers. They eventually changed their minds and ran the Shawnee off. This began a generational feud, as the Shawnee had already fled the Iroquois and the famed Beaver Wars, now they had formed new enemies in Southern Illinois.

Lines were drawn. The Kaskaskia believed that all the land between the Ohio and Mississippi Rivers was theirs to hunt and live upon, and the Shawnee began using all land east of the Big Muddy River as their own. Many skirmishes and battles happened as a result.

Generations went by and hatred grew. In 1802, the Kaskaskia Indian tribe had crossed over the Big Muddy River and was encroaching on Shawnee territory. Some Shawnee Indian spies had discovered the Kaskaskia on their territory in Townmount Prairie. Tradition has it that an Indian girl was seen going over the old Frankfort hill at sunset. By the next morning a large number of warriors were at Frankfort Hill ready for battle.

A great battle now seemed inevitable. Preparation began and breastworks were thrown up in anticipation of the upcoming battle. It was fierce and lasted quite some time. The Kaskaskia tribe slowly retreated westward toward the Big Muddy River. Crossing the Big Muddy, they finally reached the Little Muddy River which was flooded and difficult to cross. Many of the Kaskaskia warriors met their death at this location.

A few of them managed to survive the attack and succeeded in crossing the river to safety only to be overtaken near where Old DuQuoin is located. The tribe was almost wiped out. John Baptiste Du Quoin, of French-Indian descent, was the Chief of the Kaskaskia tribe. He managed to escape with a small band of warriors, women, and children. The spot where the Kaskaskia Indians were massacred was named DuQuoin in honor of the Indian Chief.

The battle in which the two fierce tribes met must have been a horrible sight. The Shawnee were victorious. It is said that the surviving Kaskaskians were chased all the way to the Big Muddy River where many more where slaughtered along the banks as they attempted to swim to safety on the other side. Even more accounts were told of the Shawnee chasing Kaskaskians to their death into what is now called Old Du Quoin, Illinois.

The battle was the end of the Illini reign. John DuQuoin escaped and managed to find protection for his tribes on reservations located downriver from Brownsville near what is now Sand Ridge, Illinois and at Fort Kaskaskia. Today, all that remains of our state's namesake is a small tribe of less than 500 inhabitants, all now called the Peoria, on a reservation in Oklahoma.

Today the site of the battle that took place at Townmount Prairie is a corn field. An old public well that is now capped over marks the crossroads near to where the battle took place. A historical marker is located in front of the Town Mount Prairie Baptist Church about three miles west of West Frankfort, Illinois on Rt. 149. This marker would not exist if not for the fact that a few centuries earlier no self-respecting European would be caught dead without a beaver skin hat.

The Townmount Prairie Indian Battleground monument is located at 10468 State Hwy 149 in West Frankfort, Illinois.

— ● — ● — ● —

Silkwood Inn

By Kale Meggs
Mulkeytown

As most of Southern Illinois historical stories seem wrought with violence and tragedy (Bloody Williamson Feuds, Herrin Massacre, 1925 Tri-State Tornado, Birger/Shelton/Young wars, Trail of Tears, Reverse Underground Railroad, etc...) it's nice to hear a good story come out of the area history occasionally. The Silkwood Inn, a museum in Mulkeytown, is one such good story. Basil Silkwood ran the Inn (known as the Halfway Inn in the early 19th century because it was a stagecoach stop "halfway" between the Ohio and Mississippi on the Shawnee Trail). He and his wife were known as generous and loving people. In fact, on Basil's tombstone it says "Pillar to the Poor."

As the story goes, while on a business trip in Georgia, Basil befriended several slaves on a plantation there. One was Priscilla. Priscilla was a house slave who loved Hollyhocks. Soon after Basil left

Georgia the plantation owner died and all his assets were sold, including slaves. Priscilla was bought by a Cherokee Chief and when the Cherokee were rounded up for the notorious and tragic Trail of Tears, Priscilla was forced to march with her master. When the thousands of Indians trekked and died through Southern Illinois and made it to Jonesboro, Priscilla spotted Basil Silkwood on the porch of the Willard Hotel there.

Basil recognized her and purchased her away from her strife and probable death from the Chief for 1000 gold pieces, hoping the money would help the Cherokee, and help Priscilla have a better life as a freed slave in Southern Illinois. She lived with the Silkwoods for the rest of her life and helped them raise sixteen orphans.

It is said that Priscilla, who brought hollyhock seeds from Georgia and planted them in front of the inn, is responsible for that particular plants start in Illinois. There is even a children's book called "Priscilla and the Hollyhocks", by Anne Broyles. Priscilla attended the local church until she died and is buried right next to Basil and his wife at the

Reid-Kirkpatrick Cemetery just north of Mulkeytown. You can still visit the Silkwood Inn today and we highly recommend you do.

The Silkwood Inn is located at 7570 Mulkeytown Road in Mulkeytown, Illinois.

The Phantom Voice
West Frankfort

The Tri-State Tornado of March 18, 1925 was the deadliest tornado in U.S. history. The path of the tornado that crossed Missouri, Illinois and Indiana left at least 695 people dead in its wake. West Frankfort was hard hit with 410 injured and 148 dead. The total killed in West Frankfort could possibly have been higher if not for a strange and unexplained incident.

Children tend to be more sensitive to the paranormal than adults. They are able to sense things that we as adults cannot. Lawrence, a schoolboy eight years of age sensed something. He told his mother that he heard something in the living room heating stove that told him not to go to school that day. The mother was very superstitious and decided to heed the warning of the mysterious voice.

Lawrence and his oldest brother were kept home from school. A few hours later, the mother noticed an enormous black cloud skimming the ground that was rapidly approaching from the west by southwest. She rushed out to the well to fetch some water to douse the fire in the heating stove.

The wind kicked up, lighting flashed and thunder roared. The windows in the house started breaking. The sky was so dark that it was difficult to see. The house was lifted three times by the force of the tempest. The house was nearly destroyed but at least the schoolboys were alive although somewhat battered.

Did the mysterious voice from the heating stove save the schoolboys? Only Fate and the killer tornado of 1925 know for sure.

Charlie Birger's Gallows – Lost, But Finally Found

Benton

On April 19, 1928, Charlie Birger was the last man to be publically hanged in Illinois. George Phillip Hanna presided over his execution, a man who was a Southern Illinois banker, farmer, and volunteer hangman. The hoods used to cover the head of the person to be hung were sewn by Hanna's wife. The prisoner was given their choice colors: black or white. Hanna would visit each prisoner before the execution and tell them, "I am here to help you." He told them that he would try to spare them any misery and assured them that their death would be painless. Charlie Birger was offered the customary choice of either a white or black hood by hangman Hanna. Birger's reply was "I'm not a klucker" (referring to the Ku Klux Klan, which he had fought in the Klan War). Birger was hung wearing a black hood.

Birger remarked to a guard that he wanted to be buried in a Catholic cemetery because the devil would not look for a Jew there. Instead he's buried in Chesed Shel Emeth Cemetery in University City (St. Louis County), Missouri under a gravestone with his given name – Shachnai Itzik Birger.

Jackson County loaned the gallows used for the hanging of Birger. Shortly before the hanging, Illinois state law on executions changed with the punishment for new defendants sentenced to death by the electric chair. Since the gallows would no longer be used (and sadly for Phil Hanna the ever-eager hangman) it was returned to Murphysboro in Jackson County and placed into storage in the courthouse basement. Forgotten for several decades, the gallows resurface sometime in the 1970s, when the county cleaned out the courthouse basement for new

office space. At that point the sheriff's department moved dismantled pieces to the Jackson County Highway Department. The gallows were last seen during a reenactment of a historical event in Grand Tower. For the next 40 years, its whereabouts were a mystery.

In 1995, the Franklin County Historic Preservation Society built a reproduction of Birger's gallows next to the old county jail in the exact spot as the original. Many Birger fans travelled to the Franklin County Historical Jail Museum to view the gallows and other Birger items on display. Still, many people wanted to see the real deal. Where was it? No one seemed to know. It was a mystery that would not be solved until recently. Then, in early 2013, the long lost gallows were discovered in a rural Grand Tower barn. Now after 85 years the Birger gallows have been returned to the place it made famous. The macabre historical artifact is now on display in the old Franklin County Jail for all to enjoy.

The Old Franklin County Historic Jail Museum is located at 209 W. Main Street in Benton, Illinois.

Gallatin County

The Old Slave House

Equality – Gallatin County

John Hart Crenshaw built this three story southern plantation style mansion on top Hickory Hill near Equality in the 1830s. Crenshaw rented salt wells from the State of Illinois and began making salt. This business venture made him a rich man. The work at the salt wells was performed mainly by slaves from Kentucky and Tennessee. The Illinois Constitution of 1818, Article VI, Section 2 reads: "No person bound to labor in any other State shall be hired to labor in this State, except within the tract reserved for the salt works near Shawneetown; nor even at that place for a longer period than one year at a time, nor shall it be allowed there after the year 1825. Any violation of this article shall effect the emancipation of such person from obligation to service."

This legal loophole enabled John Hart Crenshaw to become even wealthier. Crenshaw would lease slaves from Livingston Co., Kentucky across the river from Shawneetown for $150 a year. Being a shrewd businessman, Crenshaw was always on the lookout for new ways to increase his profits. His solution was to create a "reverse underground railroad." Slaves who escaped to the "Free" State of Illinois were captured by Crenshaw and put to work at the salt wells. Some of these slaves were sold back to plantation owners in Kentucky and then leased from the new owners to work in the salt wells. Although the slave-napping business was a very good source of labor and income for Crenshaw, it was still not enough. There was a special breeding room on the third floor where a huge black slave named "Uncle Bob" would be bred with selected females in order to produce a stronger breed or strain of worker that would be of exceptional strength for the salt wells.

To prevent prying eyes from spying on his new business venture, Crenshaw had a secret passageway built into his house so that the wagons containing the kidnapped slaves could be driven inside the mansion and unloaded at night. They were then taken to the third floor slave quarters of the mansion. The third floor contained several narrow cells that measured 6 feet by 2 feet. There was an area that contained a whipping post, shackles, and heavy balls and chains.

On one occasion when Crenshaw was whipping some "uppity" females, several other slaves attacked him with an ax, severing his leg. This understandably angered Crenshaw even more and resulted in even harsher treatment of the slaves.

Today, John Hart Crenshaw and his slaves are long gone. What remains, however, are the stories of cruel and inhuman treatment, and of ghosts. The third floor of his manor in particular is known for many stories of hauntings. There have been reports of shrieks, groans, and the sound of slaves crying in the night. Other sounds manifested were that of chains rattling and whips cracking over the naked backs of the slaves. Misty forms would be seen just out of the corner of one's eyes. The third floor quarters have a very malevolent and sad feeling to them. Many years ago, visitors were allowed to spend the night in the third floor slave quarters to experience the ghostly activity for themselves. In the 1920s, an exorcist came to spend the night with the intent of ridding the mansion of its ghosts. During the night, the exorcist came running out of mansion and collapsed on the lawn. He had died of fright. In the 1960's, two Marines (both Vietnam War veterans) tried to spend the night in the third floor quarters, but fled in terror.

Today, the Old Slave House is owned by the State of Illinois. It is closed to the public.

The Old Slave House also known as Hickory Hill Plantation is located at the end of Crenshaw Lane just south of Route 13 and west of Route 1.

The Old Slave House Stud

Equality

"Uncle Bob" Wilson was one of the slaves known to have lived at the Hickory Hill Plantation, now known as the Old Slave House outside Equality, Illinois. Crenshaw was infamous for his "Reverse

Underground Railroad." He would kidnap free negroes and sell them across the river in Kentucky as slaves.

The supply of kidnapped slaves was not enough to supply slave trade, so Crenshaw used the services of "Uncle Bob" as a stud on his plantation. Whenever Crenshaw had young female slaves, he would have them chained to Uncle Bob's bed for breeding purposes. This "slave factory" produced hundreds of children to be sold as slaves.

During the Civil War, Uncle Bob Wilson joined the Confederate Army and proudly served with the 16th Virginia Infantry as an orderly to a Confederate Officer.

After the war, he became a Baptist minister. In the 1920s he moved back to Gallatin County. Then, sometime after the 1937 flood that nearly destroyed Shawneetown, he moved to Chicago. In 1942 he was moved to the Elgin State Hospital and was the oldest resident at the veteran's home there. Uncle Bob Wilson lived to be 112 years old and said that the secret to his long life was, "I never drank, chewed or stayed out late until I was 111 years old."

Meeting Uncle Bob

By Debbie Goetz
Equality

It is said that children are more susceptible to the paranormal and seeing ghosts. I truly believe this to be true. I have experienced this myself and would like you to hear my story.

One of my experiences as a child was of the Old Slave House. My dad and mom took my brother and I there as a youngster back when you could go all the way in and around it. It was a very steamy summer day. I can remember it like it was yesterday. We walked around down stairs, looking at the antique furniture and items. Then we went to the second and third floors. The third floor/attic was a dirty, dusty place. I remember thin planks of wood against the walls of small cells. I remember one plank in particular. There were shackles on the narrow wall all along the side of the plank.

All of a sudden the stifling room seemed cooler. I looked at what was a large black man, so clear I could see the beads of sweat on him. He was attached to the shackles. We just kept staring at each other. I remember him not being mean or scary at all. He had old torn pants that were too short. His face was so sad. His eyes contained so much sorrow. It was as if he looked to me to help him but as a child he knew I couldn't and that it was hopeless. That's what I felt sorrow and hopelessness. It was probably only moments, but felt as if we had seen into each other's souls for an hour.

Many years went by. I became an adult, got married and had forgotten about the chilling moment from childhood. At least until I went to Alton one day. My husband at the time and I took a road trip to Alton, Illinois. Mainly because I had heard of it being very haunted and I wanted to explore. We ended up in a bookstore and met Troy Taylor. While flipping through some of the books I saw a picture of a slave... THE SLAVE! Waves of emotion flooded me. I exclaimed to my husband, "Oh my God! That's him!" Of course, I had to explain who "him" was. The man that I saw as a child was the main slave, Uncle Bob, who fathered so many children. The man that allowed me to see him that steamy summer day now had a name. All of the feelings of sadness and desperation enveloped me one more time as I saw the picture. The memories of that day will be forever in my mind.

The Great Salt Springs

Equality Township

Salt was very important to the Indians and early settlers near Equality. In the early 1800's salt became commercially important. One

spring of historical significance was located on the Saline River about four miles down from present day Equality. The earliest records called it the Great Salt Spring, but later as it was operated by enslaved laborers by the early 20th Century it was ugly remembered only as "Nigger Spring," "Nigger Well," or "Nigger Furnace."

A strong sulphur spring and a fresh water spring were located nearby. Up the river about a half mile from Equality on the north side of the Saline River a giant buffalo lick known as Half Moon Lick was where dozens of wells were drilled to find saltwater. Together this was known as the U.S. Salines during territorial days and the Gallatin Salines after Illinois became a state in 1818. Amazingly the Land of Lincoln's first constitution legalized the use of slavery for these saltworks until 1825 when indentured laborers, who were all but slaves, became the main labor force for the next few decades. Each spring or well fed saltwater through pipes to a furnace site where the water would be boiled off to leave a pan or kettle with salt in the bottom. John Hart Crenshaw of the Old Slave House legitimately earned at least part of his wealth from his leases of the salines.

The Great Salt Spring was an important source of salt in the centuries before European settlement. Pottery fragments left behind by early Indians are still in evidence at the spring. A short distance to the south and across the road are located many Indian graves.

This ancient salt spring has been the location of much tragedy and violence stemming from hundreds of years of use. Battles and feuds have been fought of the possession and use of the salt. Many murders occurred there along with beatings, floggings and even mutilation of the slaves that worked at the site. Many times the brine would flow red with the spilled blood of innocent and not so innocent victims.

The springs were known to the Shawnee Indians that lived in Southern Illinois. The first recorded use of the salt springs by white men was in 1778 when a group of men from Kentucky used the springs to produce salt. In 1803 the salt springs were leased to Captain Bell of Kentucky for the production of much needed salt. Slaves and indentured servants from Kentucky were brought in to work the salt mines.

The Great Salt Spring is located west of Illinois Route 1 and south of Illinois Route 13 and the Old Slave House. It's difficult to find from the lonely gravel road that passes by it. If you look closely enough you might be able to catch a glimpse of the timbers that frame the hole in the ground that forms the Old Well.

Once you find the well, you will immediately be overcome with sulfur like, rotten egg stench and the smell of decaying vegetation. Once you venture off the gravel road and into the blue mud of the creek bed, you will be immediately attacked by thousands of hungry mosquitoes.

There is a very eerie and haunting feel that will envelope you as you peer into the bluish, bubbling waters of the salt well. Many people have reported feeling like they were being watched by unseen eyes from the surrounding forest. It is like you are being watched by the spirits of the ancient Indians, slaves and maybe even the mastodons, buffalo and murdered souls who once paused at the very spot that you are standing on.

Salt and Ghost Hunting

Salt has a long history of being used for magical and protective purposes. Ancient Indians and early settlers believed that salt could offer protection from evil spirits, ghosts and witches. Throwing salt across doorways and windows is thought to prevent anything evil from entering a house or other building. Some ghost hunters use salt during their investigations to create a "safe haven" or "circle of protection" while conducting late night vigils in search of the paranormal. It is best to use a raw, natural salt for protection from evil spirits. If you live in southeastern Illinois you are very near to an ancient source of natural salt that actually comes from a haunted location.

The best source for this magical salt is the Old Salt Spring located just south of the Saline River. To find the spring, take Illinois Route 13 to the intersection of Illinois Route 1. Turn south onto Route 1 and cross over the Saline River and go through a narrow gap in the hills. At the three mile mark you will see the first crossroads. There, turn back west onto Salt Well Road which will immediately turn back to the north and then fork at the base of the wooded Wildcat Hills. Take the right fork and keep going straight in the woods. Almost immediately the road will fork again. The branch to the right is part of the old highway alignment and runs to where an earlier highway bridge crossed the river. The branch to the right is the true Salt Well Road, and is the oldest road in the region. From this branch it's just 0.5 miles down the road. If you look to the right just inside the tree line you will see a ten foot square, log lined well. This is the source of the brine to make salt.

Once you locate the salt spring, you will immediately notice the evil smell of sulfur. Mosquitoes will swarm you by the thousands to draw your blood. The spirits of tortured and murdered spirits will seem to fill the air. Be brave and venture to the edge of the brine pit and fill containers with the salt filled water. Take the brine and either boil or evaporate it in an iron kettle. Four gallons of the brine water will yield about one pound of raw, unprocessed salt. You can now use this magical salt to keep ghost, witches and evil spirits away while you ghost hunt.

Never go to this place alone!

The coordinates are 37.705000, -88.295278. The well is between the road and the river, and will be underwater if the Saline River is out of its banks.

— ● — ● — ● —

Birthday Party or Necktie Party?

Old Shawneetown

It was a great day for one man and not so great for another. On this date Joe "Peck" Smith of Ridgeway was the last man legally hung in Gallatin County. What made the day extra special was that it was the 53rd birthday of Phil Hanna of Epworth. Most people celebrate their birthdays with a cake with candles, family and close friends. Not Phil Hanna. He was a man who had a hobby of hanging condemned prisoners and this was to be the 53rd hanging that he presided over. What better way to celebrate the double 53s than to combine his birthday with a "neck tie party"?

Joe "Peck" Smith was convicted of killing his wife, Orpha, with a 12 gauge shotgun filled with #6 shot fire at very close range. The shot took off her head leaving brains and skull scattered all over the walls, floor and ceiling. It was gruesome.

After a very short trial, he was convicted of murder and the sentence of the court was that the "said Joe Peck Smith be taken from the bar of this court to the common jail from whence he came, and there be safely and securely kept and confined until the 16th day of

February A.D. 1927, and on that day, between the hours of ten o'clock in the forenoon and 2 o'clock in the afternoon be by the sheriff of Gallatin County, according to the law, within the walls of said jail or enclosure adjoining the same be hanged by the neck until he is dead."

At exactly 11:25 a.m. on February 16, 1927, Joe "Peck" Smith climbed the 13 stairs to the platform of the gallows where Phil Hanna waited at the top with the fatal hangman's noose held behind his back. After a few words of encouragement a black hood was adjusted over Smith's head and the noose was fitted around his neck and drawn snug. Hanna gave a nod to the sheriff and the trap door was sprung open. Smith plunged to his death and was pronounced dead 13 minutes later. Two minutes after that, he was cut down from the hangman's rope and carried to a hearse.

— ● — ● — ● —

Greene County

The Hanging of Doctor MacCauliffe

Carrolton

The southeast corner of in Carrollton, Illinois, is the location of the haunted grave of Dr. Charles Macauliffe.

In 1879 the doctor was having drinks with his brother-in-law, James Heavener at a tavern in Wrights, Illinois. A drunken brawl broke out and Dr. Macauliffe shot his brother-in-law with a shotgun. The man was dead before he even hit the floor. A panicked Dr. Macauliffe fled the scene. A posse of angry men soon formed and took off after the doctor. After a short chase, Dr. Macauliffe was captured, bound tightly and placed on horseback for the ride to the Carrollton Jail.

The road to the jail went past the Hickory Grove Cemetery. When the posse came to a large oak tree they had an inspiration....why not hang the doctor then and there and be done with the matter? The decision was quickly made and a rope was thrown over a suitable limb. One end of the rope was tied to the tree trunk and the other end was tied into a hangman's noose.

This noose was placed over the head and around the neck of the terrified doctor. One of the posse let loose with a shot from his Colt Army .44 revolver and the horse that the doctor was sitting on took off in fright. The doctor was jerked from the horse and left kicking, and jerking at the end of the rope. In a few minutes it was all over and the doctor was dead. The posse rode off leaving the doctor swinging at the end of the rope.

The next morning, passersby found the dead doctor, cut him down, and buried him in the southeast corner of the cemetery. Some townsfolk went to Dr. Macauliffe's office and took the metal sign from the office door and embedded it in concrete to make a gravestone for the doctor.

It is said that if you go to Dr. Macauliffe's grave at midnight when the moon is full, you will see the ghost of Dr. Macauliffe with the hangman's noose around his neck.

The Whipping Post in 1832

Carrollton

This story is from the *Carrolton Patriot*, Friday, February 2, 1906:.

In view of the present agitation for the establishment of whipping posts Dr. Willard's account of the first and lonely public legal whipping administered in Carrollton as he saw it, is apropos. After telling of the first hanging, he says:

Another infliction of punishment which would now be more revolting in public than a hanging would be, I saw on the public square in Carrollton in 1832. There was then no penitentiaries in the state, hence other penalties had to take the place of confinement. Near the court house on the public square there was set a strong post, an unhewen log, ten feet high, with a crosspiece near the top. I saw a man brought from the jail by the sheriff and a constable, to be whipped thirty lashes for the theft of a horse. He was stripped naked to the hips, his hands were tied and the rope was carried to the crosspiece and drawn as tight as it could be without taking his feet from the ground.

Then Sheriff Fry took that terrible instrument of punishment and torture, a rawhide. Probably many of you have not seen one. To make it a taper strip of soft, wet cowskin was twisted until the edges met, and the thing was dried in that position. It was hard, ridgy, and rough, but flexible as a switch, three-quarters of a yard long. The sheriff began laying strokes on the culprit's back, beginning near his neck and going regularly down one side of his backbone, the former sheriff Young counting the strokes aloud.

Each stroke made a red blood-blister. When fifteen blows had been counted, the officer paused and someone ran to the poor wretch with a tumbler of whiskey. Then the other side of the man received like treatment. Then the man's shirt was replaced and he was led away to the jail. One of the bystanders said: "O, Lord! He isn't as bad cut up as G. H. was when L. M. flogged him three or four years ago." Boy as I was I did not know what a dreadful infliction it was. The whipping post remained there 2 or 3 years, but I never heard of any further use of it.

*NOTE - Jersey County was part of Greene County in 1832.

Hamilton County

Good Morning, Mrs. McCoy

McLeansboro

The McCoy Memorial Library was originally constructed in 1884 by banker Aaron G. Cloud as a family home for himself, his wife, and two daughters. The wife died, but part of her never left. Mr. Cloud remarried to a woman from out east and brought her to this home. She did not like living there due to her feeling of a presence of the first wife, so Mr. Cloud built her another mansion nearby. Shortly after that, he died. The new wife, having never liked McLeansboro, returned east.

Mary E. Cloud McCoy, the daughter of the first wife, donated the house to the town for their library, with several of the family's things remaining on the second floor (now Hamilton County Historical Society), including the first Mrs. Cloud's wedding dress. One condition of the donation is that the library must ensure that flowers are put on Mrs. Cloud's grave every year. Library staff often hear odd noises, and see a form on the staircase, and will just say, "Good morning, Mrs. McCoy!"

The McCoy Memorial Library is located at 118 S. Washington Street in McLeansboro, Illinois.

Strange Energy at Knight's Prairie Church

By Michael Farmer
McLeansboro

While the Knight's Prairie Church near McLeansboro holds a lot of tales, one of the most interesting things that ever happened to us occurred there. My wife and I as well as others have visited the cemetery and the old church on several occasions and have had a multitude of experiences. Esther has always had someone following her around there. If anyone else approaches they are gone. One night in particular, she claimed she felt cold. I popped a photo which showed a mist surrounding her. Not just surrounding her, but appeared to have moved through her. While this in itself makes for an interesting story, another night there proved even more so. We were inside the church trying to get a response with an EVP session. Later, the session revealed nothing, but the feeling we had while inside was very strange. The atmosphere was very heavy and thick. It was hard to breathe. We all felt claustrophobic. We really didn't think much of it, but did take serious note of it.

A few days later, I was researching the interments in the cemetery and noticed a particular name that seemed to reach out and grab me. The Rev. Thomas "Uncle Tom" Hunt stuck out on the list. When looking at his story, there were a couple of photos that really made me think. One in particular shows the congregation several years back. There must be around 70 people in this picture and I thought how crowded the tiny church must have been. Could there be something to the feelings we experienced and the crowded church? Some residual energy left behind that shows itself at certain times and not others?

Knight's Prairie Church is located 7.5 miles southwest of McLeansboro, in Section 1, Flannigan Twp., on the Old Goshen Road.

Ghosts in the Attic

By Marci Kane
Hamilton County

The house I grew up in Hamilton County was haunted. It began before I was born with stories from my cousins. The house was two stories with an unfinished attic room attached to the upstairs bedroom. When I was old enough to remember, my cousin Roger told me of hearing footsteps on the stairs leading up to the bedroom and of a woman in a long dress standing at the bottom of the stairs. My mother would always laugh whenever he told us. As a child I often heard bells ringing behind the attic door crawlspace after the attic room was remodeled & became my bedroom.

I returned to live in the house at age 30. This is when I started seeing blinking kitchen lights and hearing other odd noises. Then one night while I was sleeping on the couch in the living room on a winter night I heard a loud creak in the corner of the house at the bottom of the staircase there she stood, the woman in the long dress!! I told my cousin Roger at our next visit. We had both seen her. My sister refused to ever stay in the house alone. The house had been relocated up to the road from the field behind & was built in the late 1800s.

Hardin County

Rose Hotel

Elizabethtown

This is the most haunted place the Little Egypt Ghost Society has ever investigated, and we consider the Rose Hotel to be one of the most haunted places in America. We have conducted several overnight searches for the spirits still lingering at this historic and famous hotel.

In 1813, James McFarlan received a license to operate a tavern in Elizabethtown. The McFarlan family charged 25 cents for breakfast, dinner or supper, lodging for 12 ½ cents, a gallon of oats or corn cost 12 ½ cents, a half pint of whiskey went for $1.25, a quart of beer was 12 ½ cents. The tavern was famous for drinks such as taffia, cherry bounce and cider royal.

The McFarlan family operated the tavern until 1890 when it was purchased by Mrs. Sarah Rose. At that time the name was changed to the Rose Hotel. Mrs. Rose operated the hotel for 55 years with the help of Frankie and Tote Woods.

The oldest wing of the hotel was built about 1830, with additions built about 1848 and 1866. Today, the exterior is restored to its 1866 appearance. In 1972, the Rose Hotel was added to the National Register of Historic Places. The Rose Hotel is now owned by the Historic Sites Division of the Illinois Historic Preservation Agency and at the time of our visit was operated by Sandy Vinyard as a bed and breakfast.

Sandy invited the Little Egypt Ghost Society to investigate reports of the paranormal activity that has been occurring at the hotel on a regular basis. Sandy and many of her guests have reported sounds coming from parts of the hotel (it only has six guest rooms) where no one is present. These noises are said to sound like there "is a party going on up there." Objects have been mysteriously moved, only to reappear sometime later in a different location of the hotel. Pennies, in groups of three, are found on a continuous basis throughout the hotel.

Our team captured the image of one of the former servants, Tote Wilson, in a mirror in the McFarlan Suite. The image was positively identified by Sandy Vinyard using the hotel scrap book containing old photographs of thee hotel and staff. We tried to debunk our photo, even going so far as to video tape the entire process, but could not reproduce the image.

We conducted several EVP experiments while at the hotel with very interesting results:

Q. "Are you alone?" A. "YES"

Q. "How do you feel?" A. "FINE"

Q. "Where are you now?" A. "RIGHT BEHIND YOU"

Another EVP captured with our camcorder said: "WE ARE YOUR BEST FRIENDS"

We set up motion detectors throughout the hotel. At approximately 3 a.m. the motion detector in the Charlotte Room went off repeatedly with corresponding EMF reading of 2.3 to 2.6 milligauss.

In the front lobby we took a photograph about midnight that showed the face of a young lady looking in the front window. There was no one outside at the time. This photograph was positively identified by Sandy as one of her former workers who was killed in a car crash about a year earlier.

On several occasions, our group would smell the scent of cigars, bacon cooking, lavender and logs burning when none of those items were present in or near the hotel. We heard voices and the sound of a small dog barking as well as footsteps and doors creaking open and shuts upstairs when no one was up there.

There is a small graveyard behind the hotel where several members of the McFarlan family as well as some of the servants and guests are buried. Many of the graves are unmarked.

On October 5, 2009, I was standing in the center of the McFarlan Suite in total darkness and took this photo with my digital camera and flash. I was the only living person in the room at the time. Note the image of a man looking out of the far left corner of the mirror. We went back to this room Feb 11, 2010 and tried to debunk this photo. No matter what we did, we could not recapture Tote's image in the mirror. This photo is positively paranormal.

Sandy positively identified the man as "Tote" from a photograph in the hotel scrapbook. Tote was a servant at the hotel many years ago.

The night before this photo was taken; I conducted an Electronic Voice Phenomena (EVP) experiment. One of the questions I asked was "will you join us for breakfast in the morning." We believe these orbs could be the spirits of Frankie, Tote and Mammy Rose.

This is a close up view of Tote's ghost in mirror in the McFarlan Suite.

In early spring 2010, the Little Egypt Ghost Society went to the Rose Hotel to film a TV commercial. After we finished filming, we decided to do a little ghost hunting in the McFarlan Suite. Sandy was present with us when she heard the floor start to "creak." At that

Illustration of Tote's ghost at the Rose Hotel.

moment, Lisa and I started getting readings on our K2 and Ghost Meter

EMF meters. We were able to trace the EMF field to a location near the center of the suite. We quickly realized that the EMF field was confined to an area the size and shape of an adult human! When we placed our hands into this EMF field, we discovered that the temperature was 15 to 20 degrees cooler than the surrounding area. At that point, the EMF field moved and we tracked it to an area near the fire place. Once again, the temperature inside the EMF field was noticeably cooler than the surrounding area. At this point the electric power went off in the McFarlan Suite, but not in any other area of the hotel. After we exited the suite, the power mysteriously came back on. We then rechecked the entire suite and could not relocate the EMF field. We firmly believe that this was the spirit of Tote Wood once again playfully letting us know that he still keeps watch over the nearly 200 year old Rose Hotel.

The Rose Hotel is located at 92 Main Street in Elizabethtown, Illinois.

— ● — ● — ● —

Haunted Book Signing

Elizabethtown

After we published first book, *History, Mystery, and Hauntings of Southern Illinois* we went back to the Rose Hotel in the summer of 2011, to have our first official book signing and spend the night there with some select ghost hunters.

This stay at the Rose Hotel was the most active one at this historic and famous site to date! We think the large crowd and excitement from our book signing got the spirits all stirred up.

Starting about 11 p.m. we heard the voices and giggles of two little girls below the bluff and along the river bank. When we went down to investigate, there was no one there! When we went back to the gazebo, we heard them again. Each time we went looking for the little girls, no one was around!

The PX Device was extremely chatty in the McFarlan Suite.

We detected a strong scent of camphor in the suite and had several unexplainable EMFs. We got a strong EMF coming from a doll's eyes. A little while later, the EMF moved from the doll to the left side of the desk that the doll was sitting on. A while later the EMF moved once again to the frame around a mirror in the room. After that we heard several voices and the smell of smoke coming from the dining room. We all rushed out of the suite and down the stairs to the dining room. No one was there and the smell of smoke was gone. Courtney had the key to the McFarlan Suite forcefully jerked out of her hand by unseen means. We then heard footsteps stomping up and down the staircase to the dining room when no one was on the stairs. The coat hangers in our room kept swaying and clanging together even though no one had touched them and there was no breeze to make them move. At 2:10 a.m. all of our motion detectors were activated and would not turn off. At the same time we had EMF readings in the 2-4 miligauss range.

Ghost Hunter Spirits (of the other kind)

Elizabethtown

This is the secret recipe for Cherry Bounce that was once made and served at the McFarland Tavern (Rose Hotel) during the 1800s in Elizabethtown, Illinois.

One gallon of good whiskey, one and one-half pints of wild black cherries bruised so as to break the stones, two ounces of common almonds shelled, two ounces of white sugar, one-half teaspoonful cinnamon, one-quarter teaspoonful cloves, one-quarter teaspoonful nutmeg, all bruised. Let stand twelve to thirteen days, and draw off. This, with the addition of one-half gallon of brandy, makes very nice cherry bounce.

The Ghost of Dr. Anna Bigsby

Rock Creek

Hardin County is infamous for river pirates, highwaymen, murderers and various other miscreants. However, Hardin County is also known for kind hearted, hardworking and respected people as well. Anna Bigsby was one of the latter.

When Anna was 16 about years old, she came to Southern Illinois from Philadelphia in a covered wagon with her parents. Anna was well educated and became a teacher. She was strong, fearless and able to take care of herself. According to legend, Anna once killed a man who attempted to attack her. Soon afterward, she returned to Philadelphia to study medicine. Upon completion of medical school, Anna returned to Southern Illinois as a doctor, teacher and church worker. She married a farmer's son named Isaac Hobbs.

Anna's medical practice was an extensive one and she was very well respected and sought after as a healer. Many of her patients referred to her as Doctor Anna. The acclaim for Anna continued to grow. About this time there was a deadly sickness known as milk sickness. It occurred in late summer and early fall each year. Many people and cows sickened from the disease and died. No one knew the cause or the cure. Many of the superstitious, backwoods folk of the area believed that the sickness was caused by the magic potions of witches. Anna, being much more educated than the average person at the time, did not believe in witches. A local Indian squaw and she set out to find the remedy for this deadly disease. They believed that it was caused by something that the cows were eating. After many weeks of observing cattle, Anna and the Indian squaw observed the cows eating White Snakeroot and determined that this was the cause of the mysterious disease. Armed with this knowledge, men scoured the woods and pastures on a mission to eradicate the weed. The mysterious and deadly milk sickness was defeated.

Soon after Anna discovered the cause of the milk sickness, her husband died of pneumonia. Several years later, Anna married a ne'er-do-well timber thief by the name of Eson Bigsby. He had only married Anna for the vast amount of money he thought she had. One dark and stormy night, as Anna was going to call on a patient, Eson and some of his criminal buddies seized her and bound her in chains. They then pushed her off a cliff and set fire to the woods. Anna got caught in tree branches during her fall from the cliff. A storm quickly brewed up and the torrential rain fall drenched the flames. Anna was saved from the flames, managed to free herself from the chains, climbed down from the tree and made good her escape.

There is a cave near Rock Creek in Hooven Hollow that is known as Bixby Cave. Legend has it that this cave is the hiding place of Anna Bixby's fortune. Many intrepid souls have sought to find the missing gold and silver coins. While no one has admitted to finding the Bigsby treasure, many have reported weird happenings in and around the cave. Strange, glowing balls of light have been sighted in the area. These lights are said to be a lantern held by the ghost of Dr. Anna Bigsby as she goes about her rounds to guard her treasure and to tend to her beloved sick and injured patients.

Good Hope Church Cemetery

Karbers Ridge

Good Hope Cemetery is located off Karbers Ridge Blacktop in Hardin County. There have been numerous reports of paranormal activity at this location that include ghosts, weird lights and strange noises. The cemetery is considered to be very haunted.

A headless ghost with chains around his neck has been seen walking along the road in front of the cemetery. There is also a mysterious nameless horror that stalks night time visitor to the cemetery. Many glowing balls of light have been observed in the cemetery and near the church.

One man reported that he and two friends decided to spend the night in the cemetery and church grounds just to see for themselves what type of paranormal activity they would encounter. During the night, two things happened that they could not explain. First, they heard strange hollow sounds of rapping on wood coming from a location near the center of the cemetery and then a deep snarling growl that came from the woods next to the church.

Courtney Barnard McKinley told us:

"People have experienced strange things there such as 'shadows.' One thing that creeped me out once was when I was standing there late evening by myself (went to visit for memorial day since I was out of town when the rest of my family went and I didn't wanna leave it out) and it was starting to get dark. I am so certain I heard footsteps behind me several times... I would turn around quickly and no one was there. It gave me chills. I haven't been back alone since. It really scared me. I've also heard stories of people seeing apparitions there, following them and then they disappeared. Along with the usual stories of unknown noises, etc. I believe there's definitely something to it, along with every other cemetery. There's just too much thickness in the air there for there not to be something going on."

No one knows for sure what may be causing the paranormal events at Good Hope Church Cemetery, and most likely never will. Good Hope Church is located at coordinates 37.57394 and -88.36532.

Ahab Gullettt

Karbers Ridge

Legend has it that, if you go to the small creek at the far end of Pleasant Hill Cemetery near Karbers Ridge in Hardin County at night, you will hear bells ringing and the sound of a gate opening and closing. There is a spirit there that allegedly haunts the cemetery. The name of the spirit is Ahab Gullett. His tombstone, located near the entrance of the cemetery, reads: "Friends beware as you pass by, as you are now so once was I. As I am you soon shall be, prepare for death and follow me." If you read this aloud, it is said that spirits will appear before you. My group of paranormal investigators decided to investigate this site one tranquil fall evening.

We started at Ahab Gullettt's gravestone and read the inscription aloud. We then headed to the back side of the cemetery to the creek. As we approached the edge of the creek, the wind began to pick up and the trees began to sway. The water was very shallow and crystal clear with a solid rock bottom. As I stepped to the edge of the water a horseshoe appeared right in front of my eyes along the bottom. I reached down into the water and retrieved it. Seconds later, another horseshoe was found by another investigator. We had a total of five investigators present that night. How many horseshoes did we find? Five. These horseshoes have been estimated to be over 100 years old.

Pleasant Hill Cemetery is located in a remote, wooded area off 225E, about 4 miles east of Route 34.

Pleasant Hill Cemetery Never Rests

by Tracey Todd Bragg
Hardin County

Pleasant Hill Cemetery sits deep in the heart of Hardin County. Many unusual stories, pictures, and incidents have been reported here, leading to its listing as "The Most Haunted Cemetery in Southern Illinois." A creepy epitaph on the grave of Ahab Gullettt (Friends Beware as you pass by, as you are now so once was I; As I am now, you shall soon be, so prepare for death and follow me), reports of creaking gates, smells of roses where there are none and the Shadow Man all bolster the claims.

Ben (not his real name) had heard the stories, believed them, but had no idea what could happen to someone untrained to be dealing with spirits. A late night excursion turned into some of the most terrifying events of his life. Unfortunately, he didn't learn his lesson the first time; he went back.

A late night in the winter months lead to a common hobby of many in this rural area: gravel road cruising. Many of the roads in the county interlace with each other, leaving many options as to direction of travel. This particular night, the road led to Pleasant Hill. Ben was oblivious to the risks involved in taunting spirits, especially since the legends of this haunted location require one to "knock on the headstone of Ahab Gullettt three times," read the epitaph, and see what happens. Ben and his companion did so. They also called out to the spirits, daring them to come out. He had a new cell phone and proceeded to snap pictures in the dark, sure that nothing would appear. To his surprise, two of the pictures were dark, but obviously contained the image of the infamous Shadow Man, standing near the steps that lead down to the gravel road. Ben was excited—spooked—but excited. I received a text telling me he had some evidence to show me.

The next day, I received a phone call from Ben. He needed to talk to me and it had to be in person (this made me a little concerned). He came in my door, his cell phone in his hand. I asked to see the pictures, thrilled at the prospect of viewing the elusive Shadow Man. "They aren't there" he said.

"What do you mean, they aren't there?"

He replied, "I mean they aren't there. The pictures disappeared when I tried to look at them after I left last night, and now, today, the phone won't even turn on, I'm freaked out." We went through the usual—was the phone properly operating prior to today? Has it had any malfunctions? How old is the phone? (It was two weeks old.) No answers, other than the ominous feeling Ben was having. He threw the phone in the river.

A few months later, a friend convinced Ben to return to the cemetery with him. Ben was reluctant, knowing what had happened the last time, but he went along, camera in tow. Ben was cautious this time, only taking pictures and not risking stirring anything up. His friend was less believing and despite Ben's instructions not to do anything, his friend taunted the spirits, daring them to come out. Once again, my phone rang. Ben was much shaken again. He had no idea if he had captured any evidence in the photos, because the camera wasn't working! This camera had been purchased just a couple months before and also had no prior issues.

I asked about trying to pull the photos off the memory card; Ben said he already tried. The memory card had about 300 pictures on it before, from a family event, and even those were missing. The memory card was wiped clean. He sent the camera off to be repaired only to find it was not repairable. And it didn't stop there. Later that week, Ben and his friend had been involved in two serious accidents at work (I cannot elaborate on these incidents, lest I reveal Ben's identity), both occurring only when the two of them were working together.

I received another call from Ben a few days later. He had returned to the cemetery on my advice, to apologize to whatever he had stirred up, telling the spirit to leave him alone and that he was leaving now and they were not to follow. Ben left the cemetery and as soon as he got about a mile from it, his low air pressure light came on. His tires were new, he was apprehensive, but he realized there was a chance he had picked up a nail or something. By the time he arrived at a service station the tire was flat. There was nothing wrong with the tire that would explain the sudden loss of air pressure.

Ben has not returned since to Pleasant Hill Cemetery, and says he never will.

Pleasant Hill Cemetery is located in a remote, wooded area off 225E, about 4 miles east of Route 34.

Scared to Death

Karbers Ridge

Goodhope Cemetery located south of Karbers Ridge Road near Garden of the Gods, has been known for many years as a haunted location.

Late one evening in 1934, a young man was riding his horse across the Rose Creek ford that crossed the lonely country lane near Garden of the Gods. About half way across the creek, he saw a ghostly lady dressed in white rising out of the water. To his absolute horror, the lady jumped out of the water and landed behind him on the horse.

The apparition grabbed him around the waist and started speaking in tongues. The startled horse and rider both tried to dislodge the phantom lady. The more they struggled, the tighter the ghost held on and the louder she rambled. The horse was running at full speed when finally they reached a gully and the unwanted, ghostly passenger was thrown off the horse. After a short while, both horse and rider made it back home.

The next morning, the young man's mother found the horse in the barnyard fully saddled and bridled. When she went to her son's room to ask him about it, she discovered him hiding in the corner unable to speak. He had been severely traumatized and was still in a panic. After much questioning, the young man finally told what had happened the previous night. Just one week later the young man was dead. Many superstitious people in the area thought that the apparition of the young lady was an omen of impending death. It is widely believe that the young man died of fright.

Good Hope Cemetery is located near Karbers Ridge at coordinates 37.57394 and -88.36532.

Illinois Iron Furnace

Shawnee National Forest

According to legend, before the Civil War slaves were used to fill the Illinois Iron Furnace with iron ore and charcoal to make pig iron. During one very hot day, one of the slaves was overcome by the intolerable white hot heat from the top of the furnace and fell head first into the inferno and was burnt to ash. It is said that the spirit of this unfortunate slave would be see in and around the old iron furnace screaming in  agony for many years afterwards. The Illinois Iron Furnace is located in the Shawnee National Forest near Elizabethtown, Illinois. It is the only remaining iron furnace structure in Illinois.

The Illinois Iron Furnace was built in 1837. Some of the pig iron smelted there was used at the Mound City Naval Shipyards to clad the gunboats they built. The furnace fell into disuse in 1861. It worked sporadically throughout the 1870s and 1880s. Then, in the 1930s, members of the Civilian Conservation Corps dismantled most of the furnace. The stones were used to build the embankments of the Hog Thief Creek bridge, so what stands today was rebuilt in 1967.

To get to Illinois Iron Furnace from Harrisburg take Illinois Route 34/145 south 6 miles, then continue on Highway 34 south for 16 miles to Highway 146. Go east on Highway 146 for 3.5 miles to Iron Furnace road, turn north and follow the directional signs to the historic site.

1811 New Madrid Earthquake, Lost and Never Found

Hardin County

The earthquake of December 16, 1811 made many changes in Hardin County. The entire topography of the county changed almost overnight. Hills appeared where there were once valleys and valleys became hills. Many land features were lost forever.

About two miles east of the village of Lamb, there was a cave known as Brown's Cave. During the five days that the New Madrid Earthquake of 1811 lasted, the ground at the cave was pushed up so far that the cave was now located on top of a hill. The opening of the cave actually ran straight down into the ground. The cave was then renamed Brown's Hole.

Before the 1811 earthquake, there was a sink hole known as the Lead Hole. The settlers of the area would go to this hole to dig out the soft lead to make bullets for their muzzle loading rifles and pistols. After the earthquake the Lead Hole was nowhere to be found.

At the mouth of Haney Creek where it runs into the Ohio River was a sandbar known as the Big Sandbar. The sandbar reached almost all the way to the Kentucky side of the river. Settlers and trappers wanting to cross the river between Kentucky and Illinois would cross at this point. After the 1811 earthquake this sandbar disappeared under the raging waters of the Ohio River.

Duff's Cave was located near the Little Saline River. This cave was named after John Duff, a veteran of the Revolutionary War. Duff decided to become an outlaw like the infamous Squire Potts and James Ford. Fed up with the criminal actions, Duff's neighbors dressed up like Indians and attacked and burned Duff's tavern and inn. They then dragged Duff outside and hanged him. Duff's Cave disappeared after the 1811 earthquake and is now called Duff's Hill. Legend states that the ghost of John Duff still haunts the hilltop where he was hanged.

Cave Hole located at Cave-In-Rock was the location of an underground stream called the Sinks. According to legend, the underground cavern ran for two miles. After the 1811 earthquake the underground passage was completely blocked off.

Counterfeiters would use Bigsby Cave as a center of operations. The cave was located in Hooven Hollow. To get into the main chamber of the cave, a person would have to climb down a ladder. The counterfeiters hid molds for making coins, gold and other treasure in the cave. A giant retarded man would often run errands for the counterfeiters. Shortly after the earthquake it was noticed that entrance to Bigsby Cave and the retarded giant were both missing. It's believed that if you could find the entrance to Bigsby Cave you might also find the counterfeiters treasure and the skeleton of the retarded giant guarding it.

The Bloody Harpe Brothers

Cave-in-Rock and Potts Spring

In the late 1790s, the Harpe brothers, Micajah, known as Big Harpe and his brother, Wiley, known as Little Harpe left a bloody trail of at least 28 people in Tennessee, Kentucky and Southern Illinois.

After the especially brutal murders of Major William Love, Moses Stegall's wife and baby, the Harpes were hunted down by a posse of men lead by Moses Stegall. In the ensuing chase, Little Harpe escaped but Big Harpe was shot and captured. Big Harpe was shot through the body and was losing a lot of blood. As he was lying helpless on the ground, Moses Stegall took a knife and severed Big Harpes head from his body. Stegall took the head and placed it in the fork of a nearby tree. The location of this revolting, and gruesome head was near Highland Lick in Henderson County, Kentucky. Today it is known as Harpes Head Road.

Little Harpe hid out in an area known as Natchez and took up with another highwayman known as Mason. There was a large reward offered for the head of Mason. One dark night when all the other bandits were away getting drunk, Little Harpe took the opportunity and killed Mason. After killing Mason, Little Harpe cut off his head and placed it in a bag. He took the head to Natchez to claim the reward money, but was recognized for who he was. The sheriff arrested him on the spot. After a quick trial, Little Harpe was condemned to death and then hanged.

Hick's Dome

Hicks

Hick's Dome in Hardin County has a long history of strange happenings. Some people believe that Hick's Dome was created in ancient times when a large celestial body broke apart in Earth's atmosphere leaving a string of craters along a latitude of roughly 38 degrees north between Rose Dome in Kansas, five sites in Missouri and Hick's Dome in Southern Illinois. Other people theorize that Hick's Dome was created by volcanic activity which created fluorspar deposits in the region.

During its recorded history, Hick's Dome has been noted for various earth lights. Earth lights are known as spook lights, ghost lights, corpse lights and will-of-the-wisps. While there is probably a scientific explanation for these mysterious lights, most people are quick to associate them with supernatural happenings.

Many old-time travelers during the horse and buggy days saw what they thought was someone on foot carrying a lantern in the woods. When the lights would emerge from the tree line, the travelers would be terrified when they noticed that the lights were not lanterns being carried, but were in fact only the lights themselves bobbing just a few feet above the ground.

Southern Illinois Indians would avoid the area in and around Hick's Dome if at all possible due to these variously colored nocturnal lights. The Indians associated them with evil spirits. The sightings of these strange lights have been the source of many tales of spirits, ghosts and sometimes aliens and UFOs.

What is the source and cause of the mysterious earth lights of Hick's Dome? We don't know, but we dare you to go some dark and lonely night to discover for yourself.

Hicks Dome is located at N 37.53144 and W -88.36837.

Dead or Hypnotized?

Cave-In-Rock

Henry Blakley (1860-1912) had mastered the art of hypnotism. His talent made him very well known throughout Southern Illinois and the surrounding area. Mr. Blakley believed that he could communicate with people beyond the grave. He would light candles and place them in the center of a table to conduct séances.

Once the atmosphere was suitable for conducting the spirits he would blow out the kerosene lamp and have everyone sit around the table gazing into the lit candles. The table would jump and make all manner of sounds as Blakley asked questions about dead friends and relatives.

Mr. Blakley was such a powerful hypnotist that he feared that he might accidentally hypnotize himself and be mistaken for dead and his family would accidentally bury him alive. He instructed his family that when he died, he wanted a 2-inch pipe run from the top of the ground down into his casket, so he could breathe. Mr. Blakley further instructed his family that someone was to go to the cemetery each day for three days to be sure that he was dead. The family faithfully carried out his final wishes. It seems that Mr. Blakley was really dead after all.

Many teenagers would venture to the grave late at night and drop coins down the airshaft onto Mr. Blakely's dead face. The air shaft to Mr. Blakely's coffin was eventually capped off to prevent the emission of noxious fumes (corpse gas) from the body that was actually dead and decaying and not buried alive.

Premature burial alarms of the era consisted of a metal tube connecting the coffin to the above ground fresh air. This tube also contained a cable attached to a bell that a person who was unfortunate enough to be buried alive would tug on to attract the attention of the graveyard caretaker (this is the origin of the term "Graveyard Shift").

IMPROVED BURIAL-CASE US Patent No. 81,437 Issued: August 25, 1868

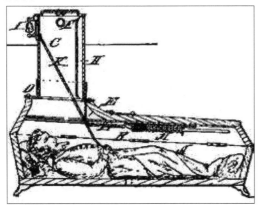

Inventor: Franz Vester, Newark, NJ

"The nature of this invention consists in placing on the lid of the coffin, and directly over the face of the body laid therein, a square tube, which extends from the coffin up through and over the surface of the grave, said tube containing a ladder and a cord, one end of said cord being placed in the hand of the person laid in the coffin, and the other end of said cord being attached to a bell (this is where the saying "Saved by the Bell" came from) on the top of the square tube, so that, should a person be interred ere life is extinct, he can, on recovery to consciousness, ascend from the grave and the coffin by the ladder; or, if not able to ascend by said ladder, ring the bell, thereby giving an alarm, and thus save himself from premature burial and death; and if, on inspection, life is extinct, the tube is withdrawn, the sliding door closed, and the tube used for a similar purpose.

Henry Blakley is buried at Mt. Zion Cemetery. It is located at N 37.551994 and W -88.180033

— ● — ● — ● —

Hamp Mine Monster

Rose Creek

Hardin County has its fair share of strange happenings and the Hamp Mine located near the Rose Creek valley is no exception. The Hamp Mine in the late 1960s was the location of various sightings of what became known as the Hamp Mine Monster. This crypto-creature was described as being a hairy man-like biped that stood about ten feet tall.

Several area residents reported seeing this Bigfoot or Sasquatch lurking around the Hamp Mine late at night. When spotted, the creature would lumber off into the mine. One night, a Hardin County Deputy Sheriff was on routine patrol near the mine when he spotted the monster. The deputy was a very large and intimidating man, but the monster was even bigger and more intimidating. The deputy and monster locked eyes and then the monster took off toward the mine. Grabbing his 30-06 rifle, the deputy started tracking the monster down the dark and lonely mine road.

After a short distance the deputy sighted the monster as it took off at a run towards the mine pit. The monster jumped over the edge and disappeared into the darkness. As the deputy cautiously stepped closer to the edge of the mine pit, he shined his flashlight into the pit hoping to locate the monster. The deputy was mystified when the beam on his flashlight only showed that the only thing in the pit was mine equipment. There was no sight of the monster.

Where did the monster go? No one knows for sure. There are still sightings of Sasquatch like monsters in Hardin County to this day.

The Hamp Mine is located on private property in a wooded area off 1100N, west of 250E, south of Karbers Ridge Road.

The Gates of Hell

By Tracey Todd Bragg
Rosiclare

On a lonely narrow road in Hardin County, near the town of Rosiclare is a single cemetery, small and dark. Divided into two parts, the old and the new, by a wrought iron fence, this cemetery has sparked feelings of unease and fear in many local residents. Moore Cemetery, or The Gates of Hell as the kids call it, sits on the side of the road known as High Water Road. The newer part of the cemetery, surrounded by the fence, has seen burials as late as the 1970s, the old part, who knows?

Many of the graves sit either marked with a small wooden cross, uncarved sandstone markers, or not marked at all. This is the part of the cemetery that has created whispers and rumors among the youth of the county, spurring some to unwisely venture there at night, some regretting the visit.

Stories have been told of teenagers, thinking it fun to roam the cemetery, upturning the wooden crosses, and taunting whatever spirits may lurk there. Some have wished they never went. Some have claimed to have had rocks thrown at them while at the cemetery, some have heard unexplainable noises, and others had the sides of their cars beaten on by no visible person or entity as they pulled away. At least four youths in recent years have experienced events after their nights of fun that made them sure something, possibly evil, had followed them home.

One chooses to ignore the hauntings, laughing it off as nothing, despite the fact he can describe what exactly followed him (the father of an entire family that is buried there) and the vicious things it whispers in his mind for him to do. Another refuses to discuss it, stopping anyone at the very beginning of any story or question regarding the occurrences. Another was very willing to tell someone who would believe him.

After a night at the cemetery, Joe (not his real name) was fearful. His friends had been calling to the spirits, daring them to do something to them, turning the cross-markers upside down. Joe did not participate, but he was there nonetheless. For the next 6 months, he felt as if he were living in hell. He immediately felt a weight, an uneasy feeling, come over him that would not go away even after he got home. He spent many restless, sleepless nights, dealing with being touched, his bed shaking, and the sensation that something had climbed into the bed with him.

The more he tried to ignore these events, the more intense they became. Five and six times a night, he was awoken by some incident that kept him shaken. The only way to stop the events was to acknowledge them.

A dark shadow figure was seen in the house on many occasions, a friend saw it numerous times in the corner of Joe's room while he slept. Joe remembers sitting on his futon one evening, talking to a friend, when he felt a breeze go past, then felt and watched the cushion next to him go down as if something was sitting next to him. He jumped up and went into the living room, catching a glimpse of the dark shadow person dart out of the room and across the hall. His dogs often would bark at the ceiling, following something around that wasn't there. His mother was awakened by a scream in her ear in the middle of the night when everyone was sound asleep.

Joe no longer lives in that house, and the hauntings have stopped. Or at least he hopes they have.

— ● — ● — ● —

The Night the Sky was Moving

By Tracey Todd Bragg
Cave-In-Rock

A friend and I used to love to camp. As long as the night temperatures were above 50 degrees, we were in a tent or camping in the van somewhere with a big fire, tunes on the radio, and checking out the stars.

One particularly warm October night in 2008, we decided to load up the van (commercial work van type) and head to Tower Rock Campground near Cave-In-Rock. It was one of our favorite places and usually not crowded. We chose our favorite spot, one near the entrance that had a clear, open view of the sky. We were just enjoying being able to relax, outside in the night air. It was getting late, but the sky was so beautiful and full of stars that we couldn't give up the view for sleep. We needed this calm after a long work week.

My friend had walked to the east side of our campsite and was standing just staring at the stars, when he finally said rather urgently "Tracey, come here!" I walked cautiously, unsure of what was waiting for me. Knowing him, he would have done the same if he'd just seen a mountain lion in the trees. He pointed to the sky and said "look at that star, it's moving." Of course, my first reaction was that the object was a plane or helicopter. But it just 'did not seem like either. We watched it for some time, moving from one direction to another, slowly at times, more rapidly at others. We soon noticed another light moving just above it in the sky. And then another and another.

We really 'were not sure what to make of it all. It was unlikely to have that many planes or helicopters floating about in such haphazard patterns in the sky. Eventually these lights worked their way above us, and then to the west side of the camp. These lights were very high up, more like stars, but moving. As they made their way to the west, we began to notice many more moving stars, or lights.

We had been watching for over an hour and we now found ourselves showing each other new moving objects that we 'could not explain. We soon began to notice that the lights were moving in unison, as if they were attached to the same object. Some remained just small, single lights; while others were three or four lights moving together. We noticed differing speeds of movement, some very slow, some very fast. Some would move toward one of the larger groupings that were moving together and then turn at a 90 degree angle and shoot into another direction. It was then that we realized that these were not planes or helicopters or weather balloons or any other explanations we had heard for moving lights and objects in the sky! There 'were not just a few. We estimated hundreds of them.

We began to be able to decipher shapes of some objects. Two in particular were identical, except one was lit with approximately 20 lights, the other was dark, no lights at all, yet we could see it tumbling, end over end across the sky. These were very large, and nearly bell shaped, with a pointed end. The unlit object continued to tumble across the sky until it left our field of vision beyond the tree line. The lighted object remained in the sky, moving slowly in what seemed very deliberate directions, sideways, and turning direction at least once.

Other shapes that 'were not nearly as clear seemed to have lights moving out from them from time to time. The single lights moved in all directions. Some would start out in a direction very slowly and then suddenly accelerate, coming near another light and then angling away.

We watched these lights and shapes for at least four hours. At one point, my friend got out his mag light flashlight and shined it up into the sky. One of the lights brightened up in response and then faded. Thinking it just a fluke, he did it again. The light once again, brightened and glowed, then faded, as if answering our call.

At this point, I decided I had had enough. It was scary. I quickly grabbed up whatever we needed to go in for the night, and barreled into the back of the van, closing and locking the doors. It was one thing to watch whatever it was, it was another if it was responding to us.

We never saw this again. Not to this extent, never with hundreds of lights moving about the sky. 'I am not sure 'I would want to.

Ghosts, Werewolves, and Banshees

Lamb

The village of Lamb had what was called the Ghost of Blind Hollow. Dr. George Stevens was a prominent physician that came to Hardin County after the Civil War. The doctor had a very successful medical practice and was often seen in his buggy going on house calls. One homestead that Dr. Stevens was seen going to two or three times a week was that of a widow woman and her six children. Many townsfolk began to gossip that something must be going on between the doctor and the widow. One man decided that he would be the one to protect the good name of the widow.

The man called on Dr. Stevens and told him what many in the village thought was going on. Angry words soon came to blows. Dr. Stevens was married and had five children. He was not about to let rumor and innuendo ruin his medical practice and reputation.

Dr. Stevens pulled a gun on the man and shot at him. The man ran for his life.

Tempers were still running hot on June 27, 1896, when Dr. Stevens was shot and killed by ambush near Blind Hollow while returning from the widow's house to tend one of her sick children. No one was ever arrested for the murder.

For many years after the murder, travelers along the road through Blind Hollow would report sightings of a man riding a buggy or horse. When they got closer the ghostly man and buggy would fade away into thin air.

A trail running from Frayser's Ferry on the Ohio River to the Salt Works at Equality was known for sightings of the Werewolf of Brookmire Hill. Many salt merchants were murdered along this trail. Travelers would tell stories of meeting a ghostly dog in the middle of the trail at Brookmire Hill. The dog seemed to be friendly and calm until approached. Whenever someone would come near to it, the dog would become vicious and attack. When the traveler would kick at the dog, his boot would pass right though the animal without making contact.

For over 150 years, a story of the Banshee has been known in the village of Lamb. It all started in the early 1800's in Ireland when Hugh McConnell saw a little girl with her clothes on fire running out of a church house. Before he could catch the girl she ran back into the flaming building and burned to death. The girl's spirit became a Banshee and her screams would warn the McConnell family of an impending death in the family.

In 1811, McConnell and his bride settled in Hardin County and started raising a family. One of his daughters married a man by the name of Jonathan Brown. Whenever a Brown family descendant died, the wailing cry of the Banshee would be heard. When Old Granny Brown was dying she tried to fight off the Banshee as it tried to get in bed with her. It was thought that only the dying could actually see the Banshee and only the family members could hear it.

Lying in State

By Tracey Todd Bragg
Rosiclare

I felt that familiar uneasiness in my stomach. The woman had just told me her father had laid in rest beneath those double windows. Those double windows where one of the encounters had occurred. I was a teen working at a local restaurant, and we were recounting ghost stories during a slow time. I discussed the house I had lived in until I was nearly 10 years old, only to find there may have been a very good reason for the stories.

Yes, I was young, but I remember some things about the house. I didn't like being in the house alone, it didn't feel right. I'm sensitive, suppose I was from birth, and that house triggered those odd feelings I get. In the basement, there was an old coal room, where coal was stored after being loaded through the coal shoot until it was needed for heating. The house had long been converted to natural gas, and the room was then used for storage. I didn't like that room. Even with the light on, I would not go in that room. I remember standing at the doorway when Mom would be getting a box or some old toy we wanted, but I would not go in. I did not like that room.

I've heard many stories over the years about that house. My dad worked at a quarry, and came home covered in lime dust. He always came in the back door, heading straight down the basement stairs to the small shower stall to clean up before supper. One evening, Mom, my sister, and I weren't home when he arrived. During his shower, he distinctly heard footsteps in the kitchen above, and he leaned out of the shower, calling for Mom, thinking we were home. No answer; because we weren't there. When we did get home, I remember Dad telling Mom the story and was visibly shaken. Apparently, this wasn't the only occurrence. Other instances included him hearing a ball roll down the basement steps and land, only to find there was no ball.

The story that shook me when the woman told me about her father's wake involved one of my older brothers. While visiting one summer, he was asleep on a pallet on the floor under those double windows (we only had two bedrooms; one for my parents, the other for my little sister and I). He was awakened during the night to footsteps coming across the living room floor; very loud and distinct footsteps that stopped right at his head. When he looked up, no one was there. He covered his head with the sheet and slept fitfully the rest of the night. Slept fitfully under the double window where the woman's father had laid in state many years before.

I have been told these are only a couple of stories of the many unusual and unexplainable events in that house. We moved when I was in the fourth grade. Once after we had moved, Mom was talking to our former neighbor who informed her that immediately after we moved, the ghost moved to their house. They had never experienced anything in their house before, and suddenly, they heard footsteps and had other weird occurrences. My mom recently spoke with the current resident of our former neighbor's house who confirmed the ghost is still there.

— ● — ● — ● —

The Legend of Potts Inn

By Tracey Todd Bragg
Potts Hill

River Pirates, the Harpes, Mason and Bixby; these are the stories that come from this little community along the Ohio River. But no recounting of tales from Hardin County would be complete without the Legend of Billy Potts and Potts' Inn.

Along the Ford's Ferry Road, near what is now known as Illinois Route 1, sat the infamous inn; sometimes referred to as a tavern, as many such establishments in the mid-1800s provided not only a place for weary travelers to lay their heads at night, but food and drink, and occasionally the company of a young lady. The road was a path for many traveling north, crossing the Ohio on a ferry operated by Jim Ford. Ford was less than a respectable citizen, conducting business of a more criminal kind with Potts, the spoils split between them. As legend goes, Ford would size up the travelers, determining the worth of the prey and sending ahead a messenger to Potts at the inn. Billy would welcome the wayfarer to his establishment, feed him, and  provide stabling for the horses, all the while telling of a wonderful spring just to the back of the inn.

The water was cold and refreshing, especially on hot summer nights in the muggy heat of the Ohio valley. Potts proudly showed his guest the fount, offering a taste from the drinking ladle already present. As the unsuspecting traveler would bend down to drink, Billy attacked, murdering without conscience, and taking possession of the deceased's valuables and money. Whoever escaped the escapades of the Harpe brothers in Kentucky was fair game for Ford and Potts.

Billy Potts had a son. Some say he took the lessons of murder and robbery his father taught him to other parts of the country, others that he went a legitimate way, but both stories conclude he moved away from Hardin County during his young adulthood. At a point some years later, he decided it was time to return and visit his home place. Arriving at the ferry, age and a beard made him unrecognizable to his father's business partner who mistook him for a wealthy traveler. He sent a message to Potts to await the arrival of their next conquest. Potts proceeded to charm his guest, also unable to recognize his own son. The son decided it would be a good joke to go along, only to spring on his father his identity at the last minute. His last minute came a minute sooner than he expected, and he went to meet his maker by the same hand as so many others.

The next day, another traveler who was an acquaintance of the son arrived at the inn asking for his friend. Potts, bewildered, went to the shallow place he had hidden the body, exhumed it, and to his great distress identified the body of his own son by a birthmark not noticed soon enough to prevent the killing of his own offspring.

The story of Billy Potts usually ends here, no explanation for where he went, what he did or how he punished himself for such a travesty. At least, the story ends for Billy. Despite the lack of documentation of the existence of Potts or his activities, due in part to the loss of the courthouse in Hardin County twice to fire, the legend is accepted as fact; as well as the evil presence in the area where the long-gone inn stood. Many have visited the bottom of the bluff where it stood, only to recount that they would never return. They believe something evil exists there. Does Billy Potts still walk the ground, lamenting his terrible crimes and murder of his son?

Geology and Ghosts

By Tracey Todd Bragg
Hardin County

Why does it seem some areas are so active with the paranormal? One theory rests in the geology of an area. Many paranormal researchers believe that certain minerals, particularly limestone and quartz, enhance the activities in a location. Quartz has properties that make it piezoelectric: that is, able to produce an electric charge across crystal faces when placed under a strain or stress. The Tectonic Strain

Theory states that stresses in the crust of the earth could result in electromagnetic disturbances near the surface. Quartz can also be electrically charged and scientists have developed quartz glass capable of storing digital data.

Hardin County is one area that has seen more than its share of ghostly and ghoulish activity. Of all the research and interviews I have done, Hardin seems to have a wealth of stories. Areas such as Hicks Dome, Pleasant Hill Cemetery and Potts Inn carry legends and lore that have been passed down from generation to generation. What is the cause? Settled in 1800, it certainly has age and history to add to potential activity, but Hardin County also has several geologic characteristics that make it prime for paranormal activity. Hardin County's terrain is made up of a great number of minerals, namely quartz, limestone, and fluorite. Fluorite, the state mineral of Illinois, can be fluorescent. It is also a halide mineral and bears a negative charge. Limestone, like quartz, has certain electromagnetic properties. Interestingly, limestone is a sedimentary rock that often made up of the bone fragments of small marine animals.

Another source or conductor of energy is water. Water is used to produce electricity in many places, providing power to great numbers of people. Water also conducts electricity, primarily through the minerals and impurities that it contains. Hardin County rests on the banks of the Ohio River, largest tributary of the Mississippi River. Many small creeks branch off of the Ohio throughout the county, and, in some cases, under it. Moving water seems to be the primary catalyst, and the Ohio River is certainly moving water.

Paranormal researchers feel that spirit activity is electrical by nature and anything with energy can be used by spirits as a source of the energy needed to manifest. Manifestations can occur as apparitions, lights, or even smells and sounds. Many have told of summer nights walking along rural roads, only to be spooked by the mineral lights bouncing just inches above the ground. Some think them to be the spirits of ancestors and settlers long gone. Others attribute the activity to the high mineral content of the soil, coupled with the humid climate and a slight electrical charge in the air. Whatever may cause it, spooky is probably a mild word.

Another interesting feature, mentioned before, is Hicks Dome. This geologic feature is a crypto volcano—a volcano that never emerged through the surface. Igneous rock and minerals such as thorium make up the mound. Rumors abound about ancient Native American burial grounds dotting the dome. Ancient Indians may have actually avoided the area, their superstitions leading them to believe it was inhabited by evil spirits. If not haunted, it is certainly impressive.

Next time you hear of a certain area being highly haunted, ask yourself: what is under foot?

— ● — ● — ● —

Conversations with a Ghost

By Tracey Todd Bragg
Shetlerville

My grandpa, Clyde Damron, was a fox hunter, as were many men in Hardin County in the mid-1900s. Fox hunting required the use of some type of hound, and between hunting trips, the dogs required exercise. Grandpa was proud of his beagles, and took good care of them, letting them run whenever he got the chance. The farm was an excellent place for the dogs, the expanse of wilderness surrounding it ideal to stretch their legs and practice their tracking skills.

Grandpa kept his dogs in a pen near the garden at the farm at Shetlerville. Founded in 1866, Shetlerville was once a town with businesses and family homes. At one time, it was the largest shipping port in Hardin County, essential for a community that relied on the Ohio River for transportation and commerce. By the 1940s and '50s, much of the town stores had closed and houses were moved to nearby

Rosiclare. What remained were a few farms, one of which was home to my grandparents.

On a warm evening, as was his practice, Grandpa went to the garden to let the dogs run. Whenever he ran the dogs, he would remain in the yard, squatted down, listening to them as they sprinted through the woods, howling and barking. The garden area was fairly distant from the house, down past the barn, and Grandpa was alone as he listened. Or so he thought. After he released the dogs and was in position, he heard someone walk up behind him, but remained squatted facing the woods. "What ya doin'?" my Grandpa heard someone ask, and without turning he merely replied, "Just letting my dogs run." For a short period of time they chatted, about the dogs, the weather, things that men-folk generally spoke of. He continued to listen for his dogs, lest they get too far and he need go after them, while conversing with the unseen stranger. After a moment of quiet, Grandpa finally stood and turned to face his visitor… only to find he was still alone.

My mother and Grandma were in another part of the yard hanging clothes on the line. They saw someone run into the house, so fast they couldn't see who it was, the screen door slamming shut. Curious, they went inside only to find my Grandpa sitting at the table, visibly shaken and he wouldn't move from that spot for a very long time. No one else had been in the yard or garden. No one had come up to the house. No one ever questioned what Grandpa heard, nor would he speak of it.

The farm house burned down some time later and my grandparents moved "to town" (Rosiclare). They kept the barn and surrounding area, as well as the dogs. Grandpa spent very little time with his dogs in the years to come. In my lifetime, I don't recall him ever fox hunting, he had given it up. For many years after, when I was a child, I remember Grandpa saying he had to go feed the dogs "before it got dark."

Did Shetlerville ever really cease to exist? Or just shifted to another realm?

Samuel Mason – Outlaw Extraordinaire

By Tracey Todd Bragg
Cave-in-Rock

On the banks of the Ohio River, near the town of Cave-In-Rock, is the namesake of the town. Often called The Cave Hole, or simply The Cave by locals, it was discovered in 1729 by French explorer M. DeLery. The name he gave it, Caverne Dans LeRoc, sounds so much more romantic than the deadly history it holds. Its 55 foot wide entrance is easily seen by passing boats on the river, and to the rear of the cave, a 100 foot vertical fissure through the top creates a natural chimney, making the cave technically inhabitable. In the late 1700s, one man took advantage of this den, to the great misfortune of many who stopped by.

Samuel Mason was born in Norfolk, Virginia to an honorable family. As Captain of the Ohio County Militia, Virginia State Forces during the Revolutionary War, he was given command of Fort Henry. Following the war, Mason served in Pennsylvania as a Justice of the Peace, followed by an appointment as an Associate Judge in Kentucky. Credits such as these would lead one to believe Mason would become the victim of our story. In truth, Samuel Mason became one of the most infamous river pirates the Midwest had ever seen.

What would make such a seemingly respectable man become a cutthroat and robber? Records of his life after the Revolutionary War are nonexistent, but one could suppose the harsh conditions of living on the frontier may have led to his life of crime. Around 1790, Mason moved his family and settled on Diamond Island, a land mass in the Ohio River west of Henderson, Kentucky. This was where his transgressions began. As travelers sailed west on the Ohio, looking for a new life in the territories yet unsettled, pirates found them vulnerable in the rocky and sometimes shallow waters. Whether through ambush or deception, they often found themselves liberated of their valuables and often their lives.

Mason moved his base of operations to the shelter of Cave-In-Rock. A sign posted that stated "Liquor Vault and House of Entertainment" proved desirable by boaters, who would dock their boats for the night, enjoying a meal and shelter. While their guests slept, Mason and his band of outlaws would pilfer the boats, taking inventory of what rewards could be reaped. The next morning, as they rounded the bend of the river, the crew of the boats would be ambushed and robbed. A quick slice to the belly, the deceased would be filled with rocks and hurled overboard to the bottom of the river. Of interesting note, Mason was briefly acquainted with the Harpe brothers, Micajah and Wiley, the murderous bandits from Kentucky.

In 1799, Mason was expelled from Southern Illinois by a band of bounty hunter vigilantes from Kentucky known as the Exterminators. Mason was arrested in what is now southeast Missouri, but escaped. A generous bounty on his head became too tempting to his gang, and he was beheaded by two of them, one of which was Wiley Harpe, traveling under an alias. When Mason's head was delivered to authorities, they discovered who Harpe was and promptly arrested him.

Samuel Mason had become one of the most notorious criminals of his time. The films *Davy Crockett and the River Pirates* and *How the West Was Won* were both not only filmed at Cave-In-Rock, but also portrayed characters loosely based on Mason. The television show *In Search of History*, on The History Channel, also told the story of Mason in the episode "River Pirates."

Jackson County

Mystery of the Woodlawn Sarcophagus

Carbondale

Located on the east side of a hill at Woodlawn Cemetery in Carbondale, Illinois, there is a stone sarcophagus raised a few feet above the ground. The sarcophagus and the two pedestals it rests on were carved from Boskeydell sandstone. Any inscriptions on the stone have long since been obliterated by the ravages of time.

There are several stories about who the sarcophagus contains. The best known and most believable one to me is that it contains the remains of a Confederate woman from Vicksburg, Mississippi, who moved to Carbondale with her husband shortly after the Civil War. She

hated the Union so much that she made her husband promise never to bury her in Union soil. When she died, the promise was kept by raising the sarcophagus a few feet above the ground. Some people believe that this was done simply because the ground was too hard to dig the grave to bury the woman.

One other version involves Lieutenant Colonel John Mills, a Union soldier who died just after the Civil War. The Colonel's family sealed him in the sarcophagus. Upon learning that a Confederate soldier was to be buried in the cemetery, the family removed the Colonel's body, leaving the sarcophagus empty. Personally, I do not believe this version because the sarcophagus is very short and doubt it could accommodate a full size man.

Woodlawn Cemetery is located at 405 E. Main Street in Carbondale, Illinois.

The Old Carbondale Train Depot

Carbondale

Carbondale Main Street asked the Little Egypt Ghost Society to conduct a ghost hunt at the old Carbondale Train Depot as one of their Halloween events. Several months prior, we had conducted an initial investigation of this historic location.

There have been reported sightings of passengers dressed in clothes from the 1880s boarding a train at the Old Carbondale Train Depot. The sightings are an example of residual ghost activity, the kind normally found in Carbondale, in which spirits are just going on with their everyday lives. In residual ghost activity, they do not realize they are dead, and they are not really paying any attention to the outside world. As far as they are aware, it is still 1882.

The Old Carbondale Train Station was constructed by the Illinois Central Railroad (ICRR) in 1903. The depot on Carbondale's Town

Square served as the city's primary point of departure and arrival well into the 1940s. The depot was constructed of brick and limestone with a slate roof at a cost of $15,900 and contained baggage rooms, ticket and telegraph offices, and waiting rooms.

The first addition, the Van Noy Lunch Room Building, was completed in 1905. It stood about 40 feet north of the depot. In 1925, a mail room enclosure measuring 20 feet by 40 feet was added to the depot. In 1930, the baggage room at the north end of the building was expanded. The mail enclosure was widened at this time as well, and the separate men's and women's waiting areas were remodeled to provide general waiting and depot offices. A total of $4,100 was spent on these 1930 additions.

There were 12 people present for our Halloween ghost hunt at the old train depot. Just before we started the EVP session, the PX device we were using said "LIGHT" and then the lights in the office went off. No one was in the office at the time. We used our short list (25 questions) of questions for the EVP session in the office where the lights went out. We got responses to a couple of the questions, but what they were will have to be determined through further analysis. During one of the EVP responses, several members of the group stated they heard something "strange" and the floor felt like it was vibrating the way it would if a train was passing by. No trains passed the station at any time during the EVP session.

The PX device was silent for over an hour until just before our EVP session when it said a few things that made sense in the context of where we were and what was going on.

It is very common for batteries and other electrical items to be drained of power during paranormal investigations. As we were starting our EVP session trying to make contact with "Allen," all the power in the train depot went off. In fact, all the power in the west side of Carbondale went off at that same time. We continued our EVP session and other activities for some time when we decided to call it a night and pack up our equipment. After we stowed all our equipment and made preparations to leave, the power came back on in the main office area where we were standing. The alarm system should have sounded off 30 seconds after the power was restored, but did not. The rep from Carbondale Main Street said that really creeped her out.

At least we warned her that something like this would probably happen.

The Old Carbondale Train Depot is located at 131 S. Illinois Avenue in Carbondale, Illinois.

— ● — ● — ● —

The Haunted Video Game

Carbondale

The Cellar in Carbondale is your typical hole in the wall bar. What makes this place so special is that it is the home of the very best Bloody Mary in town. The Cellar is also the home of a haunted video game.

During the Halloween season, we conduct historic ghost tours of Carbondale. While researching some of the historic places near the Illinois Central railroad tracks, we decided to stop by The Cellar and ask the owner if there were any hauntings in his bar. He told us that there have been some reports of paranormal activity. The door to the ladies restroom is known to lock of its own accord. Many times employees have been asked to check to see if everything is OK in the ladies room only to discover that the door is locked with no one inside. It got so bad that the door had to be removed from the door frame and replaced.

Each morning when the bar owner would open up, he noticed that the "hunting" video game had been unplugged. Each and every morning it was the same. Finally, one day the owner asked the night janitor about it. The janitor replied that he unplugged it every night. When the owner asked him why he did it, he sheepishly replied that he was afraid of it. He said the game would make strange noises and would even call him by name!

The Cellar is located at 101 W. Monroe Street in Carbondale, Illinois.

— ● — ● — ● —

The Sound Core Ghosts

Carbondale

This single-story commercial building, which is divided into two stores, has been the site of numerous businesses since its original construction in the 1890's. A circa 1900 photograph reveals the building originally exhibited an elaborate stamped metal façade.

That photograph also shows the south half of the building was occupied by Booney Furniture & Undertakers and the north half contained the Peak & Storm grocery store. Between 1906 and 1913, the original metal surface was removed and the façade re-bricked. A c. 1912 photograph shows the building's elaborate pressed tin façade removed and a modest brick façade in its place.

At that time, the south half of the building housed the Book Store, and the north half contained the "E Five 7 Ten Cent Store." By the late 1930's, the building's façade had been covered yet again with glazed tile. A c. 1940 photograph revels the north half of the building housed the "Carbondale Café," which displayed a large, overhanging sign

advertising the café's "candy and sodas." Both buildings appear to have been re-bricked again in the 1950's and 60's.

Today, this building is considered haunted by many. Employees and customers of Sound Core have reported unexplained cold spots in certain areas of the building along with the feeling of being watched by unseen eyes. Some females have stated that "something" touched them when no one was nearby. It is believed that these paranormal events date back to the days when this building was a funeral home. The son of the funeral home owner was a spoiled playboy who liked ladies, booze and money. On one summer day, the owner's son was partying at Giant City Park with some lady friends. The liquor was flowing freely and the partiers became quite drunk. While hiking along one of the bluffs, the young man fell to his death. His dead body was brought back to the funeral home that his family owned for embalming and the funeral. It is believed that his spirit never left the building.

The Sound Core is located at 122 S. Illinois Avenue in Carbondale, Illinois.

— ● — ● — ● —

DCI Biologicals

Carbondale

Treasury Secretary A. W. Mellon the old Carbondale Post Office was in 1931. Over the years it's served as a hub of activity for the city both as a post office and F.B.I, offices, then later as DCI Biologicals.

Over the years this former postal building acquired a reputation of being haunted. It is said that a postmaster died at his desk in the building. The ghostly image of this long dead postmaster has been seen on the second floor at various times. Employees of DCI  Biological have reported being afraid to be in the building alone at night. A former manager of the facility said that she did not believe in ghosts until she had worked in the building for awhile and experienced ghostly activity firsthand. A night janitor quit his job after being frightened by intense and frequent poltergeist activity. The janitor had been working alone one night in the basement when he was locked into a closet by an unseen force and a chair then flew across the room and lodged behind the door effectively trapping the terrified janitor until morning when other employees arrived for work.

Many employees have said that doors mysteriously open and shut of their own volition. A radio will turn on and off at night with on one near it. There is a beautiful chandelier in the lobby that will swing back and forth at certain times. One employee took a photograph of the chandelier and later noticed the ghostly image of a lady in a white flowing gown nearby. The ghostly lady has been seen at various times floating around the lobby near the chandelier.

Several employees have reported hearing the sounds of a telephone ringing in the basement. What makes this strange and very eerie is the fact that there are no telephones there. This fact was confirmed during the 2012 Halloween season. For 20 years Scott Thorne, owner of Castle

Perilous Games, had hosted an annual walking ghost tour of Carbondale. After so many years, Scott encouraged Bruce Cline and Kale Meggs, directors of the Little Egypt Ghost Society to establish the Big Muddy Walking Tours in October of 2012. These tours featured the history, mystery, and hauntings of Carbondale. A patron of one of our tours was a telephone installer.

When we told the group about strange telephone ringing in the basement of DCI Biologicals, this man informed our group that it was a fact that were no telephones in the basement, that is until he installed some telephone lines in the basement just three months earlier. So what about the ringing sounds heard from the basement? Was it a phone call from the dead postmaster?

DCI Biologicals is located at 301 W. Main Street in Carbondale, Illinois.

The Strange Death of Carbondale's Founder

Carbondale

Daniel Harmon Brush was the founder of Carbondale, Illinois. In his memoirs, Daniel Brush stated that "it struck me very forcefully as THE spot I was looking for."

In an ironic twist of fate, Brush struck that spot very forcefully and was killed instantly when he was hurled through the air and splattered on the ground.

On February 10, 1890, Daniel Brush was in his study writing his memoirs. The property outside his window was being cleared for Brush School. He left his writing to supervise some improvements to the school ground and offer assistance in removing a tree. A tree was being sawed down and to direct its fall a rope had been attached to it. Brush tied the rope around his body to assist. Unexpectedly the tree fell in the opposite direction hurling Brush into the air and then slamming him into the ground. The fall to earth killed him instantly.

The Brush School burned in the 1970s. In 1982, its remnants were removed and the Carbondale Public Library now stands on the site. There have been sightings of an older gruff man dressed in 1890s clothing wandering around the grounds of the Carbondale Public Library. Patrons of the library have reported that books have mysteriously flown off the shelves as they passed by. Could this be the ghost of Daniel Brush come back to haunt the land he lived and died on? We have located a tree stump on the grounds of the former Brush school. While this is probably not THE stump from the tree that played a factor in the death of Brush, it is located very near to where it would have been.

Our intent is to try to find some residual traces of the last moments of Brush's life as he was hurled through the air and then forcefully struck the ground.

— ● — ● — ● —

The Hundley House

Carbondale

J. Charles Hundley and his wife Luella built the Hundley House in Carbondale in 1907. Hundley was a very prosperous businessman and one-time mayor of Carbondale. Just two weeks before Christmas in 1928, J. Charles Hundley was shot in the head as he was getting ready for bed in his 2nd floor bedroom on the northeast corner of the house. It is believed that his killer was hiding behind the headboard of the bed that sat at an angle in the bedroom. Luella Hundley was shot in kitchen area near the rear of the house. Both Hundleys were shot with a .45 caliber handgun. The killer escaped without a trace and was never found.

Many people, including the police, suspected J. C. Hundley's son from a previous marriage, Victor, as the murderer. In the weeks before the murder, J. C. Hundley and Victor had dissolved a mining contract they held. Victor was to inherit $300,000 from Luella upon her death. It seemed that Victor had much to gain with J. C. and Luella out of the way. Police searched Victor's house and found a shirt and coat covered with bloodstains. Victor claimed that the blood was from one of his hunting expeditions. Lab tests conducted in St. Louis proved that the blood was not human. The Hundley murder remains unsolved to this day.

Dan Jones, the current owner of Hundley House, operates it as a bed and breakfast. We met with Dan to discuss the Hundley murders and reports of paranormal activity at the house. Dan has a theory that the Hundley's daughter, not son, was the actual murder. She had the motive, opportunity and possibly the means to do it. He shared some of his personal experiences with us. Dan said that the front porch swing would move without anyone being in or near it. At first he thought it might be the wind causing the motion, but one evening when the swing started moving, he went on the front porch to investigate and discovered that there was no wind what-so-ever. The air was dead calm. On various occasions he said that the computer in the office area would start doing weird things. The computer would turn on by itself and obscene words would start to appear on the computer screen.

Previous residents and visitors to the Hundley House would report strange sounds throughout the house and feelings like someone unseen was in the room with them. One of the creepier areas is the rear stairway near where Luella was shot. People have reported hearing the sound of the wooden stairway creaking, when no one was on the stairs. A .45 caliber bullet hole can still be seen on this stairway. It was made by one of the bullets that passed through Luella Hundley's body the night of the murder.

The Hundley House is located at 601 W. Main Street in Carbondale, Illinois.

The Professor's Ghost

Carbondale

A house on the corner of West Oak and North Poplar Streets is a house of death and hauntings. The house was owned by a Southern Illinois University marketing professor. He subdivided the house and rented it out to students attending nearby SIU. Today, the professor would be known as a slum lord. The house was not well maintained and when the tenants would complain, the professor would have all of their belongings removed from the house and thrown to the curb side while they were away attending classes. The professor was very peevish and was allegedly involved in some dubious international activities that resulted in criminal investigations by state and federal law enforcement agencies.

In April of 1982, the professor was murdered. His body was found inside a laundry bag in the basement of the house on W. Oak Street after someone noticed that the laundry bag smelled far worse than someone's unwashed laundry. The bag contained the professor's decomposing body. He had been stabbed multiple times. It was obvious that the professor had made some enemies and that they wanted him dead beyond doubt.

As short time after the murder the house was once again put on the market for rent. The new tenants were three female and five male SIU students. The girls lived upstairs and the guys took the downstairs. Spending her first night at the house, Marie Bennes reported that a hanging basket started swaying back and forth. There were no windows open. The baskets started swaying more and more and were hitting the walls next to them. Mary bolted out of the room and ended up sleeping on the floor between the guys' rooms downstairs. Another time, Mary happened to be laying on the couch in the living room, watching soaps and a strong breeze came through the house.

It came from the kitchen, knocked a clay potted plant off the kitchen table and exited out the back bedrooms. Mary's roommate witnessed this. Mary told the other roommates about it and they were not surprised. At various times the TV upstairs would change channels. The guys downstairs had experienced the TV channels changing or the lights turning off or dimming.

Overtime, there were other things that happened that really made Mary wonder about the history of the home. Many times during the middle of the night, she would be awakened by an odor of cigar in her bedroom. She found out that her roommate also smelled this odor. Her room was right next to Mary's, the only thing separating it was a wall.

The house dog refused to stay in the basement, he would go crazy if the door to the basement closed. The house was a beautiful home. It had lots of space. There was a fenced in area in the yard. It had a white picket fence surrounding the built-in seating. Mary and her roommates decided to make it into a beer garden. Mary remembered asking the landlord if she could scrape the flaking wood off of it and repaint it. He told her that if she did that and it turned out good, he would take some off the rent. Mary jumped at that. Long story short, there was an area on the fence that would not take the paint. Mary could put a whole gallon of white paint on this spot and the pinkish color would come through. Not sure what the story was behind that.

Mary's time was cut short at that semester. She fell and dislocated her elbow and had to return home for major surgery. Mary considered it a blessing. She did return the following semester, but did not live at the house on W. Oak Street. In fact, there were only two people left from the group of roommates. The others had moved away because of the eerie things that happened there.

In September of 2010 there was another tragic death at the house on West Oak Street.

Like so many parties at SIU, this one involved alcohol and illegal drugs. Witnesses who attended a party at the residence said some people had gone up to the roof to sit and talk with friends. The next morning, there were reports of people running from the building. One of the students that attended the party was found dead on the driveway next to the house. He had apparently fallen from the roof to the ground, a distance of about 30 feet.

Was the student intoxicated and accidentally fell to his death or did someone or something with evil intent push him to his death? Maybe it was the residual evil from the murder in 1982 that continues to visit the house that played a hand in the tragedy.

The house is located at 412 W. Oak Street in Carbondale, Illinois.

Oakland Cemetery

Carbondale

Oakland Cemetery is located on North Oakland Street in Carbondale. The cemetery is known for various supernatural happenings. Some of the creepy things that have been reported there include the apparition of a beautiful young lady in a flowing white gown

that makes her nocturnal rounds on the east side of the cemetery. There is a mausoleum whose doors mysteriously unlock from time to time seemingly to allow the unaware or foolhardy to enter. Wispy vapors and glowing balls of light have been reported along the north side on the cemetery near where the railroad tracks used to run by. Strange cryptozoological creatures have also been spotted along the path where the railroad tracks used to run.

There is an old mausoleum in Oakland Cemetery in Carbondale that appears to be illuminated from the inside when viewed from Oakland Street at nighttime. However, when you approach the mausoleum, the "lights" mysteriously vanish. We decided to investigate the strange happenings one evening. The mausoleum has massive bronze and glass doors at the front and a stained glass window on the back. While standing at the front doors and peering through the window at the crypts, we heard an unearthly "whirring" sound that seemed to surround us. There was no wind or anything nearby that could have made the sound. In fact, the entire cemetery was deathly quiet. At the base of the mausoleum I noticed some "vents."

I decided to shine my flashlight in the vent to see what was behind the screen. I was surprised to see a casket a couple of feet inside. I called my wife over to look inside and just as she did, she started

coughing and gagging and almost vomited. I jokingly told her that she must have been a victim of "corpse gas." We walked back to the truck so my wife could recover from whatever had made her sick. While driving away from the mausoleum, something "unseen" opened the passenger door of the truck. Even though it was a very warm evening the temperature seemed to drop about 20 degrees as soon as the door was flung open. What is the source of the mystery light? What was the strange "whirring" noise? What was the "corpse gas?" Who or what opened the door of the truck? The investigation continues.

The old and musty record books that are maintained in the cemetery sexton's office hold many interesting and sometimes mysterious facts. The oldest recorded burial at Oakland Cemetery in Carbondale is that of James Roberts who was buried in what is now Block 22, Lot 20, and Space 5 on March 31, 1863. The oldest known gravestone at Oakland Cemetery is that of Henry G. Hamilton located in Block 30, Lot 6, and Space 1. The interesting and mysterious fact about this burial is that there is no body buried there. Cemetery workers have probed all around the gravestone without any indication of anything buried there. They even used dowsing rods to locate the body with negative results. The gravestone was moved to its present location from some unknown site.

Until the 1940s, Oakland Cemetery was segregated. The record books contain the names and locations of people buried there under the headings of "White People" and "Colored People." Sections 1, 2, 3, 4, 5 and 6 were reserved for "Colored People." The old records were written on various scraps of paper including a page off a 1941 calendar. A hand drawn map indicated locations of graves with markings such as "next to red oak tree." The cemetery workers say that the trees used as landmarks are no longer there and the graves are now missing.

The Illinois Central Railroad used to run along the north side of Oakland Cemetery. Back in the steam train days, whenever a transient died on the train, the bodies were wrapped in a sheet or tarp. When the trains passed Oakland Cemetery, the train slowed down and the bodies were unceremoniously dumped off the train into the cemetery and they would be buried the next morning. Blocks 80, 81 and 82 became the Potter's Field burial site for these transients. Block 80 contains 115 burials, but only 12 of them are marked. If you visit this section after a heavy snowfall, you can see the depressions in the ground where many of the missing graves are located.

Oakland Cemetery is known for various earth lights and swirling mists throughout its north side. Could these mysterious lights and mists be the spirits of the unknown transient dead from the old-time steam trains?

Oakland Cemetery is located west of Oakland Avenue and north of W. Rigdon Street in Carbondale, Illinois.

Murdered by Unknown Hands

Carbondale

One grave in Oakland Cemetery had mystified the members of the Little Egypt Ghost Society for quite some time.

It was the grave of Thelma Wise, age 26, who according to her grave stone was "Murdered by Unknown Hands."

Just who was Thelma Wise and what really happened to her? After extensive research, we discovered that she was not murdered. According to the Coroner's Certificate of Death, she committed suicide. Many years ago there was a social and religious stigma attached to suicide, but not murder. We think it was the family's way of covering up a tragic family secret.

There have been sightings of a spectral lady in a long, white, flowing gown that seems to glide among the grave stones in the area where Thelma Wise is buried. Is it possible that this is the spirit of Thelma who is remorseful over taking her own life and the anguish that it caused her family?

The name on this Coroner's Certificate of Death was Thelma Mason, though it was later corrected with the state to read Thelma Wise. The cause of death was suicide by strangulation due to hanging, not "murder by unknown hands" as carved on her grave stone.

— ● — ● — ● —

1888 Train Wreck

Carbondale

We found some interesting information while conducting research at the Carbondale Public Library. On March 31, 1888, there was a horrific train wreck near Oakland Cemetery in Carbondale, Illinois. Further research revealed that the ICRR was cited for unsafe conditions less than 2 weeks prior to the train wreck.

John Chapman, the engineer of the Illinois Central Railroad train was killed in the wreck on Sunday morning, March 31, 1888. A native of England, he had been born in Lincolnshire, on Oct.  9, 1854, and was just 33 years, 5 months and 22 days old when he died. Funeral Services were held at his residence, Sunday, April 1, at 2 o'clock p.m. by Rev. F. Stolz. Interment at Oakland Cemetery occurred under the auspices of the Masonic Fraternity. The undertaker charged $40 for the casket and other expenses.

Until the 1990s railroad tracks ran along the northern boundary of Oakland Cemetery. On many occasions, earth lights have been seen along the tracks. Photographs taken near the north boundary of the cemetery show various wispy vapors among the gravestones. We wonder if the train wreck of March 31, 1888, has anything to do with paranormal sightings at Oakland Cemetery.

Oakland Cemetery is located west of Oakland Avenue and north of W. Rigdon Street in Carbondale, Illinois.

— ● — ● — ● —

House on West College Street

Carbondale

John Carter (names have been changed to protect privacy) killed himself in his home on West College Street in Carbondale. The previous year Carter's mother died. Carter never married and lived all his life with his mother. Upon the mother's death, Carter's siblings got a court order evicting Carter from the only home he had known. The siblings only cared about the money they would get from the sale of the home (less than $5,000) and caring little where their brother would go. Before killing himself, he told a friend: "I'm not going to leave this place." Carter was to be evicted from the home on West College by police acting on a court order.

Nine officers went to the home to force Carter out. They broke into the locked house and found Carter dead of a gunshot wound. He apparently shot himself several days prior. Carter was sitting in a chair in his bedroom. The wound under his chin apparently was inflicted by the .410 gauge shotgun nearby. The old, single-shot gun had been fired once. He apparently killed himself rather than be forced from the house he refused to leave. When the court proceedings to evict were begun, Carter told a friend: "I'm not going to leave this place." His ghost never did leave and still haunts the house to this day. He is buried in Oakland Cemetery.

Got Reiki?

Carbondale

Little Egypt Ghost Society was recently recalled to a home in Carbondale, Illinois whose owners have been troubled by the spirit of a man named "Sam L." who was a WW II veteran and previous owner of the house. The couple was so terrified of unexplained sounds, objects moving, and unexpected temperature changes in their bedroom that they were forced to sleep on couches in the living room. The family dog would lie on his back and act as if someone was rubbing his belly. The couple was terrified and wanted the spirit gone! Rich McLevich, our Reiki master and Kale Meggs, our Historical Researcher went to the house to try to determine what was causing the disturbances.

We had previously investigated this home, finding various unexplained EMF spikes and temperature changes in certain locations of the home. Rick was able to use his Reiki skills to make contact with the spirit of "Sam." There had been numerous break-ins at the home and "Sam" was concerned for the safety of the couple who lived there. "Sam" indicated that Rick and Kale should go to certain locations outside the house to view vulnerable areas that burglars could use to gain access to the home. After that, "Sam" communicated that everyone should go back inside the house to view a painting of lions.

According to Reiki, everything has a certain energy and power imbedded inside. "Sam" wanted the painting of the lions moved from one wall to a location near the bedroom door. He said the energy from the lion painting would help protect the occupants and possessions in the house. Rick and Kale then performed a smudging with white sage and Reiki Protection on the house to clear any negative energy from the home. After further communication with "Sam," it was determined that he was not a threat to the safety or wellbeing of the couple living in the home. "Sam" was in fact their protector. The couple was very relieved to learn this and is now happily living with the spirit of "Sam."

778 Bullets for the Carbondale 6

Carbondale

Early on Thursday morning November 12, 1970, residents on the northeast side of Carbondale were awakened by gunfire. A rental house located at 401 N. Washington Street was surrounded by Carbondale Police, SIU Police, and Illinois State Police. Inside the house were members of the Black Panther Party. Unlike other raids against the Black Panthers, these Carbondale Black Panthers (later known as the "Carbondale 6") shot back. By the time the Black Panthers surrendered, a total of 778 bullets had been fired into the house by police officers. The number of shots fired by the Black Panthers is unknown.

Events leading up to the standoff and gun battle started about 5 a.m. on November 12, 1970. Carbondale Police officers on routine patrol in the vicinity of Illinois and Grand Avenues noticed a Volkswagon van parked near the railroad tracks. The police officers shined their spotlight into the van and observed a man lying down who appeared to be sleeping. The driver of the van started driving off at a high rate of speed heading north on Illinois Avenue. The police pursued the van for several blocks before it stopped. A man with a pistol jumped from the rear of the van and fired five or six shots at the police officers. One of the officers was shot in the hip. A radio call for backup was made by the police officers who had been fired upon. All Carbondale police officers were told to be on the lookout for a black male wearing a trench coat who was armed and dangerous.

A Carbondale police officer spotted the suspect on the north east part of town near Marion and Oak Streets. The suspect shot the police officer with a shotgun, causing pellet wounds to the face. A short time later the suspect was traced to a house located at 401 N. Washington Street. Forty-five minutes after the first shots had been fired at police on Illinois Avenue, at least four Black Panthers barricaded themselves by sandbagging windows on the second floor of the house.

The ensuing gun battle and standoff lasted for about three hours. A total of 778 bullets were fired by police officers with an undetermined number of shots fired by the Black Panthers. An innocent bystander across the street at 402 N. Washington was shot in the shoulder when he stepped out on his front porch to see what all the shooting was about.

Police fired tear gas into the house in hopes of forcing the Black Panthers out into the open. Some of the suspects could be seen climbing out upstairs windows to get fresh air and then they would go back into the house.

The Carbondale Postmaster, who was African American and knew some of the suspects, convinced police to let him go into the house to see if he could get the Black Panthers to surrender. After about three hours of negotiation between the Black Panthers, the postmaster, and three other community members, the men inside the house surrendered and were arrested for the shootings. Ten people had been shot (five with serious injuries) during the gun battle. No one was killed. Several houses and cars along North Washington Street were damaged by gunfire.

The Black Panthers, now known as the "Carbondale 6," were each charged with six counts of attempted murder. During the trial, neighbors testified that police attacked the house in the middle of the night and started shooting without any warning. The Panthers defense was that they were shooting back in self-defense. An all-white jury decided that it was impossible to identify who inside the house had fired any shots. In addition, the jury determined that the police began shooting first, unannounced, in the middle of the night and that the Black Panthers had acted in self-defense. The jury found the defendants innocent of all charges.

One radical group summed up the events of November 12, 1970 as follows: "On Thursday, November 12th, the combined forces of Southern Illinois University, Carbondale and the State, Attacked the Black community of Carbondale. They say they were looking for a still unidentified 'black male in a trench coat.' The pigs tore into the community shooting up a two block area for over 45 minutes and then attacked the home of a group of Black Panthers for an hour and 15 minutes. In the midst of their mad dog attack, the pigs totaled the homes on the street. One family had to move out, since their newly remodeled home had been over ventilated by the insane wanton shooting of Carbondale's finest chumps."

"The shooting was finally ended when the people of the community realized that these crazy pigs weren't interested in justice, but wanted to kill 'all those Black Panther Bastards.' Three hundred people stood as a wall between the pigs and the Panthers and said that if you think we're gonna let you kill off our beautiful young brothers and sisters, you're crazy - you'll have to kill us too. The pigs, faced by the power of the people, stopped shooting but they started busting people left and right. The community got it together and started interviewing witnesses, one is a 55 year old man who walked out on his porch and was hit by a pigs bullet. They're starting a boycott of the racist businesses in Carbondale and raising the $50,000 ransom for the people's warriors who were busted."

The Black Panthers are no longer in Carbondale. The house at 401 N. Washington was demolished long ago. However, the echoes of gunfire can still be heard in the north east section of Carbondale by a certain criminal element that chooses to live violently, firing guns indiscriminately in the neighborhood.

Southern Illinois University and its Ghosts

Carbondale

Southern Illinois University was founded in 1869 as a teachers college. The first class at SIU had only 143 students. Over the years, SIU attracted more and more people seeking a higher education and now boasts over 20,000 students. According to Scott Thorne, owner of Castle Perilous Games and local ghost historian, SIU (like many colleges and universities) is home to a few resident ghosts.

The Student Center has been reported to be the home of mischievous ghost who moves items, mysteriously closes doors, and causes footsteps to be heard during late night study hours. The Arena which was constructed in 1962 seems to be the host of the same ghosts that inhabit the Student Center.

Faner Hall, constructed in 1971-74 is an enigma. After the anti-war riots at SIU in 1969 and the burning of Old Main by arsonists, it was decided that new building designs would be needed to prevent violent student takeover of classrooms in the future. Faner Hall is without doubt the most confusing building on campus. This massive concrete building was designed with dead-end hallways, multiple entrances, and maze-like construction. It is very easy to get lost in this building and legend has it that shortly after construction was complete a female student got lost in the building late at night and became so frightened by her experience that she died. This may account for the apparition of a girl that lurks the halls of this building. Faner Hall is home to the ghost of a girl wearing a striped shirt and blue jeans. This ghostly girl has been observed on many occasions walking through closed doors and then will vanish. This same phantom has been seen entering various classrooms and then vanishing into thin air.

Wheeler Hall, constructed in 1904, has been the scene of poltergeist activity. A woman who was working late one night was attacked by a poltergeist that threw chairs at her.

Anthony Hall is the administrative building for the campus. During the 1960's, one of the female employees suffered a heart attack and died on the job. For many years afterwards, the sounds of typing and file drawers opening and closing were heard in the area where the deceased employee used to work even though no one was sitting at the work area at the time.

The Mortuary Science and Funeral Service classroom and lab hosted at least one ghost. We were conducting a ghost hunt training session on the lawn between the Mortuary Science classroom and Campus Lake on a night in 2008. One of the experiments that we conducted was to use our "Ghost Meters" to make contact with any spirits that might be near. The Ghost Meter is a type of meter that measures electromagnetic fields that may be produced by paranormal activity. It has an analog dial that indicates the level of EMF in milligauss as well as a red flashing light and audible alarm that indicates the intensity of the EMF. My wife Lisa, and co-founder of Little Egypt Ghost Society, was able to make contact with the spirit of a female cadaver in the embalming lab. Lisa asked this spirit many questions and got several responses in a special code using the light and sound alarm of the Ghost Meter.

One of the questions that Lisa asked was "how many of you are there in the lab?" The spirit responded with several flashes of the light that would correspond with how many cadavers were in the lab. One of our close friends is an SIU employee and he confirmed that exact number of cadavers that were present in the lab on that night.

Henry, the Ghost of Shryock Auditorium

Southern Illinois University

Located in the heart of the old campus at SIU the auditorium began in 1917 for the state teacher's college features the strong Roman architectural influences of Neoclassicism in its design. It's known today at Shryock Auditorium after the university's fifth president, Henry William Shryock, who served from 1913 to 1935. In addition to the auditorium, the building also housed Shryock's office. On the morning of April 11, 1935, just prior to a convocation in the auditorium, the university president suffered a massive heart attack and died in his office. While he wanted to go home he didn't want his aides to summon an ambulance for fear of the excitement it might cause as some 1,400 students and faculty members had already gathered in the auditorium. The orchestra played weakly, its conductor and some of the students had already heard the news of the heart attack, but not of the death.

"To those who knew, the music was empty and almost that of a dirge. At length it ceased," reported the *Carbondale Free Press* a few hours later. It was left to Professor W. A. Furr, the presiding officer at the assembly to slowly rise, gaze forward and motionlessly announce, "I have the saddest news of all. President Shryock has passed away."

A silence dropped upon the gathered and the students and faculty quietly left the building, but what's uncertain, is whether President Shryock ever left as ever since his death there have been reports of supernatural activity in the auditorium.

Staff members and students have reported items that go mysteriously missing, doors that open and close of their own volition and unexplainable footsteps. Like many old time auditoriums and theaters, Shryock Auditorium has a "ghost light." The ghost light is nick-

named "Henry" and is usually located at stage center. The light is continuously lit. At times, workers in the building turn the light off only to have it suddenly turn back on. Sometimes the light turns off by itself.

A majestic Reuter pipe organ is located on the north balcony. This organ was built by the Reuter Organ Company of Lawrence, Kansas. It has fifty stops with fifty-eight ranks of pipes, totaling more than 3,000 pipes. There have been reports of a "Phantom of the Opera" entity near the pipe organ as well as occasionally on stage.

The Little Egypt Ghost Society was invited to conduct a "ghost hunter" program at Shryock Auditorium for the local Girl Scouts by Castle Perilous Games owner Scott Thorne for Halloween. The group was granted exclusive access to the auditorium for this special event.

There was a large turnout of Girl Scouts and their parents. After being seated in the auditorium, staff locked the doors so that we would not be disturbed. We conducted a "show and tell" of our ghost hunting equipment and had a question and answer session.

During the program we used "Ghost Meter" and K-2 EMF meter in an attempt to make contact with any spirits that might be present. Suddenly we heard a very loud "BANG" from a door slamming shut somewhere off to stage left. We looked out into the audience and noticed that everyone was accounted for and sitting in their seats. There was no one lurking anywhere in the shadows. Kale and I went to investigate. Every door we came to, we tried to slam shut to reproduce the loud bang.

Every door that we tried had a damper on it preventing any sudden slamming of the doors. We noticed that all doors leading to the outside were securely locked.

We obtained the door keys from a staff member and unlocked a door off stage left that exited to the front sidewalk. When we opened this door we were able to make it slam shut with a loud BANG. However, we noticed that door was barricaded from the outside to prevent anyone from using it. Was this door slammed shut by the spirit of Henry Shryock leaving the building because he did not approve of such nonsense as Girl Scout ghost hunters?

Sunset Haven

Southern Illinois University

One of the creepiest and mysterious buildings in Carbondale is the Vivarium Annex, also known as Building 207, located at Sunset Haven. Many people have mistakenly called it "the Insane Asylum." Originally, it was the Jackson County Poor Farm. It became a home for the destitute, mentally ill and severely retarded. In the 1940's its name was changed to Sunset Haven and converted into a nursing home. In 1957 Southern Illinois University purchased the property, changed its name to Building 207 and used the building and surrounding land for agricultural programs.

Sunset Haven has long been known as one of the major haunted spots in Carbondale. It is well known for paranormal activity such as disembodied voices, doors that open and then slam on their own accord, sounds of moaning, cries, chains being dragged, animal sounds, cold spots, lights that turn on and off as well as the creepy feeling of being watched by unseen eyes.

The Little Egypt Ghost Society was intrigued by the history, mysteries and hauntings of Sunset Haven. This was one location we needed to investigate and contacted a reporter with the Daily Egyptian at SIU to see if she could help get us inside. After negotiations with authorities at SIU, we finally had the long sought after permission.

Just hours before our scheduled walk thru, the Chief of the Southern Illinois University Police Department denied all access to the property. Members of the Little Egypt Ghost Society investigation team along with a reporter from the Daily Egyptian went to the SIU Police Dept to speak with the chief of police. We were denied access to the chief and met with the director of the department of public safety instead. We once again asked permission to conduct the investigation stating that Sunset Haven had a reputation of being haunted and that we wanted to check it out for ourselves.

At that point, the director expressed his skepticism at the reputation of the location as being haunted. I then produced copies of books by three of my favorite authors, Michael Kleen, Troy Taylor, and Jim Jung, all of which contained stories about Sunset Haven and the reputed hauntings that occur there. I went on to explain that there are several websites devoted to the hauntings of Sunset Haven. The director then stated that the location was too dangerous for us to be there and my reply was, "why then, do SIU Army ROTC and the Carbondale and SIU police departments conduct tactical exercises there?" He was at a loss for words and just reiterated that it the chief's decision not to allow us access.

The bottom line was that ghost hunters and paranormal investigators are "persona non grata" at Sunset Haven in Carbondale. The area is patrolled by police on a regular basis and all trespassers will be arrested on sight.

All this secrecy makes us wonder... just what is SIU trying to hide?

UPDATE: Just before Halloween 2013 SIU administrators ordered that Building 207 aka Sunset Haven be demolished. Wrecking crews

bulldozed the building into its basement and backfilled the hole with dirt from the nearby farm. The only traces of this historic and haunted building are a few random bricks and an old rusty water tank with "Bldg 207" stenciled on the side.

Caverns of the Unknown

Southern Illinois University

Mysterious, secret places exist on many college campuses, and Southern Illinois University in Carbondale is no exception. One evening our ghost hunting group was conducting a training exercise near the "Old Main" area of campus. We each had a Ghost Meter and were scanning the area for EMFs (Electro-Magnetic Fields). I was walking west along the sidewalk on the south side of Woody Hall when I discovered an EMF that ranged from ground level to just a couple of feet above ground. This EMF ran the entire length of the sidewalk. There were no overhead electric lines and no visible source of electrical devices nearby.

What was the cause and source of this unexplained EMF? I discovered that there is a complete network of secret tunnels underneath the SIU campus. There are several hidden access points to the tunnels, some of which are: a pump house at the west end of the pedestrian overpass from Brush Towers, a pump house near one of the turnarounds at Thompson Point, a manhole in the woods behind the Center for Public Policy, a manhole on the south lawn of the AG Building, a manhole at the south end of the Student Center, a grate at the southwest corner of Life Science II. Some of these tunnels are guarded during final exams to prevent their use by "test thieves."

Upon entering the tunnels, strange echoes can be heard. Graffiti such as "WILDMAN AND CREW" and "CREO'S LAST STAND" may have been left during the anti-war riots of the 1960s. A Physical Plant supervisor once stated that "Some parts of the tunnel have not been checked out since the Berlin Wall fell. If anyone was trapped down there, we wouldn't even know today."

An official at the Office of Student Life at SIU stated that many years ago a maintenance man left one of the access gates to the tunnels open. A student saw the open gate and decided to go exploring. The student was alone when he ventured into the vast underground reaches of the tunnels. Shortly after the student entered the tunnel, a maintenance worker noticed that the gate was unsecured. He immediately secured the gate with a heavy duty pad lock and chain. The student became disoriented in the labyrinth of passages but finally found his way back to the gate where he had entered the tunnels. To his horror, he found the gate locked. There was no way around it and no other exit. The student's dead body was found several weeks later when workers noticed a foul stench and went to find its source.

Could the strange echoes that are heard from time to time in the tunnels be coming from the ghost of the student whose rotting corpse was discovered so many years ago?

Roll Call of the Dead

Sunset Haven

Just before Halloween 2013, Sunset Haven also known as the Jackson County Poor Farm, Building 207, Vivarium Annex and the "old insane asylum" was razed to the ground. Sunset Have was one of the last remaining almshouses in Illinois.

A spokesman for the SIU administration stated that the building "had been vandalized. The windows had been broken out. It was spray painted. The building really wasn't structurally sound. We couldn't keep it locked up."

The two-story brick building started out as the county poor farm before becoming a nursing home known as Sunset Haven in the 1940's. In 1957, the property was turned over to SIU which used the area for agriculture programs.

After many years of use and disuse, the building fell into disrepair and acquired a reputation as being haunted. Thrill seekers, ghost hunters, druggies and other trespassers would risk being arrested by law enforcement officers in order to see for themselves what the hauntings were all about.

There are 87 known burials in two separate areas at Sunset Haven. Both grave sites are located in wooded areas, one to the west and the other to the east of where the building once stood. The burials took place between 1877 and 1943 and included a former slave and veterans from the Civil War, the Spanish American War and WW-I. None of the graves were ever marked. SIU has no plans to place any kind of historical or memorial marker at the site.

Here is a roll call of the known dead who are buried at Sunset Haven. May they rest in peace and never be forgotten.

- Abernathy, Jeremiah Addison "Jack," b. 1829 d. Apr. 17, 1917 He is in the 1860 Slave Census for Perry County

- Adams, Nelson, b. 1854 d. Nov. 23, 1911
- Arnold, Richard, b. 1794 d. Dec. 5, 1877
- Behr, Mary, b. 1872 d. Nov. 25, 1922
- Bennett, George, b. Nov., 1870 d. Apr. 9, 1905
- Brock, Henry, b. Dec. 19, 1874 d. Jan. 4, 1878
- Brooks, Fred, b. 1857 d. Sept. 29, 1910
- Burket, Aaron, b. June 9, 1847 d. Feb. 5, 1927
- Burns, Joseph, b. 1861 d. Aug. 29, 1908
- Butler, Newton, b. 1850 d. July 26, 1929
- Campbell, Thomas M., b. 1829 d. Feb. 3, 1878
- Chasm, Fred, b. 1860 d. Mar. 6, 1925
- Cook, Dora, b. 1845 d. May 14, 1925
- Cook, George, b. 1835 d. Dec. 25, 1914
- Cross, Jonathon R., b. 1843 d. Feb. 14, 1923
- Crutcher, Lucy, b. 1825 d. Apr. 23, 1915
- Davis, Charles, b. 1829 d. Apr. 16, 1909
- Denny, John, b. 1842 d. Feb. 22, 1905
- Dolin, John, b. 1830 d. Oct. 25, 1906
- Duncel, Thomas, b. 1883 d. Aug. 11, 1907
- Easton, Ollie, b. 1872 d. 1907
- Feltman, Susie, b. 1849 d. May 1, 1909
- Foster, William, b. 1861 d. May 23, 1942
- Galliger, Robert, b. 1851 d. Aug. 30, 1906
- Gilroy*, Thomas George "Gilroyd," b. 1836 d. Oct. 8, 1897
- Golza, Frank, b. 1852 d. Sept. 24, 1912
- Green, James, b. May 10, 1829 d. Sept. 22, 1909
- Gregory, Campbell, b. 1847 d. Feb. 25, 1905
- Harper, Thomas, b. Nov., 1854 d. July 21, 1928
- Harrel, James, b. 1857 d. 1915
- Harris, Carrie Dixon, b. 1892 d. June 30, 1931
- Harris, Ed, b. 1846 d. Dec. 1, 1881
- Hawkins, Jane, b. 1828 d. 1906
- Haynes, Mike, b. July 7, 1842 d. Aug. 26, 1924
- Herron, George, b. 1857 d. Nov. 12, 1922

- Holbrook, May, 1874 d. Nov. 14, 1904
- Hughes, Mandy, b. 1843 d. Nov. 28, 1918
- Hughes, Patrick, b. 1815 d. Feb. 29, 1880
- Jeremiah, William H. "Jerry the Bootblack b. 1843 d. Dec. 17, 1905
- Johnson, William, b. 1831 d. Jul. 19, 1910
- Keifer, Edward, b. 1832 d. Dec. 19, 1904
- Kelly, William, b. unknown d. Nov. 26, 1922
- King, Amos, b. 1886 d. Jun. 7, 1908
- Knox, Charles, b. 1851 d. Feb. 13, 1908
- Maxwell, William C., b. 1849 d. Mar. 25, 1878, listed as a "tramp"
- McBride, John, b. 1848 d. Jan. 6, 1928
- McCloud, Daniel, b. 1850 d. 1880
- McCoy, Allen, b. 1853 d. Julr 4, 1908
- McFord, Hugh, b. 1864 d. Mar. 23, 1928
- McLaughlin, Rebecca, b. 1842 d. 1922
- Milligan, Hugh, b. 1826 d. Nov. 2, 1906
- Moore, John, b. 1876 d. Nov. 29, 1914, Spanish American War Veteran
- Morgan, Francis Scott, b. unknown d. Oct. 19, 1937
- Murden, William, b. 1885 d. Jan. 25, 1907
- Norton, Wallace, b. 1858 d. Aug. 5, 1934
- Ovat, Ann, b. 1839 d. Aug. 30, 1879
- Peterson, John, b. 1846 d. Aug. 21, 1904
- Raymond, Augustus, b. 1863 d. Aug. 24, 1879
- Reed, Henry, b. 1866 d. Jan. 28, 1924
- Rein, John A., b. 1861 d. Mar. 23, 1924
- Richeson, Elijah, b. 1840 d. May 26, 1912
- Riley, George, b. 1879 d. Nov. 12, 1879
- Roe, Mary Lula Waddington, b. Oct. 31, 1882 d. Nov. 7, 1916
- Schrumm, Phil H., b. Feb. 6, 1879 d. Mar. 13, 1936
- Shaw, Lewis, b. 1831 d. Mar. 7, 1915
- Sloan, Dan, b. Jun. 11, 1862 d. Sept. 14, 1924
- Smith, George, b. 1848 d. Sept. 16, 1906
- Smith, Joe, b. May 9, 1853 d. May 1, 1930
- Smith, Rachel, b. 1866 d. Apr. 8, 1908

- Sorrels, Dick, b. 1838 d. Aug. 26, 1925
- Specie, Sigmon, b. 1822 d. Feb. 19, 1909
- Stephens, Jasper, b. Nov. 30, 1847 d. Jan. 30, 1934
- Storm, John, b. 1879 d. Nov. 8, 1904
- Stradley, Capt. E. V., b. Nov. 27, 1834 d. Jul. 8, 1925, Capt. Civil War
- Taylor, Edward, b. 1846 d. Oct. 29, 1921
- Tobin, Andy, b. 1836 d. June 9, 1929
- Unknown Male, b. 1839 d. Jan. 16, 1882
- Vickroy, William C., b. unknown d. Mar. 25, 1878
- Vowell, John, b. 1854 d. Sept. 9, 1912
- Walbridge, Anthony, b. 1855 d. June 20, 1878
- Wars, Jasper, b. 1859 d. Sep. 7, 1904
- Weidert, John, b. June 15, 1856 d. Dec. 8, 1933
- Weston, Baker, b. 1862 d. Dec. 9, 1936
- Weston, Caroline, b. Dec. 26, 1858 d. July 28, 1940
- Williams, Charles, b. 1878 d. Oct. 15, 1908
- Williams, John, b. 1834 d. Feb. 28, 1909
- Zimmerman, Alfred, b. July 15, 1884 d. Jul. 29, 1921, WW-I Veteran

Jerry the Bootblack

Sunset Haven – Carbondale

Could the old burying ground at Sunset Haven be haunted by the wandering spirit of William "Jerry the Bootblack" Jeremiah? (b. 1843 d. Dec. 17, 1905)

As the old papers described, "Wm. Jeremiah, known to nearly every resident in this section of the country as "Jerry, the Bootblack" died at the county farm, southeast of this city at 2pm Sunday. Dec. 17, 1905. No especial cause of death given other than as the result of his well known and careless and improvident manner of living and traveling. He was in Carbondale Saturday on his way to the county farm and told several that he was awful sick and that he was nearly 'all in.' Twenty-four hours later he was a corpse. He was about 62 years old.

"His burial took place at the burying ground at the county farm this afternoon, being interred in the potter's field. While he always posed as a veteran of the civil war we understand he was not generally recognized as such and belonged to no G.A.R. post.

"Jerry" was a very familiar character in these parts. His early history is unknown, but years ago he had quite the collection of medals, curios, etc picked up in his travels, as he claimed, in all parts of the world. During the past few years he has tramped from town to town, with his boot-blacking outfit, without a home, and seemingly with no other purpose in life than to keep himself fortified with "booze" for which he had a great capacity for a little man.

"'Known to thousands, yet mourned by none' is the epitaph which could appropriately be placed on the headstone marking the grave of 'Jerry, the Bootblack.'"

The Coydogs of Chautauqua Bottoms

Southern Illinois University

The Chautauqua Bottoms area on the southwest side of Carbondale is home to mysterious creatures known as Coydogs. They are coyote dog hybrids that are produced when coyotes and stray dogs breed.

The origin of these hybrids can possibly be traced to animal experiments conducted at the Vivarium Annex (Sunset Haven) on campus. In the 1960s a research doctor at SIU conducted animal research. Some rumored that the doctor conducted unauthorized experiments and was eventually fired for mental instability. One of these experiments was the breeding of coyotes with domesticated dogs.

It is believed that some of research animals escaped into the Chautauqua Bottoms area where they still can be found. On very calm nights under a full moon, the sounds of the coydogs can be heard throughout the area.

Chautauqua Bottoms is located on the north side of Chautauqua Road, between Emerald Lane and Tower Road.

— ● — ● — ● —

WSIU-TV Interview with Little Egypt Ghost Society

Carbondale

Danielle, a reporter for WSIU-TV, was looking for an interesting news story when she came across the Little Egypt Ghost Society website on Facebook. Intrigued, she made contact with our ghost hunter club and asked if we would consent to an interview. Of course, the answer was a resounding "yes!" A date was decided on when she could interview the club officers.

The interview was conducted with co-founders Bruce and Lisa Cline. During the interview, we were asked what got us interested in ghost hunting and what some of the most interesting encounters were. After that a demonstration was made of all the official Little Egypt Ghost Society equipment. Danielle's interest was now at an all-time high. She asked if she could go on a ghost hunt with our group and film it. Once again the answer was, "yes!"

Our group had been asked to conduct a paranormal investigation of an old two-story house on North Almond Street in Carbondale. The upstairs apartment in the house was shared by Josh, his girlfriend and another female roommate. They stated that the house was over 100 years old and had once stood on the land where Crab Orchard Lake is now located. When work on the lake was started in 1936, it was decided to move the house to Carbondale.

Josh said that he found an old guitar in the attic of the house and decided to add it to his collection of vintage guitars. He hung the old guitar on the wall near some of the others. Each night, the old guitar would fall off the nail that held it up. No matter how many times he re-hung it, it would always fall off the nail. He also said that he and his girlfriend and roommate would hear sounds of a small animal in the hallway by the bedrooms and would see the shadow of it on the walls. This in itself was not strange except for the fact that they had no pets!

We all agreed on a date for the TV crew to film the investigation. After the investigators and TV crew arrived at the house introductions were made and the background of the strange happenings was made known to all present. Danielle checked all of the equipment to be used for the investigation to make sure that the batteries were fresh and that everything was in good working order. Just as we went into the room where the guitar had been falling off the wall, the TV camera stopped working.

Danielle rechecked her equipment and could find no logical reason why it would not work. I explained to her that sometimes during a paranormal investigation, electronic equipment would fail whenever spirit activity was nearby. Fortunately, I had my SONY NightShot Camcorder with infrared lighting enabling us to continue to film the investigation. We took several temperature readings with our pyrometers and Kestrel Weather Monitor and found an area in the back bedroom that had a temperature drop of 14 degrees in one small area near the center of the room.

The dowsing rods we were using would cross at exactly the same spot. After two hours, we decided to end the investigation. Just as soon as we turned on all the lights, Danielle's TV camera mysteriously started working again. It seemed like whatever spirits were in the house did not want her to document what was going on.

We did not see any guitars flying thru the air and did not hear or see the spectral animals. All we had to show for our efforts was one cold spot, crossed dowsing rods, a TV camera that mysteriously stopped working and one very scared TV reporter.

Murphysboro Mud Monster

Murphysboro

Contrary to published accounts by famous cryptozoologists and other so-called experts, the "Big Muddy Monster," aka "Murphysboro Mud Monster," is a fabricated hoax. How do we know? We know it to be a fact because we are personally acquainted with the perpetrator of the hoax. "Willy" has revealed to us the complete and true details of what the "mud monster" was and how he did it. Complete details are on file in the archives of the Little Egypt Ghost Society.

What follows is the generally accepted account of the Big Muddy Monster.

The first recorded sighting of the Big Muddy Monster took place on June 25, 1973, near Murphysboro, Illinois. According to the Murphysboro Police Department, the Big Muddy Monster remains one of two open cases in the history of the department. Two visitors to Riverside Park in Murphysboro were parked in a car when they heard a loud screaming sound in the wooded area and observed a large creature approximately 7 feet tall. The creature appeared to have light-colored hair matted with mud. The creature appeared to be walking on two legs and was proceeding toward their car.

Police searched the area with flashlights and spotted tracks in the mud approximately 3 to 4 inches deep, 10 to 12 inches long, and 3 inches wide. While officers were searching the area they reported hearing another scream coming from the woods. The next night, two teenagers sitting on a porch reported a tall, white-haired, hairy creature in a field just to the edge of the woods. Using a police dog, officers followed the creature making note of a discernible foul smell and slime on the branches. The dog tracked the creature to an empty barn.

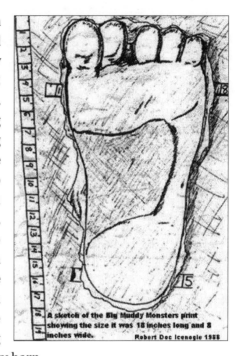

A sketch of the Big Muddy Monsters print showing the size it was 18 inches long and 8 inches wide. Robert Doc Icenogle 1988

This is the real story:

On a warm summer night in June of 1973, two young lovers came face to face with a creature that has baffled crypto-zoologists for almost 40 years. On that fateful night, the young couple was "parking" at Riverside Park alongside the Big Muddy River in Murphysboro, Illinois. As they were watching the stars, they were startled by some movement they saw in the woods next to the river. As they strained their eyes in the darkness to see what it was, a 7 foot tall creature covered in mud matted fur emerged from the woods. Just as they were nearly overcome by an overpowering stench, they heard a blood curdling scream come from the creature that was walking erect like a man.

The young couple hurriedly started their car and went straight to the Murphysboro Police Department to report what had happened. Police were dispatched to Riverside Park and the surrounding area to search for the creature. When they arrived, all they found were some very fresh and very large footprints made by an unknown creature. While at the scene the police reported hearing a bellowing scream come from the woods.

The Jackson County Sheriff Department sent a K-9 unit in hopes of locating the creature. The police dog tracked whatever it was to a barn, but the dog refused to enter it. Once again there was an overpowering stench in the area. The Big Muddy Monster is an open police case in Murphysboro to this day because they just don't know what it was.

The hoax was perpetrated by "Willie" (His real name is in the case files of the Little Egypt Ghost Society) and two of his associates. Willie is a science fiction, paranormal and zombie fanatic. He is extremely skilled in theatrical makeup, costume design and film making. In early summer of 1973, Willie got together with his associates and they decided it would be great fun to create a large, hairy monster costume to frighten the locals who used Riverside Park as a "lover's lane." They put together a costume that was over 6 feet tall and covered it with fur that was heavily matted with mud from the river bank. They left out no detail and even made realistic, oversized feet for the costume that would leave credible footprints. Next they went to their garage lab and concocted a batch of "Eau de Sasquatch" stink juice to go alone with the prank.

The night of June 25, 1973, at Riverside Park in Murphysboro was the only time that Willie and his friends performed this elaborate hoax. Willie put on the mud monster costume while his associates stood ready with the Eau de Sasquatch stink juice. After all of the preparations were made, they waited in the woods for some "parkers" to show up. Shortly before midnight their preparations paid off as a young couple drove to a secluded spot nearby. After waiting a short time, the 'mud monster" made his presence known with grunting and loud bellowing screams, the associates quickly sprayed the area with the stink juice. Much to the delight of Willie and his associates, the young couple quickly left the park with their car tires squealing.

It seems that people liked the story about the monster and there was a snowball effect causing various other "sightings" of the Big Muddy Monster, but no further evidence of its existence was ever found. Due to all of the police and public attention that the "monster" sighting received, Willie and his associates were afraid that they would get into serious trouble if they were ever found out

(Willie is to this day, nearly 40 years later, remains fearful and reluctant to talk about the hoax).

— ● — ● — ● —

A Murder, a Hanging and a Haunting

Murphysboro

It was a hot, muggy day in Murphysboro, Illinois, on July 30, 1915. Lizzy Martin, the wife of prominent Murphysboro attorney, James Martin, was found brutally murdered in her home on North Ninth Street. She had been savagely beaten on her head and upper body. The only suspect in this horrendous crime was the Martin's live-in handyman, an African-American by the name of Joe DeBerry. At first, he denied killing Mrs. Martin. After intense questioning by the Jackson County Sheriff, DeBerry confessed to bludgeoning Mrs. Martin with a fireplace poker. The reason for this crime was never clear. Some say he had been accused of stealing and had been caught by Mrs. Martin. Others said that he killed her because she refused to give him 50 cents for a haircut.

One month after the murder, DeBerry was found guilty and sentenced to death by hanging. October 16, 1915 was the day of the execution. The *Daily Independent* newspaper reported that "fog hung over the city like a cloak of death." Jackson County Sheriff James White deputized 2,000 citizens of Murphysboro so that all could obtain a good view of the hanging. Executions were very good for business in Murphysboro. Hotels, restaurants and shops were all crowded with customers. The entire downtown had a carnival atmosphere to it.

DeBerry was hung on the same scaffold that was used several years later to hang Charlie Birger. Once the trap door was sprung, it took De Berry 16 minutes to die.

After the death of Lizzy's husband, James, rumors began to circulate that the majestic Victorian home that they had lived and died in was haunted. During the 1940s a fire destroyed the top portion of the stately Victorian home that the Martins once lived in. The two-story Victorian home was remodeled into a one story bungalow. Starting in the late 1940s, occupants of the house would report mysterious sounds. It is not known if the strange creaks and other noises were due to the brutal murder that took place there or if it was the result of extensive remodeling that perhaps the spirits of the Martin's did not approve of. Many residual hauntings have been reported wherever there was a tragic event or remodeling of an older structure.

The Cottonwood Tree

Murphysboro

The mid 1800s were violent times for Southern Illinois and 1874 would be one of those violent years. Early spring brought death to an unknown black man who was accused of robbing, raping and murdering a white woman in Carbondale, Illinois. The man was quickly arrested and locked up in the Jackson County jail in Murphysboro.

The public was outraged at this heinous crime. An angry mob of about 200 men and women gathered around the jail. When it became evident that the Sheriff and Jailer were not at their post, the mob broke down the doors to the jail and forcefully removed the black man. The crowd, hell bent for leather and wanting revenge, carried the frightened prisoner to a site near the old Mount Carbon bridge on the Big Muddy River just east of town. They hastily hurled a short rope over a high branch of a cottonwood tree and Granny Patchett, a prominent lady in Murphysboro was given the "honor" of placing the noose around the black man's neck. Many referred to her as "good old Granny Patchett."

The *Daily Independent* reported that "the best people of Murphysboro were in the lynching party, and no one was arrested, though the state's attorney made some fuss about it." After the black man had been left hanging overnight, a Murphysboro doctor cut him down and took the body to his office where he removed all the flesh. The doctor then reassembled the skeleton and displayed it in his medical office for many years. The whereabouts of the skeleton is a closely guarded secret to this day.

Thus is the story of the only recorded lynching in Jackson County, Illinois. Only the footings of the Mount Carbon Bridge remain today and the cottonwood tree has long since been swept away by floods along the Big Muddy River. Several fishermen along this stretch of the Big Muddy River report mournful cries and wispy vaporous forms along the river banks. Could this be the spectral replay of a ghostly lynching that took place there almost 140 years ago?

— ● — ● — ● —

John Henry Jones Finally Hanged

Murphysboro

John Henry Jones made his living as the city marshal of Anna, Illinois. One fine day, Jones along with a deputy went to arrest Albert Chapman for horse theft and what Jones referred to as "moon shining" with a married lady, Mrs. Mitchell. A scuffle ensued and Jones pulled his pistol and shot Chapman in the gut. Death was slow and painful.

The fine people of Anna were outraged. They did not believe that Chapman's crime warranted lethal force. Jones was arrested, tried and sentenced to six years in prison. During this time his wife ran off and eloped with another man and moved to St. Louis, Missouri.

After being released from prison, Jones tracked down his ex-wife and daughter and forced them to go back to Anna, Illinois with him. Things became very heated and Jones told his ex-wife to either "go back to St. Louis or go to Hell." His ex-wife chose St. Louis.

Three years went by and the Union County Fair was in full swing. Jones was operating a concession stand along with his sister and Susan Mendenhall. August 30, 1895 was the last day of the fair. The crowds were dwindling and cleanup was starting. An argument ensued between the two ladies and Mendenhall was ordered out. Mendenhall had not been paid for her labors and refused to leave until Jones returned and gave her the money she had earned. When Jones returned, he sided with his sister and refused to pay Mendenhall and ordered her to leave. Again, she refused at which time Jones beat the lady into a bloody pulp. An hour after the brutal attack, Mendenhall was dead.

Jones was arrested that night and locked up in the Jonesboro, Illinois jail. After two failed lynching attempts, Jones was moved to Murphysboro, Illinois for trial. On December 9, 1895, Jones and four other prisoners escaped from the jail. They were all captured the next day and locked up in cells that were more secure. On January 1, 1896, Jones managed to escape once again.

Jones made it to Cairo, Illinois where he made his way to Texas. He soon crossed the border into Arkansas and was soon beaten unconscious. After recovering he decided to return to his ex-wife and daughter in St. Louis. Police finally caught up with Jones while he was in St. Louis and returned him to Murphysboro for trial. Jones confessed his guilt and was sentenced to hang by the neck until dead. At five minutes past noon, in an enclosure on the courthouse lawn, on May 19, 1896, in Murphysboro, Illinois, in Jackson County, after ten years, two murders, and two escapes, John Henry Jones was ushered down to Hell by the Hangman. He was wearing a fine new suit of clothes from the Fair Clothing Store in Murphysboro, Illinois.

A memento from the Fair Clothing Store which distributed postcards of the handing as an advertisement.

— ● — ● — ● —

Ghostly Nuns

Murphysboro

Both St. Andrew School and the parish house across the street are haunted. An eyewitness gives the following report.

After hours, it wasn't uncommon for bathroom doors to start slamming, the water to be turned on, and toilets to flush when no one was there. We also occasionally saw shadows. This was experienced by most employees in the building including myself. The school was built where the original St. Joseph Hospital was located many years ago. Apparitions are sometimes seen across the street at the parish house too. From what I was told, many years ago, three nuns went on a mission to South Africa and were killed.

They believe it is the spirits of the nuns that remain at the parish house. When I asked why they didn't do anything to remove the spirits from the school and parish house, the priest simply replied that they were harmless, so why bother. The current priest does not admit to having any experiences, but other parish staff and former priests do.

German Afrika Korps P.O.W.s

Camp Pomona

In 1933 the Civilian Conservation Corps recruited young men ages 18 to 25 years old to join President Franklin D. Roosevelt's "Forest Army." Camp Pomona in Jackson County was used briefly in 1944 for U.S. Army training maneuvers.

In 1945 the camp housed German prisoners of war who were captured in North Africa from Field Marshal Erwin Rommel's Afrika Korps troops. They were put to work picking fruit.

Pomona Zombies

Pomona

A cemetery just west of Pomona has some creepy and interesting activity. It has been reported by a man who resides nearby that the cemetery is the host of two zombies, one slow and one fast. Other people have reported the apparition of a lady in white who glides among the graves.

The Flipping Cemetery

DeSoto

Located between Carbondale and De Soto is a small country cemetery that has long been known for strange happenings late at night. Local legend says that on certain nights the cemetery appears to "flip" into a mirror image of itself. One night we decided to go there after I got off work at 11:30 p.m. We brought along our ghost hunting kit with EMF meters, EVP recorders and pyrometers. We turned onto the lonely country lane that the cemetery is located on and parked our car in front of the main gate. There was a full moon that night and we were able to get a good view of the various gravestones.

We waited in the silence of the moonbeams for the cemetery to "flip"," and not a "flipping" thing happened. We did however get some high readings on our EMF meters just in front of the main gate. After waiting several minutes, we went back to the car and sat for a while longer. After about 5 minutes, I looked in the rear view mirror and noticed a tall, thin smoky mist like entity standing at the rear bumper of our car. Right at this moment our EMF meters detected a strong electromagnetic field. As we sat there and watched the figure, it began to move to the passenger side of the car.

The smoky mist began to evaporate into thin air as it approached the passenger door. We left the area later with nothing additional to report. When we got back to Carbondale we pulled into a lighted parking lot and I got out of the car. When I walked to the rear of our car, I noticed that there were two dusty hand prints on my otherwise clean car. These hand prints corresponded exactly with where the entity was standing. It was as if someone or something had risen out of a grave and left its mark. Normally, hand prints are left on a "dusty" car. It was the exact opposite in this case. My car was clean and the hand prints were dusty. Could this be an effect of the "flipping" cemetery with the hand prints being the reverse of what they should have been?

Boone Cemetery

Fountain Bluff

Well hidden off the highway along rural Route 3, through an uncleared pathway which treks uphill in dense woods until you begin tripping over older tombstones in the high foliage and tree covered hilltop, is Boon Cemetery on Fountain Bluff. Built by a relative of Daniel Boone's and the son of William Boon (who removed the "e" from the name), his tombstone, towering at a height of nearly seven feet, tells of his roots here in Southern Illinois.

It is faded, but says, "Benningsen Boon first white child born in Jackson Co Son of Capt. Wm Boon, first permanent settler of Jackson Co was also Capt. of Ill. riflemen in Battle of New Orleans. Elizabeth H, his wife was a daughter of Conrad Will founder of Brownsville first State Senator member First Constitutional assembly."

Benningson's father, William, led the Illinois riflemen under Andrew Jackson in the Battle of New Orleans. When Conrad Will and William Boon met with locals in Brownsville and were deciding on a name for the county a very short time after that famous battle, they decided to name it after "Old Hickory," Andrew Jackson, their hero at the time. Thus, we are Jackson County. Conrad Will became the state's first senator, William Boon the second senator. Conrad Will's daughter, Elizabeth, married William Boon's son, Benningson, and the rest is history.

Benningson, a veteran of the Black Hawk War, was the founder of Big Hill, Illinois, and named Postmaster by President Pierce. It is said he built Boon Cemetery. Buried next to him are members of his family, including a son (William, named after Benningson's father), who died of wounds received in the Civil War.

Boon Cemetery is located about 300 feet up a bluff just off Route 3 south of the Gorham turnoff.

Death Omen ESP

Jackson County

My wife Lisa has psychic abilities. Many times on ghost hunts and paranormal investigations, she has been able to "see" and "hear" things that others could not. More times than not, these psychic manifestations have proven correct to the utter amazement of our team members.

The most recent occurrence was a couple of days ago. Lisa went fishing at a Carbondale lake. Later that night when Lisa picked me up at work, she told me that she saw two dead people in the lake. She went on to state that the dead people she saw were just visions and that she could not make out any details about who they were, only that they were dead and that they had drowned. She said "someone is going to die in that lake soon."

Just one day later, the headlines in the *Southern Illinoisan* newspaper read "TWO KILLED WHEN CAR GOES INTO LAKE." The story told how two girls died after their automobile went into Cedar Lake south of Carbondale about 3 a.m., according to Dr. Thomas Kupferer, Jackson County coroner.

Lisa's psychic abilities are both a gift and a curse. Anytime she tells me about her visions, I listen closely. She is usually dead on the money.

— ● — ● — ● —

Boomer, the Three Legged Hero Hound

Makanda

Across from the boardwalk in Makanda next to a picnic shelter by the railroad tracks you will find a monument to a hound dog named Boomer. The inscription on the monument reads: "In memory of Boomer the hound dog. Tradition says he dashed his life out against the iron abutment of the railroad bridge 300 feet south of this point on September 2, 1859, while running along on three legs trying to put out the flame in a hotbox on the speeding train of his beloved fireman-master."

Boomer was the faithful companion of a fireman who worked for the Illinois Central Railroad. The railroad bosses would not let Boomer ride on the train with his master, so the hound would run beside the train every time it passed through Makanda. Soon the news got out that Boomer would keep up with the train. Other railroads began to ridicule and joke about how the Illinois Central train could go no faster than a hound dog. After much public abuse, the bosses at the Illinois Central railroad came up with a plan.

The fastest train that the Illinois Central Railroad had was brought to Makanda. Wood and coal was double loaded in the tender. The engineer and fireman were ordered to heap on the fuel and go full speed ahead. The fire raged and the pressure in the boiler rose higher and higher. The firebox door was glowing red and the rivets were about to burst. The pistons pumped harder and harder speeding the train faster than any train had ever gone. Dust, smoke and steam billowed out around the train as it flew down the tracks. People were lined up along the route to see if Boomer could keep up.

Finally, the fireman shouted out "Saints be praised!" Boomer was chasing the train and indeed was keeping up with it. The wheels of the train started to overheat and the bearings lit their grease. Flames started shooting out of the bearing boxes. The fireman yelled out "HOTBOX!" Boomer saw that the train and his master were in peril when the flames started to shoot out. Boomer quickly took charge of the situation. He ran to the hotbox, lifted his leg and pissed the fire out. Unfortunately, Boomer could not see or react in time to avoid running into a bridge that was hidden by the steam and dust and he was killed instantly. Many lives had been saved by the heroic actions of the faithful hound dog. Boomer was given a hero's funeral and an impressive monument was erected to his memory.

— ● — ● — ● —

1925 Boskydell Train Wreck

Boskydell

In 1925, an Illinois Central train wrecked in what is now the ghost town of Boskydell, Illinois just south of Carbondale. A hobo, who had hitched a ride on the train, had his legs trapped between two of the wrecked train cars. A crowd quickly gathered and watched as the man screamed in agony. No one made an attempt to move the train cars to free the man because they believed it would kill him.

After a long delay, a doctor who had been called from Carbondale arrived at the wreck. By lantern light, the doctor opened his black leather medical bag and retrieved his amputation saw and knife. After a few quick slices with the knife, the amputation saw finished the job. The man's legs were tossed to the side of the railroad tracks. The nearly unconscious hobo died on the way to the hospital in Carbondale.

On some nights people claim to have seen a strange glowing light along the railroad tracks and tell of the blood curdling screams under a full moon. Is this a residual haunting of those tragic events of the train wreck?

Big Muddy Bridge Haunting

Jackson County

The Big Muddy River railroad bridge just north of Carbondale on RT 51 was the site of an encampment of Union soldiers during the Civil War. President Abraham Lincoln personally directed that a company of militia be stationed in Carbondale to guard the Big Muddy railroad bridge.

This was the first Presidential War Order issued during the Civil War. General Prentiss deployed a regiment of soldiers and cannons to protect the bridge from the Confederates and Southern sympathizers. Although many people in southern Illinois were sympathetic to the Confederate cause, there are no recorded attacks on the Union Army stronghold at the Big Muddy Bridge.

The day to day boredom of the Union soldiers was at times almost unbearable. Every day was the same; drill, picket duty, inspections and so forth. As the days turned into weeks and the weeks into months and the months into years, the daily routine of these weary soldiers left an imprint in the land around the bridge and river.

Many years after the Civil War, travelers on the road between Carbondale and DeSoto would report seeing blue balls of light moving around the bridge at night and the sounds of a phantom drum beating a cadence, then fading away. On misty or foggy days, there have been reports of apparitions of Civil War soldiers and horses on and near the bridge.

Several years ago SIU students were going home after a night of partying on the strip. As they neared the Big Muddy Bridge, their car had a flat tire. As they were fixing the tire they were confronted by two tall, men wearing blue civil war uniforms. As the phantom soldiers approached the car, they just faded away.

The Tag-Along Ghost

De Soto

Did a ghost follow Kale home from our cemetery crawl?

While we were at the Stoddard County Confederate Memorial in Missouri, Kale's digital voice recorder kept turning on by itself and started playing back EVP music. Later that night about midnight, the Ghost Meter EMF that he had accidentally dropped at the foot of his bed a few hours earlier, started to "alarm." It indicated a very high level of EMF.

When Kale picked up the Ghost Meter, the alarm stopped, but when he lowered it to the floor it alarmed again. He experimented and discovered that the EMF level was the approximate size and shape of a dog! After about three minutes, the EMF level slowly tapered off. All he can figure is that "something" must have followed him home.

The Hot Fingered Ghost

Vergennes

Many years ago there was a very wicked and evil man who lived near Vergennes. After many years of tormenting the townsfolk of town, this bad man died. Everyone was glad to be finally rid of him. In spite of the evil reputation of the man, his family put a tombstone on his grave that had this epitaph: "He lived with the Lord and died with the Lord."

A short time after the evil man had been laid to rest, many late night visitors to the cemetery would hear mysterious and terrifying sounds coming from his grave. A group of brave men went to the cemetery to investigate the strange sounds. After waiting for a short time, the strange sounds filled the air. Looking around, the men saw nothing unusual, so they sat down and leaned against a gravestone to wait for whatever would come their way.

Soon their patience was rewarded when the ghost of the evil man appeared right next to his tombstone. The ghost told the brave men that he was haunting the cemetery because he did not approve of the inscription on his tombstone. The ghost pointed to the inscription and as his ghostly finger touched the stone there was a blazing flame as it burned a hole right through the stone. The evil man's ghost vanished and never was seen again.

Sand Ridge Indian Reservation

Sand Ridge

Sand Ridge, located west of Murphysboro along the Big Muddy River, was the only Indian reservation in Illinois. The reservation was only a half mile wide and two miles long. Members of the Kaskaskia, Cahokia, Tamaroa and Mitchigamie tribes who lived in the reservation signed a treaty with Captain William Clark of the Lewis and Clark Expedition, Pierre Menard and Clark's son, Meriwether Lewis Clark on October 27, 1832 giving up their rights to the land in exchange for some land in Kansas.

All traces of the Indian Reservation are long gone. Traces of the reservation can be found on Jackson County plat maps. The original reservation boundaries are shown as current property lines.

Brownsville Slaves

Brownsville

Brownsville was legally chartered on January 10, 1816, making it older than the state of Illinois.

Many veterans of the Revolutionary and Black Hawk Wars used their War Bounties to obtain land in this area. Brownsville was located where Kinkaid Creek empties into the Big Muddy River near Murphysboro was the location of Dr. Conrad Will's salt works. He operated the salt works using slaves imported from Kentucky. Brownsville was the former county seat of Jackson County until the courthouse burnt to the ground in 1843, exactly 27 years to the day after the its founding. By 1850 Brownsville was a ghost town.

The Haunted Indian Mound

Big Lake

In the bottoms along Illinois Route 3 in the northwestern part of Jackson Co. an prehistoric Indian mound rises among the cornfields near the intersection of the highway and Big Lake Road. Experts this mound to the Hopewell Culture of 500 B.C. to 500 A.D. It's said that this mound is haunted and protected by powerful Indian spirit forces. In the mid 1970s this mound was about to be bulldozed so that more corn could be planted.

The day of the scheduled work, all of the heavy equipment including the bulldozer and front-end loader broke down and would not work. Later that night workers heard what they described as angry disembodied voices speaking in an unknown language. The voices

always seemed to be behind them, no matter which way they faced. The workers sensed that they were being followed by hostile forces and had horrifying nightmare about impending disaster if they continued with their plans.

The next morning the workers discovered that all of their tools were missing from the locked truck where they were stored. Broken tools were found scattered around the Indian mound. At that point they all agreed that the Indian mound should not be damaged in any way. Immediately afterward, all the equipment started right up and operated as if nothing had been wrong.

The project was halted and the Indian mound was left alone to guard its interred dead in peace.

This Indian mound is located on the west side of Illinois Route 3 across from Austin Hollow.

The Ghosts of Devils Backbone and Grand Tower

Grand Tower

French priests discovered Tower Rock near the Missouri side of the Mississippi River in 1698. The local Indians believed that evil spirits lived on Tower Rock. To dispel the fears of the Indians, the priests erected a wooden cross on top of the rock to show that the Christian faith was stronger than any evil.

This area of the Mississippi River is thought to contain evil spirits. This is reflected by the various names associated with landmarks nearby; Devil's Backbone, Devil's Bake Oven and Devil's Tea Table.

One legend of the area is about an Indian brave named Woncasta and the tribal chief's daughter named YaRohNia. The two of them were in love, but the chief had promised his daughter's hand in marriage to a brave of another tribe named YeWongAte. The two braves fought over the girl until a medicine man appeared. To settle the dispute, the

medicine man instructed the two braves to climb to the top of Tower Rock and smoke the medicine pipe. Whoever blew the smoke the highest would win the girl.

YeWongAte won the contest and was entitled to the girl. Unbeknownst to everyone, the girl had observed what had happened. She was grief stricken, and instead of going with the brave that had won her, she leapt off the top of Tower Rock, falling 100 feet to her death in the river below. Woncasta was also grief stricken. He took the plunge and followed the girl he loved in death.

During the full moon passersby purport to see the two lovers united in death with smiles of happiness and contentment on their faces.

A Tragic Wedding

Grand Tower

A very tragic wedding occurred at Grand Tower on April 9, 1839. The wedding party crossed the river to hold the ceremony on top of Tower Rock. After the ceremony, the wedding party was leaving Tower Rock, when their boat got caught in a whirlpool. The only survivor was a slave. On the same day, the bridegroom's niece was born. For her twentieth birthday on April 9, 1859, a party was held on Tower Rock and the slave who survived the whirlpool was her special guest. During the party the doomed original wedding party appeared to rise from the depths of the Mississippi River and the priest handed the niece a parchment scroll.

The ghostly wedding party then sank back into the river without speaking a word. The parchments predicted a great war in which families would be torn apart and bring great sadness. Two years later, the Civil War began. One of the niece's brothers enlisted with the Union Army and another brother joined the Confederate Army. During a battle in Missouri the Union brother killed the Confederate brother, thus fulfilling the prophecy.

— ● — ● — ● —

The Day a Dead Man Hanged a Live Man

Grand Tower

In the late 1800s Grand Tower was the scene of a very macabre accident in which a dead man hung a live man. The saloon keeper in Grand Tower was a morbidly obese man. In fact, he was the largest man in Jackson County at the time. The town doctor always joked with the saloon keeper that he wanted to by his body he died. The saloon keeper offered to sell his body for five dollars and the deal was struck.

A short time later, the saloon keeper died and was buried in a very large coffin. The doctor had paid for the body fair and square and was determined to take the body to his medical office for study.

The doctor hired a man to help him dig up the dead man's body. After they dug it up, they realized that the body was too heavy for them to lift out of the grave. They went a got a team of horses and some chain to pull the body out of the grave. The doctor's helper got down in the grave and put the chain around the body. The helper noticed a high fence nearby and looped the other end of the chain over the fence and hitched it to the horse team. As soon as the horses began to pull the chain, it came loose and became wrapped around the helper's neck. The saloon keeper's body was much heavier than the helper's, so the saloon keeper slid back into the grave and the helper was hoisted up on the fence. The live helper was hung by a dead man.

The doctor became frightened that he might be discovered digging up the grave and ran off. The next morning, the helper was found in the cemetery hanging from one end of a chain the dead saloon keeper on the other end of the chain. Many of the town folk said the helper got he deserved for robbing graves.

Jefferson County

Baboon Beast of Mt. Vernon

Mt. Vernon

In 1941 the Rev. Lepton Harpole was attacked near his home in Mt. Vernon, Illinois, by what he described as a dark brown, three foot tall member of the ape family. The beast jumped from a nearby tree and knocked the pipe out of Harpole's mouth and the hat off his head. The beast then proceeded to jump up and down while making "a very queer sound."

During 1941-42 several people in and around Mt. Vernon reported a large hairy crypto creature that looked like a large baboon. A posse of men went hunting for the creature after it killed a dog near Bonnie, Illinois. The beast was observed by some farmers as it jumped over a twenty foot wide ditch with ease. The posse found a trail of strange footprints that led to several dead animals but could not locate the beast responsible for the killings. It was if the creature had vanished into thin air.

Jersey County

Twin Springs Lovers

Grafton

There is an old Indian legend about twin springs that run with warm and cold water. The springs are located in what is now Marquette Park. The legend states that the chief of the Iroquois tribe did not have a son to one day take over as chief. In view of this sad fact, the chief hoped that his nephew would one day lead his tribe to great victory in battle against the hated Illini tribe.

One day the chief was shocked and angered to find that his nephew was in love with the daughter of the Illini chief. The Iroquois chief tracked the lovers to their meeting place and shot an arrow at the Illini chief's daughter, killing her before his own nephew arrived. Satisfied with his deed, the Iroquois chief returned to his camp. When the nephew found his lover lying dead with his uncle's arrow in her heart, he went mad with grief. He pulled out his hunting knife and thrust it through his own heart and collapsed in death next to the body of his lover.

Twin springs emerged from the ground shortly after this tragedy. One ran with warm water year round while the other ran with cold water year round. The Indians believed that the cold spring was in honor of the woman who was already cold in death and that the warm spring was in honor of the man whose blood was still warm when it flowed from his broken heart. The Indians believe the springs will flow forever in tribute to the power of true love.

Johnson County

Herman, the School House Ghost

Somewhere in Johnston County

Jane (not her real name) worked at a Johnson County school where it was common knowledge that the school was haunted. School staff had even named the ghost Herman. Here's how Jane's story goes:

The special education/remedial teachers were always located in a small room in the basement of the school. Adjoining this room was the janitor's room. The teacher used a program called the Herman Reading Method to teach students, so that's where Herman got his name. Whenever I was at work, I quickly learned to leave the door open that joined the janitor's room and my small classroom. Anytime I closed the door, it always opened by itself but no one was there. If I left the door open, all was well. I simply assumed Herman didn't like the door closed.

Sometimes basketballs would bounce across the gym floor when no one was there. Another teacher came in over the weekend to the smell of hamburgers and French fries cooking. However, it wasn't a school day and no one else was there, not even the cooks. One other teacher came in over a weekend and heard a loud scream in the building and quickly left. Again, no one was there.

As I was going up the stairs, I heard footsteps behind me. For the most part, Herman is harmless and school staff members have assumed he is a child but no one knows for sure. No one has any idea why Herman is in the building or where he came from. The only thing we knew for certain was that Herman, as harmless as he was, liked to play tricks, but he also gave the teachers a reason not to work late or come in over the weekends.

—•—•—•—

Ghostly Adventure at Zion Cemetery

By Flo Austin Dunning
Ozark

Zion Cemetery near Ozark has been said to be the most haunted cemetery in the area. There have been many sightings over the years. The most talked about are the ghosts of two soldiers from the Civil War era. They were brothers who fought against each other in the Civil War and were both killed in the same battle. They were buried side by side in the Zion Cemetery. They still argue about who was right and who was wrong. They have been seen several times, mainly when there isn't a moon and when the stars are clouded over.

It's on these dark nights that the boys supposedly appear sitting by a campfire in a heated argument. They aren't the only ones who come out at night to play (or fight). There is a lady nearby who wears a long white dress and has her long hair up in a bun. She seems to be looking for something. Her stride is quick and determined. Most of the sightings of her have only been partial—the skirt of her dress, a shoulder and arm, and head, neck and part of her bodice all have been reported being glimpsed. Some say that sometimes she will allow you to smell her perfume, which is light and flowery.

This could easily be explained away in the summer time when wild flowers and honeysuckle abound. Not so easily in the winter, for it's still just as sweet and flowery and it's right by her grave which is marked with a sand rock. I saw her one sunny day. Just a brief glimpse out of the corner of my eye. When I turned for a better look, she was gone. What I saw was a young slender woman in a long dress walking quickly and with purpose. I didn't know about the perfume then nor did I know where her grave was. I learned about that later when I was telling this to my friend Lynn who knew the story on this lady. Lynn then told me about the perfume and where to find her grave.

I went back to the cemetery (I have family buried there) and after visiting my sister's grave in the newer part of the cemetery, I got in my car and ventured across the road to the older part where the soldiers are buried and where the lady roams about.

Birds were singing and everything else looked very normal. I didn't feel the least bit afraid even though I had seen the lady there the last time I came. I followed Lynn's directions and found the big cedar tree that she described and the sand rock. In fact, the two were not far from each other. I was drawn to the one closest to the cedar tree. Suddenly, I smelled the perfume, strong and sweet. I looked around to see if I could see and flowers blooming anywhere but there was none.

Being left alone, I felt a shiver go down my spine and hurried to my car. I stopped by Lynn's and told her about the perfume. She seemed surprised and said, "She usually only lets you smell her perfume at night...But...then I guess she will let you get a whiff in the daytime too." There was no mistaking it, but I have stopped by there again and again when I am up that way and each time I smell the perfume no matter what the season. Lynn ran a Bed and Breakfast Inn and she occasionally hosted ghost hunting tours around the area for her guests. Since she wasn't feeling well one afternoon, she asked me if I would take a group of girls on a tour. That sounded like fun to me, and after she suggested a few places to take them and gave me printouts of the sightings and encounters that had been reported at each place, we all piled into one of the girl's truck and the adventure was on.

The girls were from Missouri and they were a brave bunch, not seeming to be afraid of anything. We stopped by the old railroad tunnel at Tunnel Hill where there had been several ghostly encounters. Right away something happened that set my hair on end. A disembodied voice spoke right behind us as we were making our way through the rock-sided cut into the tunnel. It sounded like a couple of words from a conversation had broken through the time barrier and were briefly caught in that spooky place. We looked around trying to find the source, but we were alone on that trail. Or were we? It didn't faze the adventurous girls who only shrugged and continued hurrying toward the tunnel where they hoped more exciting adventures awaited. As we walked into the tunnel's dark gaping mouth, I told them the ghostly and ghastly story about it. That is another story that I won't get into here because the voice in the rock cut was all we got out of that tunnel tour.

The next place we went to was Zion Cemetery, which was buried in a darkly wooded area. It was starting to get dusky. I had hoped to make it there before dark. The idea of being in this old cemetery after dark bothered me. Before we got out of the truck, I had told the girls the stories that refused to die about the hilly cemetery. By then darkness was settling in all around us. I'm not the type that wants to be in a cemetery at night. The stones in that ancient part of the cemetery almost glowed in the darkness. They were old, some fallen and some slanted. Some of the graves were sunken and large cedars were scattered about. The cedars had been put there as mere twigs to mark a loved one's grave and now were gnarled and twisted, bent by winters of ice and summers of storms. How different it all looked with a cover of darkness.

The four girls, all in their late teens to early twenties, were excited and showed no sign of being scared. I, their guide, was the one whose knees were knocking. They stayed near me with their cameras though, expecting me to drag out a ghost for them. It had always been my experience that ghostly encounters just don't appear on demand or expectation. The only ones I had ever seen or heard surprised me with their presence, none really scared me, mainly because they were gone before I had a chance to know if I had really seen what I had seen.

With our flashlights in hand, I took the girls first to the lady's grave near the big cedar. They were sniffing for her perfume. I smelled it immediately and it wasn't long until I heard the girls exclaim, "Oh I smell it! I smell it." They took several pictures, an eerie sight, lights flashing off dead tombstones whittled down from countless rains. They then wanted to find the Civil War graves, which I had to admit that I wasn't sure just where they were. Someone had said they were over the ridge which was far off in the black night. I couldn't help but remember the story I'd heard about a young man who had stumbled onto this cemetery by accident after dark one night and saw the two Civil War brothers by a campfire. Not knowing they were shadows from a long ago era, he approached them to perhaps get warm by their fire.

The closer he got, he began to realize something wasn't quite right or natural. When one of them leaped up and started toward him with a pointed finger and staring him down with cold blue eyes the poor guy turned and fled and never quite got over the encounter.

I led the girls a little ways to the north of the lady's grave and we all took some pictures. I then heard one of the girls whisper that she had just seen a man in what looked like some sort of uniform step out from behind a tree, but just got a glimpse of him. A glimpse of a man in uniform in the dark was plenty for me. I told the girls I would wait for them in the truck and with the help of my flashlight I got there pretty quick.

Inside the truck, I glanced back to where the girls had been. Their flashlights were already out of sight over the rise. I was alone and suddenly not feeling a bit better than when I was with them, because it hit me that ghosts can go right through things. I just hoped those girls would hurry, see what they wanted to see and come running back to the truck so we could get out of there!

I was just beginning to settle down a bit, when I saw a light out in front of the truck. There was not a house anywhere in sight, and no traffic out here in the wilderness. Was it someone hunting?" After all, the light did seem to be across the road from the cemetery. Then it began to get closer.

The light was up sort of high, too high for a person to be carrying. I searched for a rational reason for the light. Was it a reflection from something in the truck? No, that wasn't it. Frantically, I kept looking around for an answer, not the reflection of the girl's flashlights. They were not back up over the hill yet. Then the light moved closer. It was now over the hood of the truck. Before I could panic and bolt, it vanished. The girls returned shortly and as I told them about the strange light that had zeroed in on the truck they looked shaken and one of them said, "Yeah, we saw it. We were watching it too." They were now as ready to get away from there as I was.

One of their cameras picked up a strange object in the cemetery that we definitely had not seen there. It was an odd white shaped thing or figure, and there were lots of orbs, so many they were piled on top of each other. Some orbs were colored and some were white. There is some controversy about orbs which can be caused by dust, bugs, or even dew, so these alone would not have meant anything to me. But what about all these restless sightings and encounters that are happening in Zion Cemetery that cannot be laid to rest?

To visit Zion Cemetery, turn off Route 145 into Ozark. Go about five or six miles until you come to a "T." There is an old church on the left where the newer part of the cemetery is. On the right is where the ancient section of the cemetery lies. Enter with reverence and respect, and it wouldn't hurt to say a prayer for these wondering souls who may not yet realize that they are on the other side.

The Max Creek Vortex

Johnson County

The Max Creek area can be found about half way between Vienna and New Burnside, Illinois. This area is known for tragedy, violence, ghosts and earth lights. Local legend states that a group of early settlers made their home on a bluff above Max Creek. One night the wife of one of the settlers went insane and killed her husband and children. Glowing balls of light can be seen from time to time in the woods near the creek. They are said to be the restless spirits of the murdered family wandering aimlessly seeking the answer to why a loved one would turn on them in such a violent rage.

Max Creek is located near an ancient volcano known as Hicks Dome. Earth lights have been seen all around Hicks Dome. Local Indians would avoid Hicks Dome claiming that it was inhabited by evil spirits. This area has been unpopulated since it was purchased by the National Forest Service in the 1930s. It is now part of the Shawnee National Forest. If you go there some dark and lonely night, you may be fortunate enough to witness the earth lights for yourself.

Max Creek is located at N 37.443107 and W -88.7617254.

Mad Myrtle

Ozark

The tragic Tri-State Tornado of 1925 was responsible for 695 deaths. Many children lost both of their parents. Myrtle was one of the unfortunate orphans. She ran off into the woods near her home and lived there as a feral child until she became an adult and was discovered by some Civilian Conservation Corps (C.C.C.) workers.

Although Myrtle had lived a rough and tumble life in the woods, she had grown into a very beautiful young lady. Her striking beauty was noticed with much interest by one of the camp officers. Soon, Myrtle and the officer were married. She took on the job as camp cook. Life was very happy for the loving couple.

Sadly, once again, tragedy struck hard in Myrtle's life. Her husband was helping some of the C.C.C. workers in moving a large pile of dead timbers. It was a hot humid day and the strain was too much for the officer. He had a massive heart attack and dropped dead on the spot. Myrtle blamed the C.C.C. workers for her husband's death and went into a homicidal frenzy. That night she armed herself with a knife from the kitchen and an axe from the tool shed and murdered several of the C.C.C. workers. She was tracked to a waterfall near camp but jumped into the waters below before anyone could stop her. Myrtle's body was never found.

To this day, knives and axes go missing from a Boy Scout camp nearby. On some dark and stormy nights Mad Myrtle can be seen, sometimes as an old hag and other times as the beautiful young lady she once was.

Most versions of the tale take place at Camp Pakentuck owned by the local Boy Scout Council in Paducah, Kentucky, hence the name. The Egyptian Council in Southern Illinois also used it for their summer camps in the 1930s and 40s. The stories about Myrtle have circulated at least as early as the 1940s. Today the area around Cedar Falls that served as the scout camp is part of Camp Ondessonk owned by the Belleville diocese of the Catholic Church.

— ● — ● — ● —

Madison County

Cahokia Mounds

Collinsville

Cahokia was inhabited from about A.D. 700 to 1400. Built by ancient peoples known as the Mound Builders, Cahokia's original population was thought to have been only about 1,000 until about the 11th Century, when it expanded to tens of thousands.

At its peak from 1,100 to 1,200 A.D., the city covered nearly six square miles and boasted a population of as many as 100,000 people. Houses were arranged in rows around open plazas. Agricultural fields and a number of smaller villages surrounded and supplied the city. The Cahokians were known to have traded with other tribes as far away as Minnesota. The original name of the city is unknown and the inhabitants apparently never utilized writing skills. The name Cahokia is that of an unrelated tribe that was living in the area when the first French explorers arrived in the late 17th century.

These ancient Indians built more than 120 earthen mounds in the city, 109 of which have been recorded and 68 of which are preserved within the site. Many others are thought to have been altered or destroyed by farming and construction. While some are no more than a gentle rise on the land, others reach 100 feet into the sky. Made entirely of earth these ancient people transported the soil on their backs in baskets to the construction sites, most of which show evidence of several construction stages. More than 50 million cubic feet of earth was moved for the construction of the mounds, leaving large depressions called borrow pits, which can still be seen in the area.

Three types of mounds were constructed, the most common of which was a platform mound, thought to have been used as monumental structures for political or religious ceremonies and may have once been topped by large buildings. Conical and ridge top mounds were also constructed for use as burial locations or marking important locations.

At the center of the historical site is the largest earthwork called Monks Mound. At one hundred feet, it is the largest prehistoric earthen mound in North America. The mound is 1,000 feet long, 800 feet wide and comprised of four terraces, each one probably added at different times. An estimated 22 million cubic feet of earth was used to build the mound between the years of 900 and 1,200 A.D. The mound was named for French monks who lived nearby in the early 1800's and was most likely the site where the principal ruler lived, conducted ceremonies, and governed the city. Over the years, the mound has significantly eroded or been damaged by man, so that the original size is now uncertain.

Surrounding Monks Mound and the center of the city was a 2-mile-long stockade with guard towers placed every 70 feet. Thought to have been constructed four different times, each building took nearly 20,000 logs. In addition to defense purposes, the wall acted as a social barrier, separating the elite from the common people. Today, several sections of the stockade have been reconstructed.

Archaeologists have also excavated four, and possibly five, circular sun calendars referred to as Woodhenge. These evenly spaced log posts were utilized to determine the changing seasons, displaying an impressive example of scientific and engineering practices.

The area at Cahokia Mounds that we are primarily interested in is the mysterious Mound #72. Mound #72 is located about one half mile south of Monks Mound and measures 7 ft in height, 140 ft long and 70 feet wide. It covers 3 smaller mounds that were built over high status and sacrificial burials. Some of the more interesting burials are that of a man on a platform of 20,000 shell beads, built in the shape of a falcon. Underneath this man is the skeleton of another man, aged in the early 40s and about 6 ft tall. Nearby are six burials possibly sacrificed to the man on the beads. One of these skeletons is lying with arms and legs akimbo as if thrown there before death. In another area of the mound is a group of seven men and women surrounded by many offerings including two piles of arrow points; 332 aligned W-NW, and 413 aligned E-SE. 3 more burials are nearby.

Twenty-one skeletons were found on a low square platform with at least 13 of them aged between15 and 35 years. On the SE side of the mound there was a 25- 35 year old female wearing a choker with 4 strands of shell disk beads. Next to her was a 25 – 35 year old male wearing a choker with 5 strands of shell disk beads. He was found lying face down. 2 other males were found face down nearby. On the SW side of the mound there are 22 females buried in 2 layers. On the SE side of the mound there are 19 females buried in 2 layers. On another side are 24 females buried in 2 layers. 4 men, aged 20- 45 years with arms interlocked and all missing their heads and hands are in this mound. There are many burial pits surround Mound #72.

Cahokia Mounds State Historic Site is located at 30 Ramey Street in Collinsville, Illinois.

The Haunted Mansion

Collinsville

Many years ago, a stately mansion stood on Keebler Road in Collinsville. This mansion had a dark history due to the slave auctions that were held there before the Civil War. Entire families of black slaves were put on the auction block and sold individually to the highest bidder. Many husbands, wives, sons and daughters never saw or heard from their loved ones again after being taken to the farms and business of the wealthy slave holders.

After the Civil War, the mansion stood vacant and dilapidated. The mansion had acquired a reputation of being haunted. Townsfolk would only pass by the mansion on the far side of the road due to their fear of the apparitions that had been reported there. Candles would be seen floating past the broken windows of the mansion and wispy, vaporous forms of slave women were reported walking among the tombstones of the nearby graveyard.

The First Baptist Church in Collinsville is reported to be haunted by the phantom of a hooded figure accompanied by a ghostly black dog. Shadows float across the walls of the church even though there is nothing visible that could cause them.

During World War I, some citizens of Collinsville distrusted Germans so much that one German immigrant was reported to have been killed in the basement of the church. Some people believe that the murdered German is now a ghost that inhabits the church. On occasion, this ghost has been known to hit church members so hard that bruises are left on their bodies.

The Piasa Bird

Alton

The mysterious Piasa bird (pronounced PIE-saw) has a recorded history that goes back to 1673 when Frenchmen, Jacques Marquette and Louis Joliet, were exploring the Mississippi River near present day Alton, Illinois.

Marquette kept a journal in which he referred to the "monster" as "large as a calf; they have horns on their heads like those of a deer, a horrible look, red eyes, a beard like a tiger's, a face somewhat like a man's, a body covered with scales, and so long a tail that it winds all around the body."

Marquette went on to state that the painting of the monster had a terrifying meaning to the Indians. It was such that "upon which the boldest savages dare not long rest their eyes."

According to legend, the Indians of the region were terrorized by a winged creature they called the Piasa, which was an Illini word for a bird that devoured men.

The Piasa bird was so big that it could carry off a deer in its claws. Once having tasted the flesh of humans, it would eat nothing else. The Piasa would fly over the Indian village looking for tasty young Indians. Once a likely victim was spotted, the Piasa would swoop down from the sky, hook its talons into the unlucky Indian and carry them off to the bluffs along the river. Screams would be heard for a very short time while the Piasa nibbled away at the tasty Indian morsels.

So many of the tribesman were eaten by the Piasa that the Chief decided something must be done and done quickly. Ouatoga, the Illini Chief, fasted and prayed to the Great Spirit for guidance. The Great Spirit appeared to him in a dream and told him to pick 20 of his best warriors and have them take their bows and arrows to a certain spot on the bluffs. This was done and they waited for the Piasa to swoop down on the brave Chief as he was waiting as a decoy. Just as the Piasa was about to attack, the warriors let loose with their deadly arrows. The Piasa, pierced by many arrows, let out a shriek and flew across the river and died.

To commemorate the death of the feared Piasa, the Indians painted a giant image of the monster on a bluff overlooking the river.

A startling discovery was made in 1836 by John Russell who was a professor at Alton Seminary. A guide led Russell to a cave in the bluffs in which the Piasa once lived. Russell stated that "the floor of his cave throughout its whole extent was a mass of human bones. Sculls (sic) and other bones were mingled together in the utmost confusion...we dug to the depth of three or four feet in every quarter of the cavern and still we found nothing but bones. The remains of thousands must have been deposited here; and by whom, and for what purpose, it is impossible even to conjecture."

The Piasa Bird has made several appearances in more recent times. On April 4, 1948 Colonel Walter Siegmund sighted "an enormous bird about the size of a small pursuit plane" flying near the bluffs. On July 25, 1977, ten year old Marlon Lowe was attacked by two birds with 10 foot wingspans that carried him about 35 feet from his home in Lawndale. The 65 pound boy was so frightened that his red hair turned grey. On July 28, 1977, a farmer in Lincoln spotted one of the large birds in flight. Two days later "Texas John" Huffer photographed a Piasa Bird in a swamp near Tuscola. A few days later a truck driver reported a large bird carrying a pig over the highway between Delavan and Armington.

The Piasa Bird site is located 1 mile north of the Alton Visitors Center on Illinois Rt. 100 (the Great River Road).

The Haunting of Small Pox Island

Alton

Alton was the site of a prisoner of war camp that housed Confederate soldiers during the Civil War. Conditions at the prison were brutal. During the winter of 1862 and spring of 1863 a smallpox infection broke out that killed over 1500 Confederate prisoners and 300 Union soldiers.

The dead or dying prisoners and guards were taken to an island in the Mississippi River across from Alton. Soon this unnamed island had a name, it was called Smallpox Island. As a dreaded place of death and burial, the island received a reputation for being haunted.

Many years after the close of the prison, some boys who heard that the island was haunted decided to explore it and see for themselves if the ghost stories were true. They were not disappointed.

The boys borrowed an old canoe and paddled out to the lonely and deserted island for an overnight camp out. After telling stories around the campfire the boys finally went to their tent and went to sleep. The campfire embers were glowing orange as sparks flew up in the sky. Shuffling footsteps were heard near the dying fire. Mystery shapes took the form of long dead and emaciated Confederate soldiers.

The specters of the dead Confederates glared at the boys with empty eye sockets. One of the ghostly soldiers pointed a bony finger at the boys and screamed out "WHO DARES TO INTRUDE UPON OUR RESTING PLACE?"

The boys ran out of their tent, jumped into their canoe and paddled back to Alton was fast as they could go. The boys now knew that the ghostly stories about Smallpox Island were true.

— ● — ● — ● —

Hanson Home Hauntings

Alton

Alton is one of the most haunted towns in all of Southern Illinois. Many of the key sites are decades old, but some, centuries. One particularly haunted location even served as a station on the Civil War era Underground Railroad.

Photo by Gary Hawkins of www.AltonHauntedOdyssey.com.

The Enos Apartments at 325 E. 3rd St., once served as the Enos Sanatorium operated in the early 1900s for tuberculosis patients. The sanatorium expanded upon the earlier stately Hanson House built in 1857 by Nathaniel Hanson near the Mississippi River.

The house had secret underground rooms and tunnels that were made out of limestone. As all paranormal investigators know, limestone is known for its ability to store up and release paranormal energy.

These secret rooms were used to hide slaves who were running away to what they hoped would be freedom. Many slaves found what they were searching for. Others were not so fortunate and died along the way. It is believed that some ghosts remain at the site of the Hanson House where they died. During life, some of the slaves would take (steal) things that they needed from those who were so kind as to help them.

As in life, so in death spirits continue to do the same things. Residents at the Enos Apartments have reported that various items in their apartments, such as jewelry, keys, clothing, and in one case a bottle of wine, have gone missing only to reappear later. Lights will mysteriously turn off and on of their own accord. Doors are heard slamming along with unexplained footsteps. Agonized wails can be heard coming from the basement. Many people think that the spirits of the slaves are responsible for the mysterious activity at this location.

Deaf Bill, The Alton Mummy

Alton

William "Deaf Bill" Lee[1] lies at rest in the St. Francis of Assisi Catholic cemetery in Portage des Sioux. His flat, gray, granite grave marker shows his name, a figure of a fisherman and three dates: 1863, the year he was born; 1915, the year he died; and June 24, 1996, the

---

[1] Despite acting deaf, Lee's nickname was pronounced as "Deef Bill."

day he was buried. How "Deaf Bill" finally came to rest is an interesting story that was 81 years in the making.

Deaf Bill fished on the Mississippi River. Being successful at his trade, he also thought of himself as a fisher of men. He was a jack-leg preacher who was known to deliver fire and brimstone sermons on both the Illinois and Missouri sides of the river. What made his sermons especially interesting was the fact that he often delivered the sermons while rip roaring drunk! On many occasions Bill would show up unannounced and uninvited to a local church and would physically remove the minister from the pulpit and then start into his holy rant. No one dared make a move for fear of a torrent of curses or a sound thrashing by the self-proclaimed reverend.

There is some doubt about exactly how deaf Bill really was. One day, some river ruffians decided to have a little fun at Bill's expense. The leader of the group snuck up behind him and started using the worst language and curses imaginable, spoken in a very low tone thinking that Bill would not be able to hear what was said. It only took about 30 seconds for him to spin around and punch out the ruffian. Deaf Bill then spit a wad of chewing tobacco on the man's face and shouted out "Bub, there ain't nobody in this world who's that deaf!"

Even though Bill was only 5'9" and about 160 lbs, he was one tough S.O.B. After many years living the life of a destitute alcoholic, he ended up in the county poor farm where he died November 13, 1915, at the age of 52. Now most people who died at the poor farm were buried in a potter's field. Some people thought that Bill might have some family in the area who would claim the body. It was decided to have the body embalmed by Bauer and Heohn, the local undertakers. The owners of the funeral home were experimenting with a new embalming procedure that they used on Deaf Bill. The undertakers kept the body for six weeks but no one came forward to claim it. As the corpse remained at the funeral home, the air dehydrated it and turned the body into a mummy. The undertakers were about ready to finally bury

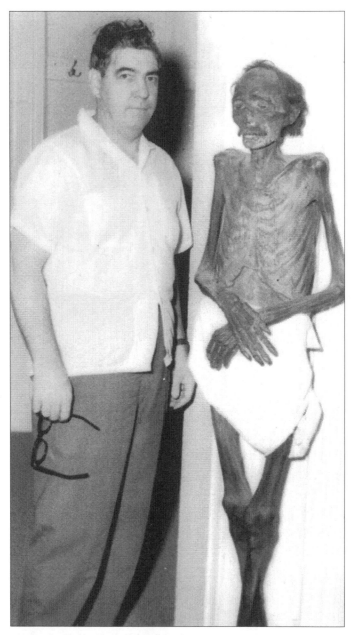

Photo provided by Gary Hawkins of www.AltonHauntedOdyssey.com

him when a traveling carnival came to Alton. The carnival owner offered $2,500 for the mummy of "Deaf Bill" so that he could put it on display as a curiosity. The undertakers refused, saying that it was illegal to sell a dead body. The carnival owner was sent on his way and the undertakers started to think about the possibilities that Bill's mummified body offered. They decided that it would be great advertisement to make Deaf Bill a permanent part of their establishment.

By now the mummy had shrunken to about 5'3" and weighed only about 60 pounds. They propped up the body to a closet, where it remained for several decades for guests to view him. It still had the mustache that Bill wore in life. His legs were crossed, and arms folded. The skin was leathery and dark and felt like wood. The mummy was a great attraction at the funeral home, especially around Halloween.

In 1948, Tom and Dallas Burke bought the funeral home, mummy included. It stayed in a closet until the owners decided it was time for it to go. They contacted the Alton History Museum to see if they would take the mummy. The board of directors turned them down, thinking it "just dreadful." Dallas Burke and Brian Fine, co-owners of the Burke-Fine Funeral Home, asked for advice from the Rev. Michael Sandweg, pastor of the West Alton and Portage des Sioux Catholic churches. He said buy him and agreed to conduct Bill's funeral.

"Deaf Bill" was dressed in a turn-of-the-century tuxedo coat and trousers with a white shirt and black string tie. His hands were crossed and held a bouquet of red and white carnations. His hair and mustache were neatly groomed. The funeral home provided a varnished poplar casket with gold trim and on June 24, 1996, Deaf Bill was finally laid to rest. Nearly 400 people attended the funeral. As the priest sprinkled holy water on the closed casket, he said, "Every person born into this world has a right to a proper and a decent burial. So we bury him today and pray for his soul."

— ● — ● — ● —

The Phantom Spectre Hunter

Madison County

In the mid-1700s, a mysterious entity was often seen on dark and stormy nights near the Cahokia Indian Mounds. When lightning flashed, frightened travelers would see a tall man dressed in sackcloth carrying a powder horn on his wildcat skin belt. They called it the "Spectre Hunter."

Some people believed what they saw was a man wandering in the woods. Others thought that it was a demon. In 1774, the true identity of the phantom was revealed. The Spectre Hunter phantom was a rich and powerful Spanish grandee by the name of Don Manuel. Many years previously, Don Manuel returned unexpectedly from a long journey and discovered his beautiful wife being ravished by a fancy-dressed cavalier. In a fury, Don Manuel drew his dagger and stabbed the rascal in the heart. To his horror, Don Manuel soon realized that he had killed his sister who what been dressed in the costume as a joke.

Don Manuel could not live with himself having the knowledge that he had killed his sister. He was arrested, tried and sent to prison for his crime. After losing his freedom and vast estate, Don Manuel went insane. After being released from prison, he ran off and hid in the wild country near the Indian mounds, living as a hunter.

Death finally freed Don Manuel from the torment that plagued him since the death of his sister. A Catholic priest conducted a funeral mass for Don Manuel, but he still could not find peace and his tormented phantom spirit is still said to appear on dark and stormy nights to frighten unwary travelers.

Massac County

Fort Massac State Park

Metropolis

Fort Massac, located in Metropolis, was built by the French in 1757 as an outpost to fight off an expected invasion by the British. The original name for the fort was Fort Ascension. Much to the relief of the locals, the invasion never came.

Local legend says that a group of French marines stationed at the fort saw some bears across the river. They quickly gathered up their muskets, knives and canoes and set out to cross the Ohio River in pursuit of the bears. The remaining personnel remained at the fort unarmed and watched the hunting party from the shore.

The French hunting party stealthily positioned themselves so that the bears were trapped between them and the river. The Frenchmen took careful aim and just as they were about to fire they discovered, to their horror, that the bears were in fact Indians that were wearing bear skins as a disguise. The Indians had laid a clever ambush for the Frenchmen. Throwing off their bear skins, the Indians took aim at the Frenchmen at the same moment that another group of Indian warriors charged out of the woods behind the startled French. There were war whoops, screams, yelling and many gunshots. Soon the woods became silent as the last of the Frenchmen were slain. The situation was not any better back at the fort. A group of Indians attacked the unarmed garrison and killed everyone they found there. After these brutal attacks, the French renamed the fort as Fort Massacre which eventually was shortened by the Americans to Fort Massac.

The fort has been considered haunted since 1818. In that year a man by the name of Dillworth was found dead by the river bank. His throat had been cut from ear to ear. The ghost of Dillworth has been seen from time to time along the river bank where he died and at the Visitors Center next to the reconstructed fort. Park employees and visitors have reported sounds of footsteps when no one was there and doors that open and shut by themselves.

Fort Massac State Park is located at 1308 E. 5th Street in Metropolis, Illinois.

The Birdman of Alcatraz

Metropolis

The Birdman of Alcatraz is buried in Southern Illinois. If you watch paranormal investigation shows like Ghost Hunters, then you are probably familiar with Robert Stroud, better known as "The Birdman of Alcatraz." Perhaps you have even seen him portrayed by Burt Lancaster as the affable character in the 1962 movie by the same name, but he was not so affable. Robert Stroud was an evil and malicious convict who was feared by inmates and guards alike. Many locals do not know this, but Stroud is actually buried next to his mother right here in Southern Illinois!

Kale Meggs, our historical researcher, had a little success while visiting the tombstone of Robert Stroud in the Masonic Cemetery of Metropolis, Illinois, by obtaining an EVP there. It wasn't what you would expect from the restless soul of a psychotic murderer, though. Instead, the recorder caught the sound of what seemed to be a playful infant somewhere off in the distance. It just goes to show you that you never know what you'll find on an investigation.

The Birdman of Alcatraz is buried in Masonic Cemetery located at N 37.169777 and W -88.730609 in Metropolis, Illinois.

The Last Legal Hanging In Massac County

Metropolis

On December 17, 1926, William Brown brutally butchered Sadie Harris and Georgianna Caldwell in Brookport with an axe. Arrested the next day Brown was indicted for the murder of Harris but not Caldwell. A jury quickly found him guilty. Execution day in Metropolis became a party with many women and children present complete with picnic baskets, ice tea, and coffee. People not fortunate enough to obtain an invitation had to remain outside the stockade. Many waited in anticipation of hearing the "click" of the trap door and the "snap" of the rope and neck. A good time was had by all... except William Brown.

A few days later on the 21st, *The Republican Herald* reported:

> *William Brown, convicted of the murder of Sadie Harris and Annie Caldwell, near Brookport on December 17, 1926, paid the penalty for his crime here last Friday. Nearly 400 persons, including several women and girls, witnessed the execution within the enclosure. There were five or six hundred others on the court house yard who did not enter the fenced-in yard. He slept soundly the previous night and when the hours of execution drew near stoically waited the arrival of Sheriff Risinger. Rev. John Grooten of Carbondale, who is the pastor of the local Catholic Church, was with him until the last.*
>
> *Shortly after 10 a.m. Sheriff Risinger and Phil Hanna, professional hangman from Epworth, Ill. and several others including physicians accompanied Brown to the gallows. He ascended the steps without a quiver and at the trap door the noose was adjusted by Mr. Hanna. After Rev. Grooten finished his fervent prayer a black cap was placed over the condemned man's head and the sheriff sprung the trap. During the time from when Brown left the jail cell to the time he was hung, he did not speak a word.*
>
> *While lying in state at the establishment of Aikens & Fleming, many curious persons, black and white, came to view the body lying silently in death. Burial was in the Kidd Cemetery. Under the new state law, this probably is the last hanging Massac County will ever see.*

A Grisly Hobby

Samoth

In 1898 Dr. Elmo made his own medical skeletons in his barn. Dr. Elmo lived in Samoth which was in Massac County, Illinois. This town no longer exists. Dr. Elmo would boil water to prepare the skeletons. He would have the dead body hanging by the neck in his barn. The clothes would be cut off and the internal organs removed. The flesh would be cut off being careful to preserve the joints. He would bury the guts and then put the dissected body into the kettle of boiling water and quicklime. After the bones were boiled they were bleached white. Dr. Elmo would then assemble the bones into a skeleton for display. It is not known where he obtained the dead bodies.

Monroe County

Indian Killer

Valmeyer

Moredock Lake was named for a family that was massacred by Indians in the 1800s. Only one son survived and he swore that he would not rest until he had killed each and every Indian that he deemed responsible (meaning *any* Indian). He spent the rest of his life doing, just that... killing Indians.

Satanic Hippie Desecration

Eagle Cliff

Eagle Cliff Cemetery is the burial place of 430 known and as many as 200 unknown people. The area just below Eagle Cliff is an ancient Indian burial ground. The land where Eagle Cliff Cemetery and Miles Mausoleum is located was owned by Stephen W. Miles.

Thousands of acres of land around the Monroe County bottoms were purchased from the government land office in Kaskaskia by Miles. Men who had received land grants from the government for their service in the Revolutionary War would stake their claims and then mysteriously disappear after allegedly transferring their land holdings to Miles. Although this sounds a little sinister on the part of Stephen Miles, there is no proof of wrongdoing. Miles had acquired so much land that it is claimed that he used to stand on top of the bluffs overlooking the river and say "For miles and miles it is all Miles."

Stephen Miles commissioned a civil engineer by the name of Major Yrasillion to build a massive mausoleum on top of Eagle Cliff. This mausoleum was to be the final resting place of Miles and his descendents. The vault was made of Italian marble that was shipped up the Mississippi River from New Orleans. The cost was a staggering $25,000 and was  completed in 1858. Miles died three months before the completion of the mausoleum. Due to the severely cold winter, his body was kept in the parlor of his family home until construction was complete on the burial vault. Legend has it that his bread grew three inches during the time it took for him to be entombed.

The completed mausoleum contained fifty-six burial vaults. There were twenty-four vaults on each side and eight in the back wall. Miles was laid to rest in the vault along with two of his wives, a few mistresses and other family members. It is said that at least one of his negro servants was also placed in the vault. An engraving inside the vault was said to have read "Fanny, a pious, honest and upright colored servant of S.W. Miles, Senior. Died October 18, 1847 aged about seventy five years." A member of the Miles family is said to be buried under the steps of the mausoleum entrance and remains there to this day. Despite grand plans for the upkeep of the tomb, Miles went bankrupt and only 11 of the 56 vaults were ever used. Unfortunately, none of the dead would be allowed to rest in peace.

As originally constructed, the Mausoleum was covered with earth. The entrance had in inscription above it that said "S.W. MILES." Marble panels on each side of the entrance had inscriptions stating that the mausoleum was built by Stephen W. Miles, Esquire, the son of the elder Miles, in 1958 as a memorial to the Miles family and their descendants. It also stated that the mausoleum was to be cared for by the eldest son of each generation and to hold it "through this succession in trust for the above family." Bible verses were inscribed on the door of the vault and a wrought iron fence surrounded the front and part of the top of the mausoleum. Both marble panels are now long gone and mostly forgotten.

Visitors to Eagle Cliff reported that in the 1930s the wrought iron fence had been removed. It was said that the right bottom vault contained the body of a black mammy with a baby on her left arm. By the 1960s, Eagle Cliff Cemetery and Miles Mausoleum had been hard hit by vandals, thieves, hippies, and Satanists. The Satanist hippies had been conducting séances inside the mausoleum and had destroyed the vaults and coffins. They stole jewelry from the dead and dragged the bodies from the smashed coffins outside and set them on fire. The Satanists believed that this macabre ceremony would bring the dead back to life. Later inspection of the mausoleum revealed the extent of the damage. All of the vaults had been broken into. The floor of the mausoleum was covered with broken glass, beer, and wine bottles, scattered bone fragments, tattered bits of burial clothing, and coffin hardware. This vandalism and desecration prompted the caretakers to wall up and seal off the two windows and door to the mausoleum.

Today, the mausoleum is just a shadow of its long ago majesty. Graffiti covers both the exterior and interior of the now burial crypt. It is said that Eagle Cliff is haunted by the desecrated dead. Disembodied voices and whistles can be heard in and near the vaults. Mysterious wisps of smoky vapor can be photographed at various times. Inside the mausoleum you will encounter cold spots and sometimes even the touch of a long dead, ghostly hand.

Miles Mausoleum is located at N 38.363109 and W -90.262338.

Perry County

The Stump Pond Monster

Pyramid State Park

Strange creatures and monsters are common in Southern Illinois. One of the oldest stories was first reported in from Stump Pond. In 1879, a man was fishing from his boat on Stump Pond when he noticed a very large submerged object was plowing through the water. The object came so close to the boat the waves from it actually rocked the boat. The man was so frightened that the paddled to shore as fast as he could. He swore that he would never again go boating alone in the evening at the pond.

In July 1880, two coal miners reported a serpent that was 12 foot long at the pond. They said it was a dark green color and had a body as large as a telephone pole. The serpent was a ways out in the lake and headed straight for them. The miners did not stick around for its arrival.

Throughout the years there were sporadic reports of the pond monster. Finally, in 1968 Stump Pond was partially drained. Electric probes were placed in the water to stun the fish. Interested onlookers lined the banks of the pond hoping to catch a glimpse of the fabled monster at last. To every one's disappointment, the largest fish to float to the top of the water only weighed about 30 pounds.

Despite a lack of evidence, many of the witnesses stuck to their stories. One witness, Allyn Dunmeyer, stated "I was in my boat fishing for bass when it happened. Something came up from the bottom, struck the boat underneath so hard I nearly tipped over."

According to Dunmeyer, there's more than one giant in the pond. He'd seen them so near the surface that their dorsal fins stuck out.

Other witnesses have reported seeing what appeared to be an alligator.

The park is located at 1562 Pyramid Park Rd. near Pinckneyville.

Ouija Board Spirit

By Danni Weinhoffer
DuQuoin

Our good friend, Danni Weinhoffer sent us this true story.

"You know about the Ouija board and my family's fascination with it, right? Well we went to see my brother at his new house a couple of weeks ago.....and they had the Ouija board out.

No one could get any spirit to come to them, so me and my sis got together, we ALWAYS bring em in. We start talking to a ghost and I ask it if it is MY ghost from home, at first it says yes, but then it couldn't answer like she normally does, so I said are you pretending to be her and it said yes ma'am.

I asked its name and its age, it spelled Jimmy and went to 4. I was like 4 what? 4 years and it didn't answer; I said forty-something like me? And it said yes ma'am.

We talked to him for a while then he got quiet and I asked if there was anyone else with him and he said yes, I asked if we could talk to the other ghost and it said yes, so we started talking to the next one, we asked its name and it went to the letters AZ, and we asked its age and it went to 0. It wouldn't talk anymore and we got tired of trying ... AZ and age 0 really!? We were non-believers in that one.

Next day my sis and her guy are driving out in the country and found something. They came flying back to the house; hey that ghost ... his name was Jimmie right? Uh yeah, why?

Come on, come on, come on they said.

About 2 miles down the road is this memorial ... HUGE memorial.... JIMMY, a BABY and another girl. CARWRECK. We came back and asked the board about it, yes it was him, died in 2005. I looked it up on the internet.... sure as heck did!"

— ● — ● — ● —

Wake House Haunting

By Jack Wilson
DuQuoin

Here is a story about hauntings in a "wake house" as told to us by Jack Wilson.

I used to live in a house at 313 N. Division Street in DuQuoin, Illinois. It was used as a wake house in the 1930-40s and we would smell pipe smoke, cigar smoke and perfume. Down in the basement where they kept coffins and bodies, I saw a kid about 8 or 9 years old in clothes from the 1930s with dark eyes looking at me from the door way looking into the basement. I set a recorder down there one night, and picked up voices, footsteps, and banging noises, and a voice that said "GET OUT I'M WORKING."

I saw a civil war soldier in the back yard. He was facing the railroad tracks. When I would be home by myself, a woman would call my name from the kitchen. I saw the boy a few times, so I put some toys down there for him, I would mark the spot with tape, and the toys were moved by morning. We had to keep our keys to the house on us all the time because when we were outside, the door would lock (deadbolt).

My daughter, who was two to three yrs old at the time, would not go into the kitchen, she would throw a fit! I liked the house, but we had to move because the land lord would not fix the basement, every time it rained a lot, the sewer line would back up and flood the basement with nasty water.

Beaucoup Creek

Perry County

In 1880, Beaucoup Creek in Perry County, Illinois broke thru the overburden of the Beaucoup Mine. The mine was flooded so quickly that some miners were trapped inside. In 1918, the mine was finally pumped out and the body of a coal miner was found face down on the muddy floor of the mine. The mineral water of the creek had completely petrified his body. The preservation was so perfect that even his pipe and tobacco were intact.

Pope County

Satan's Ghost

Herod

Satan is buried in a private cemetery near Herod, Illinois. The Evil One is not the actual corpse buried in this haunted cemetery. This burial is that of Satan Parton. Unlike the Satan of the Bible, Satan Parton was an upstanding, respected and likeable person. The ghost of Satan loves to pull pranks on visitors to the cemetery. He is in the habit of hopping into cars parked nearby, putting them in gear and driving off a short distance.

The Golconda Madstone

Golconda

In the early 1800s, Golconda was a wilderness area infected with snakes and various animals. As the settlers encroached on the natural habitat of the wildlife, some of the animals fought back by biting the unwary. Animal bites brought forth the fear of rabies. In pioneer times there was no cure for rabies, except for madstones.

The madstones could be found in the heads of toads and fish and could even be a hard object found in the stomach of a white deer. Some stones were discovered in creek beds or mines. These stones had the mysterious ability to draw out toxins from the human body.

Madstones were considered extremely valuable. There were at least three known madstones in Southern Illinois with the most famous being in Golconda. According to John W. Allen, the Golconda madstone was discovered in a coal mine and brought to Illinois from Tennessee about 1870 by Matthew Trovillion. This madstone was so valuable that it was the subject of a lawsuit in 1911.

The proper way to use a madstone was to let it adhere to the area of the bite. After about an hour the madstone would fall off the wound. The stone would be placed in water until its surface would start to bubble. The process would be repeated until the stone would not adhere to the wound anymore. As if by miracle, the patient was cured.

The Golconda madstone was used hundreds of times on all kinds of bites with only one death due to the vicious wounds not rabies. No one knows for sure how the madstones worked and their whereabouts are a mystery today.

Golconda Tragedies

Golconda

An Indian fort known as War Bluff is located near Golconda. Indians built the fort with stones that they carried to the top of the bluffs from creek beds below. Legend tells of an Indian warrior and beautiful maiden that were forbidden to marry by the maiden's father. The two love struck Indians climbed to the top of War Bluff, joined hands and then jumped to their deaths in the creek below.

Around the time of the Civil War, a German family by the name of Rauchfuss settled on a hill that bears their name near Golconda. The family was known for the fine quality lace and quinine which they sold at their store. Mr. Rauchfuss imported two especially fine lace veils for his two daughter's upcoming weddings. Tragically, one of the daughters fell through some thin ice at Lusk Creek and drowned before her wedding. The distraught family buried their daughter wearing her lace wedding veil. There have been reports that on very cold and moonlit nights during winter months, the mournful spirit of a young female wearing a lace wedding veil can be seen hovering near a certain spot at

Lusk Creek with her head bowed. She vanishes before anyone can get very near.

Murder in Golconda: In the terrible winter of 1838 thousands of Cherokee Indians were forced to march through Southern Illinois by Andrew Jackson's "Indian Removal Act," away from their homeland and on their way to their Oklahoma reservation. The soldiers pushed them along. Thousands died.

Before crossing into Illinois over the Ohio from Kentucky, many were forced to camp under Mantle Rock near Berry's Ferry, as John Berry was profiting from the tragedy by charging a dollar a head to the poor souls. This was extremely expensive, as the usual price for a white man and his entire wagon was only twelve and a half cents. Berry made over ten grand that winter, which was a huge amount of wealth in 1838. Not many folks know this part, but I have researched John Berry and he died less than one year after making his fortune, never being able to enjoy the fruits of his evil.

Unfortunately, many Southern Illinoisans weren't much friendlier to the weary and sick travelers. It's said that extortion and murder occurred on our side of the river. In fact, some Cherokee were murdered for sport by Golconda citizens, or by a similar profiteering scheme as Berry pulled. The murderers actually tried to sue the federal government for the burial of the victims of their crime, (they specifically requested $35 a body) pretending that they, the shooters, were the actual victims because of the stench of the bodies still lying in the streets. The government threw out the case and told the citizens that they killed the Indians, they could bury them.

The bodies of the murdered Cherokee were tossed into the back of a wagon, moved to what is now the Trovillion Cemetery in Brownfield, Illinois, and thrown into a dry creek bed. There is a marker at the cemetery entrance and a monument honoring the victims, however, the details just shared are left out.

Golconda Ghosts And Tokens Of Death

Golconda

Some old timers in Golconda used to tell spooky tales about tokens of death and other strange happenings. One story took place near Palestine Church on the north side of town. On a dark and lonely night, two young men took a shortcut through the cemetery on their way home. Up ahead, near some tombstones, they saw a white shimmering "something." One of the men picked up a rock and threw it at the apparition. The rock bounced off and made a sound like the rattling of bones. Both men ran the rest of the way home.

A man in Golconda used to make coffins in a little shop. Each coffin was made to order at the time of need. Sometimes late at night the sounds of sawing and hammering could be heard coming from the coffin shop. On close inspection, it would be discovered that the doors were locked, the lanterns were not lit, and no one was inside at work. Each time this happened, someone would stop by the coffin shop the next day to order a coffin. Whenever the late night sounds came from the coffin shop, it was taken as a token that death would visit soon.

The owners of the Schrenck Funeral Home were asked if they ever had any tokens of death. Mrs. Schrenck replied that one night she heard a noise upstairs and when she investigated the cause she discovered that a little casket had fallen off of its bier. The next morning they sold the casket.

Pulaski County

Murder in Mound City, Illinois—the Murderer Hung

Mound City

From an old newspaper clipping:

An 1884 Cairo correspondent of the St. Louis Democrat *says:*
On Saturday night last a desperado of considerable notoriety in that locality, named James Vaughn, in company with one of the operatives at Goodloe's foundry, name unknown, got on a spree and became inebriated to a considerable extent. Subsequently the two fell in with a carpenter or machinist from Pennsylvania, by name, John K. Charles, similarly inflicted. They continued together, and in the course of the evening's conversation, there seems to have been a clash of opinion between Vaughn's companion and Charles, resulting in a clash of arms, boots and fists. They closed, and in the ensuing struggle, Charles, proving to be the more sober man, got rather the better of the foundryman, observing which, Vaughn, who stood by, drew his pistol and deliberately shot Charles through the heart, killing him instantly.

Vaughn instantly disappeared, and crossing to Kentucky, fled. He was pursued however, Saturday, by Captain Ferrel and others, who overtook him about ten miles below Cairo. He was armed with a gun, which he presented, but was, nevertheless, captured without difficulty, taken back to Mound City, and lodged in jail, to await examination. A crowd gathered, went to the jail, armed with a log as a battering ram, affected an entrance, and taking Vaughn out, notified him that fifteen minutes would be generously allowed him to say his prayers and attend to any other matters he chose, preparatory to having his "mortal coil shuffled off." Hardly appreciating the reality of the thing at first, his cries when the truth began to break upon him are represented as heart-rendering--increasing in force and piteousness as the stolid indifference of his captors show how fixed was their purpose for blood, and how surely the retribution for his villainy was at hand.

Neither prayers nor cries could defer the appointed time, however, and at the minute he was run up a tree by the excited throng, where he hung till he was dead. He was left hanging till morning, when he was cut down by some of his friends and taken away. The thing was done determinedly, and at the scene of blood there seems to have been general unanimity of feeling. The appearance of his father, an individual enjoying considerable notoriety in the same way as his son, and his companion of Saturday night, had well-nigh cost them their lives, and they made themselves scarce suddenly.

— ● — ● — ● —

The Mound City Massacre

Mound City

On February 9, 1813, a band of Creek Indians led by Little Warrior and known to the locals as "the outlawed Indians" came to what is now Mound City. The Indians soon came to some cabins showing hostile intent. Armed with guns and tomahawks, the Indians walked up to one of the cabins and asked for something to eat. They were invited inside by Mr. Shaver. Once inside, one of the Indians felt the muscles of Mr. Shaver's legs in an attempt to judge his ability to run.

Mr. Shaver asked "Do you wish to run a race?" The Indian answered "No." Mr. Shaver then asked "Do you wish to wrestle?" The Indian answered "No." The white families started to become alarmed and hoped that the Indians would leave after eating. It was not to be. Soon after finishing their meal, the Indians attacked Mr. Shaver with a hatchet, striking him a stunning blow to the head. Mr. Shaver ran out the back door and took off on his horse with the Indians in hot pursuit.

Mr. Shaver made his getaway across a frozen bayou near what is now the former Marine Ways. The Indians stopped at the bank of the frozen bayou and shouted to Mr. Shaver that he was very brave and if he returned they would do him no further harm. Mr. Shaver used some very strong language telling the Indians what he thought of them and where they could go. He then made his escape to some Union County settlements.

The Indians returned to the cabins where they had been lunch guests and proceeded to murder seven families. The attack was extremely cruel and showed all the barbarity that could be invented. One woman was cut open and her unborn child removed. The child was then impaled on a stake. All of the other bodies were mangled almost beyond recognition. The Indians ripped up feather beds, destroyed furniture and stole whatever they wanted. The Indians crossed the river into Kentucky and were never apprehended for their crimes. A group of soldiers came down from Fort Massac to bury the dead.

Gore Monument

Olmstead

E. B. Gore was a very prominent shopkeeper and practical joker in Olmstead, Illinois. In 1933, he frightened a small boy by the name of George Britt. Here is the story in Britt's own words.

"I lived across the road here. And he came out here to the cemetery with a real pretty horse - single horse - in a buggy and had a suit on and a tall Abraham Lincoln hat I was nine years old so I walked down here.

"And they're down here working with cement mixers. So I asked him what's going on and he tells me they're going to build him a monument and they're going to put him in the bottom of the monument in a copper coffin - he's going to die in a couple of months.

"That frightened me considerably being nine years old and I don't really understand what death is and here he was alive talking about that. This was in 1933 and he said in the year twenty-hundred they could then open that up - look through the glass thing and see him."

Sure enough, E. B. Gore died that same year. After his death, Gore was placed in a copper coffin filled with formaldehyde. The coffin was then placed in a chamber in the 60 foot obelisk that was made of reinforced concrete with footings extending 18

feet into the ground. The obelisk is topped with a ball of solid lead. According to legend, there is some kind of secret treasure buried under the monument as well. The sealed up entrance to the burial chamber is located on the back side of the monument.

The E. B Gore monument is in Concord Cemetery located at N 37.20920 and W -89.11920 near Olmstead, Illinois.

Randolph County

Kaskaskia's Curse

Kaskaskia

Kaskaskia was the site of the Mission of the Immaculate Conception founded by Jesuit priests in 1673. The mission drew French settlers from Canada. The French military decided to build a fort nearby that they named Fort de Chartres. Construction of the fort started in 1750. According to legend, an Algonquin Indian fell in love with a French maiden from Kaskaskia. When it became known that they planned to marry, the maiden's father forbade the two lovers from marriage or even seeing each other again. Grief stricken, the Indian placed a curse on Kaskaskia. In 1881 a mighty flood occurred on the Mississippi River that destroyed Kaskaskia. The cemetery was flooded and caskets holding dead bodies popped out of the sodden soil and floated down the Mississippi. The river actually changed its course, forming a 14,000 acre island where the present day village of Kaskaskia is located. It is the only Illinois town that lies west of the Mississippi River.

Hexebuckel

Red Bud

Hexebuckel, sometimes known as Witches Hump, is a hill located north of Red Bud. In years past, superstitious families seeking to escape a witch's spell would go to Witches Hump hill because it was widely believed that witches could not follow them up the hill.

Burned at the Stake for Witchcraft

Randolph County

Manuel, a slave, was burned at the stake for witchcraft on June 15, 1779, in present day Randolph County, Illinois. The warrant for execution read as follows:

> *Illinois to Wit; To Richard Winston, Esq., Sheriff in Chief of the District of Kaskaskia. Negro Manuel, a Slave, in your Custody, is condemned by the Court of Kaskaskia, after having made honorable Fine at the Door of the Church, to be chained to a post at the water side & there to be burnt alive, & his ashes scattered, as appears to me by Record. This Sentence you are hereby required to put in Execution on tuesday next, at 9 o'Clock in the morning; and this shall be your Warrant. Given under my hand & seal at Kaskaskia, the 13th day of June,- in the third year of the Commonwealth. I am, sir, yr hble servant, Jno. Todd*

Note: At the time, Illinois Territory was part of the Commonwealth of Virginia No record of the actual execution has ever been found.

The Creole House

Prairie Du Rocher

The Creole House is located in Prairie du Rocher. It was built around 1800 by Dr. Robert McDonald. Two of the families who owned the Creole House lived in a mansion that stood just to the north of the house. This mansion mysteriously burned in 1867. The mansion was rebuilt and once again mysteriously burned just over a hundred years later in 1970.

No paranormal activity was reported until "haunted house" tours were started in 2005. "Ghost Effects" were set up in the Brickey Family cemetery behind the house. It almost seemed like someone or something was not very accepting of the activity. All of the electric equipment "fried." One evening, one of the haunted house actors looked in the bedroom window from outside and saw an old woman staring back at him. No one was in the house at the time. On the first night of the haunted house tour, all of the electricity shut down. An electrician was called to fix the problem. At that very moment, all of the electricity came back on. The circuit breakers were checked and none were found to have been tripped.

One of the rooms contains an old clock with a swinging pendulum that sits on the mantel. The clock was in perfect working order until the night of the haunted house tour, when it stopped on the stroke of 11:00. The clock has not worked since. When you are in the house and someone else enters, there is a very distinct, but difficult to describe sound no matter where you enter from. This sound can be heard, even when no one has entered.

Cold spots have been felt on many occasions. One caretaker came to the house one evening with four other people to take photographs of a mysterious image that appeared on the kitchen wall. The image is a bright light reflection through a window. The strange thing is that the entire window does not glare. Only the letters "I M" followed by a perfectly shaped skull.

This appears to be an imperfection in the glass. All attempts to photograph the image have failed. All types of cameras have been tried including manual and auto focus cameras, digital and film cameras, cell phone cameras, flash and non-flash. No matter what is tried, the image cannot be captured with a camera. As the caretaker and guests were looking at the wall, a nearby chair began to move. It made an impression on the seat cushion as if someone was sitting on it. There was an extremely cold area of air above the seat.

There is only one room to enter the house from the outside and a key has to be used to open the door. When the door is unlocked it easily swings open with a nudge. One evening, the caretaker came back with some guests and as the door nudged open, it slammed shut with force! The caretaker tried to reopen the door, but it would not move. It was discovered that a folding chair was lying behind the door as if thrown there. No folding chairs are kept in that particular room and no one had been in the house. The door slamming incident has happened on more than one occasion.

One evening, one of the volunteers went out back to unplug some electric cords. There were lots of dried leaves covering the ground the volunteer heard very heavy, deliberate footsteps coming from around the corner. When he went to look for them, he discovered that no one was there. Random lights have been reported in the house by locals. The caretaker receives many calls from locals telling him that the lights are on and seem to come on "magically."

Many years ago, a local person committed suicide near the Creole House. He has been seen to the rear of the house. One night, two of the volunteers joked about the suicide, saying, "that's all I need is him running around the backyard!" At that very moment some of the black lights they had set up for the haunted house, started to flicker. The volunteer said, "Ya know, the spooks are gonna have it all turned off by starting time tomorrow!" Right then, the light went out leaving the volunteers in total darkness.

A volunteer was cleaning the house one day and felt a very cold spot in the bed room. Thinking a door was open, she checked the other rooms in the house and found them to be quite warm and all the doors barred. When she returned to the bedroom, it was warm just like the rest of the house.

One room contains photos of a family from the 1830s. These photos are generally crooked when you enter the house while all the other photos and paintings are always straight. One evening while straightening a rug in front of the corner cabinet (belonging to the first Governor of Illinois), the latches on the cabinet clicked and the glass doors slowly swung open. Later a light suddenly came on in the basement. This light could be seen through the knot holes in the parlor's wood floor. The strange thing was that the only access to the cellar was boarded shut several weeks previously.

One evening, as one of the volunteers was attempting to leave, he tripped and his car keys went flying. He heard them hit the metal of his car. He proceeded to feel around on the ground in the grass for about 15 or 20 minutes. When he got up, he discovered the keys were mysteriously hanging in the door lock.

The Little Egypt Ghost Society team of investigators encountered some unexplained paranormal activity while conducting a ghost hunt at this location. A moving ghost light orb was seen in real time, zipping from the parlor and into the kitchen area right behind me (witnessed by four people). There was the sound of footsteps running across the front porch. Several team members immediately went outside and could find no one near the house and no foot prints in the snow around the house. We recorded several unexplainable EMF readings using the Mel Meters, K2 meter, Ghost Meter and Cell Sensor meter. The PX device responded intelligently to questions asked.

The Creole House is located on Market Street in Prairie du Rocher, Illinois.

— ● — ● — ● —

The Chair of Death and Pain

Chester

Illinois is home to three electric chairs. They were located at Stateville prison in Joliet, Cook County Jail in Chicago and Menard State Penitentiary in Chester. The electric chair at Menard was used for the last time on January 28, 1938 for a double execution.

Marie Poster and her lover, Angelo Giancola were convicted for the murder of Porter's brother in order to collect on a $3,300 life insurance policy. The brother was killed on his wedding day just hours before his fiancée would have replaced Porter as beneficiary.

At 12:06 a.m., Angelo Giancola was the first to die, followed 10 minutes later by Marie Porter, aged 37. At 12:16 a.m. the guards adjusted the straps and electrodes on Marie Porter. The prison warden asked Marie for a last statement. She thanked prison officials "I have no malice toward any one". The warden asked, "Is that all, Mrs. Porter?" She whispered "Yes." The warden said quietly, "good-bye Mrs. Porter," and signaled.

All present heard a sharp sizzle as her body lurched against the straps. One spectator was heard to say, "Look at her burn." At 12:19, two minutes after the 2300 volts were sent through her body she was pronounced dead. Marie Porter had the dual distinction of being the last female to be executed in Illinois and the last person to be executed in Menard's electric chair.

Today, the Menard electric chair is located at the Randolph County Museum in Chester, Illinois. John (real name on file with the Little Egypt Ghost Society) one of our Little Egypt Ghost Society members, visited the museum and located the electric chair exhibit. For many years, John has had the gift of being an "empath." An empath is a person who can tune into the emotional experience of a person, place or animal. John walked up to the electric chair and grasped two upright wooden supports on the back. These two supports would have aligned with the spinal cord of the person being executed.

The electric current from the electrode cap worn on the prisoners head would have traveled along this path to the electrodes attached the prisoner's legs. As John held on to the wooden supports, he felt a surge of pain that traveled up his arms and to the center of his chest.

At that point, he became very short of breath. John said it felt just like he was having a heart attack. John believes that he was feeling psychic pain that was a residual from the executions that had taken place in this electric chair.

The electric chair is on display at the Randolph County Museum & Archives located at 1 Taylor Street in Chester, Illinois.

The Sea Hag

Chester

Elzie C. Segar, Popeye's creator, was born in Chester and many of the Popeye characters were modeled after real residents of the town. One of my favorite Popeye characters was the Sea Hag. The Chester resident who inspired the character of the Sea Hag is a mystery and remains secret to this day. Whoever it was, she must have been a very interesting person.

The Sea Hag was one of Popeye's greatest enemies. She was the last witch on earth and a pirate who sailed the Seven Seas. The Black Barnacle was her ship. The Sea Hag had a vast knowledge of magic and was able to practice Voodoo. Her companions were a pet vulture named Bernard and an army of Goons.

Even though Popeye and the Sea Hag were enemies, Popeye's honor would not allow him to hit a woman, even someone as evil as the Sea Hag. At one point, Popeye believed that the Sea Hag was finally dead. When he discovered that she wasn't, however, he said "I yam glad she ain't dead even if she is a exter bad woman. If they wasn't no bad women, maybe we wouldn't appreciate the good ones. Anyway, she yam what she yam!"

In 2010, a granite statue of the Sea Hag and Bernard the Vulture was unveiled along the Popeye "character trail" in Chester.

— ● — ● — ● —

Miss Minnie The Library Ghost

Chester

The Chester Public library is haunted by the ghost known as Miss Minnie. Like most library ghosts, Miss Minnie is not a scary or threatening apparition. This ghost likes to play pranks on library staff and visitors. Miss Minnie will make the elevator come up from below when no one was in or near it. An elevator repairman was called in to check out the seemingly malfunctioning elevator. After an extensive examination of the mechanical and electrical workings of the elevator, the repairman reported that it was in perfect working order. He did state that while the elevator might go down by itself, it was impossible for it to come up by itself.

Other pranks that this ghost likes to play are to ring the bell on the front door late in the evening when staff members are working alone, tossing books in the aisles, and calling librarians by name when on one is around. Who is or was Miss Minnie? No one knows for sure, but she still likes to make her presence known.

The Chester Public Library is located at 733 State Street in Chester, Illinois.

— ● — ● — ● —

Richland County

Burrow's Cave

Olney

Would you believe that ancient treasures from Queen Cleopatra and King Juba II were found buried in a cave near Olney? According to Russell Burrows, that is exactly what happened. Burrows had an interesting hobby. He was a treasure hunter. On April 2, 1982, Burrows was exploring a cave near Olney looking for treasure. The interior of the cave was like many he had been in before except for one thing. At the back of the cave was what appeared to be a chamber that had been sealed up for many years.

Armed with his pick hammer he started chipping away at the back wall of the cave. After a short time he broke through the wall to discover a small chamber with carved stairs that lead down about 30 feet. At the bottom of the stairs was a hand hewn tunnel about 500 feet long that had several old time lanterns hung along the walls.

Burrows entered the chamber at the end of the tunnel and discovered a 5 foot statue of a man that appeared to be made of solid gold. A few feet beyond the statue was a sarcophagus also made out of gold. Scattered around the chamber were various swords, battle axes and spears. There were statues and carvings that depicted Roman soldiers, Jews, Christians and African sailors. Shining his flashlight around, he found piles of gold and silver coins as well as uncut diamonds.

Burrows knew he had made a major find and was fearful that someone would find out about the treasure trove. He quickly gathered up as much treasure as he could carry and loaded it up in his truck after carefully concealing the entrance to the cave with tree branches and boulders. He came back a short time later and dynamited the entrance of the cave so that no one else could loot the treasure.

So how did the treasure come to be stashed in the cave? For the answer you need to go back to the year 46 B.C. on the North African coast. The king of Namibia (present day Libya) fought the Pomsey against the Roman Emperor, Julius Caesar. After Caesar defeated the Africans, the king committed suicide rather than being captured. The king's son, Juba II was taken as a trophy by Caesar and taken back to Rome. Juba II was raised by Caesar's nephew, Octavian. Since he was now part of Caesar's family, Juba II was educated by the best scholars of the time. When he reached adulthood, he was appointed ruler of Mauritania on the West Coast of Africa. He married the daughter of Anthony and Cleopatra, Cleopatra Selene and they ruled the country from 25 B.C. to 19 A.D.

When Caligula became Emperor of the Roman Empire, he had a falling out with Juba II and his wife Cleopatra, Caligula had their son, Ptolemy put to death. This caused the Mauritanians to revolt against Rome. Fearing that the Romans would crush the revolt and execute them, King Juba II and his family gathered up Cleopatra's vast treasures and the library of King Juba II that contained vast amounts of ancient wisdom. They then built a fleet of ships and sailed west to establish a new kingdom.

It is believed that King Juba II, his family and many loyal followers eventually landed on North American soil and made their way inland. After much hardship they ended up near what is now Olney and hid their treasure in a cave located there. No one knows what happened to King Juba II, his family, or followers after that. The exact location of Burrow's Cave is a mystery to this day. If you find it, there is a vast fortune to be discovered.

Saline County

The Murder of Deputy Sheriff Royce Cline

Carrier Mills

On Friday, August 14, 1925 at about 8:45am, Sheriff John Small sent Deputies Royce Cline, Silas Rude and Hubert Hawkins to the Lakeview Settlement about two and a half miles south of Carrier Mills, where a large supply of booze was reported to be hidden. Royce Cline was a brave and fearless man. During daring raids, Deputy Cline always took the lead. It was his policy to say, "Come on, boys," and not "Let's go."

The Deputies arrived at the settlement about 11:00am and entered a thicket that was very dense with briars, brush and vines. It was impossible to see a man standing six feet away. After a short distance, the deputies found a path and followed it to a small clearing where barrels of mash had been hidden by a bootlegger.

At about 11:30a.m., as the deputies lay in wait, they heard someone coming through the thicket. Deputy Cline arose and moved in front of Deputy Rude and crouched down on one knee with his Colt .45 pistol drawn. They waited for the party to approach. The man approaching the deputies was an African-American with a .12 gauge single barrel shot gun that was cocked and in both hands ready to fire. Just as the negro saw the head and face of Deputy Cline he took aim and fired into the face of the brave lawman. Deputy Cline fell back into the arms of Deputy Rude. The negro dropped the gun and ran off. Deputy Rude fired at the fleeing negro, but missed.

Deputy Cline was horribly mutilated. His mouth, nose and ears were torn off and he was blinded in one eye. Deputy Rude helped Deputy Cline out of the bushes and onto a tree stump and then ran for help. When Deputy Rude got back to his car, he was surprised to see Deputy Cline lying in the road next to the car. Deputy Cline had walked near half a mile unassisted with his face shot almost completely off, strangling from blood running into his lungs and blinded in one eye. According to Deputy Rude, the ground that Deputy Cline traveled could not have been covered by a healthy man without great exertion.

Deputy Cline was rushed to Lightner Hospital in Harrisburg where Drs. Lightner and Gaskins succeeded in getting the hemorrhage stopped. Deputy Cline's wife, Nellie, was summoned to the hospital and arrived just a few minutes before he died at about 2:30 p.m. The body was taken to the Gaskins Undertaking Parlor where it was prepared for burial.

Harrisburg was in an uproar over the murder of Deputy Cline. Determined and angry men and law officers formed up in posses to capture the shooter, who was named Isaiah "Zebe" Taborn, age about 46, who had committed the cowardly murder. A man-hunting German police dog was brought in from Sebree, Kentucky to aid in the search. For two days and nights the hunt for the murder of the brave law officer continued.

On Sunday afternoon, the funeral for Deputy Sheriff Royce Cline was conducted at the Cline's residence at 322 West Poplar Street in Harrisburg. Rev. J. H. Davis was in charge. Rev. Whitlock read the obituary. Mrs. Bonnie Hetherington sang "Death is Only a Dream." "Jesus Savior Pilot Me" was performed by a quartette composed of Roy Staiger, Bob Hine, Bob Burnett and Charles Ferguson. Mrs. P. W. Sherman sang "I've Done My Work" and Bonnie Hetherington and her son Charles performed a piano-violin duet. The services were impressive and the throng of those attending outnumbered any ever gathered in Harrisburg to pay a final tribute. Deputy Cline was held in very high regard in the hearts of the people of Saline County and the surrounding area. After the services, Deputy Sheriff Royce Cline was taken to the old Masonic Cemetery near Raleigh for burial on the rolling hills near the cedars.

During the funeral service, "Zebe" Taborn was finally captured in a corn field. Taborn came out of the corn field after his uncle, Wiley Taborn, went in to fetch him. "Zebe" had his hands outstretched and said; "Mr. Mitchell (a deputy sheriff), I want your protection." Deputy Mitchell told him that he would protect him. Several other black men were standing nearby and one of them yelled, "Three cheers for the Red, White and Blue!" "Zebe's" father then came with some clean clothes and his mother and sister came with lunch. A white boy gave the prisoner a watermelon that "Zebe" ate ravenously. The prisoner was taken to the Benton jail and held there until brought back to Harrisburg for trial.

Isaiah "Zebe" Taborn went on trial at the circuit court in Harrisburg with Judge A. S. Somers presiding. The prosecution team consisted of K. C. Ronalds, W. C. Kane and S. D. Wise. The defense team consisted of D. F. Rumsey, H. N. Finney and Walter W. Wheatley. In the closing argument of the prosecution, W.C. Kane brought in an element of the supernatural when he stated that the jurors "need have not fear of the dead hand of Royce Cline returning to haunt them should they sign a verdict of guilty." He went on to state that "Punishment is necessary and is under God's law; you can abolish capital punishment and the crime wave will sweep the country. There is no other way to protect our homes." He made a strong plea for the death penalty.

The verdict of conviction was returned in open court. It read: "We, the jury find the defendant guilty as charged in the indictment and fix his punishment at fourteen years in the penitentiary." Judge Somers lost no time in notifying "Zebe" Taborn and his attorneys that sentence would be passed without delay. Taborn was immediately taken to the Southern Illinois Penitentiary at Chester.

Nellie Cline, the slain deputy's wife, made this remark about the verdict: "we, my daughter, his mother and I feel very disappointed. When Royce was killed I was glad the man who killed him was not lynched. I wanted him to be tried fairly and punished for his crime. I heard the questions asked the jurors, heard their answers and thought that justice would be rendered, but it seems impossible."

"It is not that I am disappointed in the officials of Saline County or the counsel for the prosecution, for they did all they could, but it does seem that fourteen years is light punishment for a man who deliberately kills another, especially when the other is an officer performing his duties, and I don't know how the public can expect another officer to risk his life by trying to enforce the law, as my husband was doing when he was killed."

I wonder if the jurors were ever haunted by the dead hand of my great-uncle, Royce Cline, for handing out such a light sentence.

— ● — ● — ● —

This is the Colt's Government Model .45 cal pistol that Deputy Cline was carrying when he was gunned down by a bootlegger near Carrier Mills, Illinois, on August 14, 1925. The nick in the handle was caused by a  shotgun slug as the gun was held in the hand of Deputy Cline.

— ● — ● — ● —

Salem Cemetery

Carrier Mills

Salem Cemetery located in Carrier Mills is, *or should I say was*, the location of a very mysterious grave. This above-ground burial contained the body of a young girl. On nights where there was a full moon the grave produced a vaporous mist that would creep along the ground. It seemed to be an intelligent mist in that it would inexplicably move toward and follow anyone nearby.

It was rumored that if you went to the grave at night and knocked on it three times and then go back to your car you would smell roses. This used to be a weekend ritual with many of the high school kids in the 1970s (myself included).

One weekend night in the mid '70s, several of my friends and I decided to find out for ourselves. We drove out to the cemetery and located the grave near the back of the cemetery. I parked the car and we all got out and slowly crept over to the grave. After arranging ourselves in a circle around the grave, we all knocked three times, turned and ran towards our car. Looking behind us, we saw a wispy mist forming along the ground. The mist was slowly undulating along the ground towards us. At that moment we all smelled an overpowering scent of roses. We got out of there as fast as we could.

As if all of this was not mysterious and creepy enough, we decided to try to locate this grave again in 2008. The grave is not there anymore. What happened to it is a mystery. Was it relocated to discourage thrill seekers? No one seems to know, or if they do, they are not willing to say what happened to it.

Salem Cemetery is located at N 37.708056 and W -88.625000 in Carrier Mills, Illinois.

Tuttle Bottoms Monster

Harrisburg

Southern Illinois has long been known for its reports of monsters and strange happenings and Tuttle Bottoms is known to have its share of strange creatures. Since at least the 1960s, the area north-west of Harrisburg known as Tuttle Bottoms has been the stomping grounds of what is known as the Tuttle Bottoms Monster. The Harrisburg Police Department has received over 50 reports of a strange big foot type of monster in the Tuttle Bottoms area since the early 1960s.

The Tuttle Bottoms Monster was first reported in the north outskirts of Harrisburg is the section of town referred to as Dorris Heights. The middle fork of the Saline River passes through the woods of this scenic area. Hunters and people who would park along the road in that area would make frantic calls to police and sheriff departments reporting a large furry animal that resembled an overgrown anteater. Others said the creature resembled a large bear.

Strange tracks were often found nearby. In the 1960s and '70s many high school kids would go to Tuttle Bottoms to drink beer and "make out." It was rumored that some murders took place in the Bottoms. Parents warned kids to stay away from that area. I remember one hot summer night in the late 1960s when our sitter took me and my brother for a ride through Tuttle Bottoms. As we crossed the bridge over the middle fork of the Saline River, a large creature that resembled a prehistoric pterodactyl swooped down at the roof of the car, circled around and followed us for a short distance. Our sitter floored the gas pedal in her old car and we flew down that dark gravel road as fast as it could go. It was quite some time until I was brave enough to go back to Tuttle Bottoms.

Brian DeNeal, editor of the *Harrisburg Daily Register* wrote an article telling how the Tuttle Bottoms Monster was researched by Virgil Smith, founder of the animal research organization Shadows of the

Shawnee. Smith believes that the creature known as the Tuttle Bottoms Monster was an actual animal released by the federal government. The creature was described as standing on two legs, covered in hair and lived near swampy areas. The creature appeared to be some type of primate and was not afraid of humans.

According to Smith, a former employee of the U.S. Department of Agriculture said that the USDA had investigated the Tuttle Bottoms Monster. It is Smith's belief that the creature known as the Tuttle Bottoms Monster was released by a government agency and that the creature had long since died.

Pauper House Cemetery

Harrisburg

The Saline County Pauper (or Poor) House is listed on the National Register of Historic Places. As early as 1819, the Illinois General Assembly enacted a "Pauper Bill" which required County Commissioners to appoint overseers of the poor. In an effort to care for the area's poor, land was purchased in 1863 and construction began in 1877 starting with a two-story Victorian style home that is now fitted with a museum of local and donated artifacts from the 1800s. Several log homes, a barn and blockhouse, an old Quaker church, jail house and a school completed the village.

Volunteers and visitors to the house have reported strange lights, voices, footsteps, cold spots and a chair that seems to rock on its own. Most anyone who has witnessed the activity of the home refuses to be left alone in the home or stay in it overnight.

The Pauper Cemetery contains some 263 crude stone markers with an estimated 60 belonging to children, dating back as far as 1849. Records indicate that not only people from the poor farm were buried here but that it was also the county burial site for unknown vagrants, rail road and coal mine victims, or abandoned children. The custom of the time was for those not having a proper funeral to be buried the same day as they were discovered dead, which did not leave a lot of preparation time for headstones resulting in some rather crude burial notes to be carved on the markers.

Some of these notes include; "Run over by a train at Wasson," "Gunshot wound," "Unknown baby found in sewer," "Gunshot wound administered by chief of Police," "Daddy," "Lithuania-wife still in Europe," "Found dead in ditch," "Carnival worker," "Murdered," "Left of Charlie Yates-O-Gara," "#3 mined accident," and "Shot by Charlie Birger at Ledford." Despite the large number of graves that have already been located the Historical Society is still searching for, and finding more unmarked graves.

The Pauper House Cemetery is located across the street from the Saline Creek Pioneer Village located at 1600 Feazel Street in Harrisburg, Illinois.

— ● — ● — ● —

Harrisburg Cinema 4 Ghost Hunt

Harrisburg

THEATER ONE – The only report of anything odd from theater one is an employee states that he saw the silhouette of a person looking out of the porthole at him.

THEATER TWO – An employee was vacuuming near the door when he felt a sudden cold chill and saw a large shadow to his right. There was nothing to his right and when he looked back it was gone. He said it was the most defined shadow he had ever seen.

THEATER THREE – By far the most reports of paranormal activity have been in theater three and the hallway leading to it. Dan Beal, the manager of the theater, has heard several stories of employees seeing a dark figure of a man near the front rows of the auditorium from

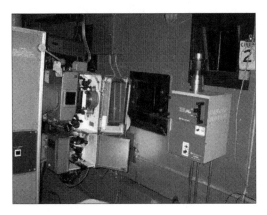

upstairs in the booth. Customers have complained about someone moving the curtains when there was no one there. There is a wooden door at the end of the auditorium that leads to an area behind the screen. This door is known to open, close and even lock itself. Dan said that he has been in the building and noticed that the door will be in a different position than it was before. Dan has worked here longer than anyone and has never met an employee that has not felt "like someone was watching me" or "like someone else was there with me."

One year he was sweeping the hallway leading to theater three and when he looked up from the floor onto the wall and the tall shadow man was on the wall right in front of me. Dan pretty much froze up and starred at it. Within seconds, he seemed to dematerialize like sand blows away in the wind. Everyone seemed to get a "bad" vibe from him. As Dan previously mentioned, there is a storage area behind the screen that leads into our warehouse. The employees say they feel like someone is in there watching them and they feel like whatever else is in there with them, seems to be behind the screen in the area. When employees have been in there alone, the area seems to have an odd "pull," like someone wants you to come back there. It is very hard to explain. Also, there is a small storage room near the entrance of the theater where we keep our posters. The light in there goes on and off by itself. The light is securely in place an there is no faulty wiring. There is one handicap seat in this auditorium that goes down by itself.

THEATER FOUR – Several employees swear that when they were in that theater they saw someone looking at them from the porthole in the booth. The theater is also known to have the areas where "cold spots" are felt.

LOBBY ONE and LOBBY TWO – Lobby one and two are hard to explain. While Dan has never heard anyone say anything about seeing something in either of the lobbies, it seems like when you are in one of them, you will hear something in the other and when you go to investigate, you just hear something in the other lobby. One thing that comes to mind is that the chandeliers have been reported to swing by themselves very slowly. On one occasion, a theater patron said he was watching them one day and a light started to turn on and then go off. He said he kept looking at it and when he looked at the light in the reflection of the front windows, there was the faint form of a small hand playing with the bulb.

RESTROOM 1 - Late one night, Dan was in the building alone standing in the concession area. He looked towards the ladies restroom near theater one and there was a little girl running out of it towards theater one. She was running the way a little kid would run to catch up with their parents. She had curly blonde hair and wore black shoes. She was faint, yet defined. One night while Dan was there with two friends conducting a ghost hunt, we heard knocking on the counter while we were in the restroom.

ARCADE – Dan has never heard of anyone seeing or feeling anything in the arcade. There are reports of employees hearing footsteps and muffled sounds of people talking in the office while the theater is closed.

BOOTHS – Booth one and two are in the same room. It is above the concession stand and it is where the projectors for theater one and two are located. It is a long room and the view is partially obstructed by the placement of the projectors. We have heard stories of people hearing things and sensing something coming from the far side of the booth.

Update: AMC Harrisburg 4 closed its doors for the final time on November 28, 2010. On January 22, 2014 the building was reopened as a gun range and gun shop called Point Blank Range. We have not heard of any recent haunted activity at this location.

AMC Cinema 4 was located at 5 S. Main Street in Harrisburg, Illinois.

The Graveyard Mystery Ball

Sunset Lawn Cemetery. Harrisburg

Located just west of the Sunset Hill Mausoleum in Harrisburg, Illinois is a large grave monument with a polished granite ball resting on top. Several years after its erection, visitors noticed that the heavy granite ball on top of the pedestal had rotated. Various irregular markings on the ball indicated that the ball was on the move. The cause of the movement of the granite ball is unknown. Some late night visitors have reported actually seeing the granite ball in motion giving off a greenish glow.

Sunset Lawn Cemetery is located north of McHaney Road, east of Leinbach Road, south or Shepherd Drive and W. Sloan Streets and west of Dennison Street in Harrisburg, Illinois.

Hungarian Cemetery

Ledford

Hungarian Cemetery, also known as Hunky Dory Cemetery, is located just north of Ledford. This historic cemetery is rumored to be haunted and plagued by Satanist activity. This secluded cemetery has been the scene of ghoulish activities such as grave robbing, grave desecration, satanic rituals, and animal slaughter and according to some rumors, human sacrifice. Blood and melted wax from black candles have been found on gravestones on many occasions.

If one is brave enough or foolish enough to enter the cemetery at night, they might be greeted by an elderly female apparition that walks the deserted road leading to it. Once seen, this phantom lady vanishes into the mist of the night. If you venture toward the far side of the cemetery, you may be able to see a glowing gravestone. Some say it glows all the time, others say it only reflects the moon light. This cemetery has a very sinister reputation and we do not recommend that you go there, even in daylight. It is known to be frequented by devil worshipers and meth users.

— • — • — • —

Demonic Forces in Eldorado Home

Eldorado

Our paranormal investigation team received a request to help rid a house of demonic activities. Upon arrival, the young couple who lived there explained that some unseen force had been attacking their baby. The baby slept in a crib in the front bedroom where the parents also slept. The parents stated that "something" unseen appeared to choke the baby as she slept and would shake the crib at times. The house was old and somewhat rundown in appearance. The ceiling sagged and the paneling on the walls was warped. A curtain served as a door between the living room and kitchen. The back bedroom had a small closet with a trap door that led to the attic. The entire house had a very depressing and oppressive atmosphere about it.

We conducted an Electromagnetic Field (EMF) sweep of the living room and front bedroom with our "Ghost Meter" EMF detectors and discovered very high EMF in the area of the crib while the rest of the room had no EMF. We decided to move the crib to another part of the bedroom that had no EMF. We then rechecked the area where the crib had previously stood and discovered that there was no EMF in that area. We then checked the crib with the EMF meters and discovered that the EMF was coming from the crib itself. We thoroughly searched the crib but could find no visible source for the EMF. Wherever we moved the crib, the EMF followed it. We then turned off all electric power to the house at the main switch to eliminate any man made sources of EMF.

Armed with flashlights, we performed another EMF sweep of the crib and found that it was still enveloped in a strong EMF field. Lisa and I went to the living room to discuss what might be causing the EMF when we both saw a "dark shape" run behind the curtain separating the living room and kitchen. Lisa and I were the only people in the house at that time and the family did not have any pets. We both ran into the kitchen to find whatever had run past the doorway and discovered that the room was empty and the back door was locked from the inside. We went outside and asked the other team members if they had seen anyone or anything enter or exit the house and they all reported that Lisa and I were the only ones that they saw.

We went back in the house with our St Benedict's Crosses and Holy Water to bless the crib, the bedroom and the entire house. We recited the Exorcism Prayer from the St Benedict's Cross and applied Holy Water to the entire area. We then went outside and blessed the four corners of the house. After the ceremony we once again check the crib for EMF and discovered that it had vanished. The entire house was free of the EMF fields. The house seemed to take on a new, brighter, happier appearance. It has been eight months since the exorcism and the family says that there have been no further occurrences of demonic attacks or activity.

— ● — ● — ● —

The Largen Family Homestead

Stonefort

The Little Egypt Ghost Society was invited by Jim Largen to conduct a ghost hunt at his old family homestead located in Stonefort, Illinois. The Largen family had lived there since the mid 1800's. The homestead, which is in almost total shambles, is located on the top of a hill, miles from the nearest neighbors. The actual farmhouse is over 120 years old. It sits on top of limestone blocks and has three abandoned wells located nearby.

Jim said that on many mornings before getting up for the day, he would smell coffee brewing even though a fresh pot had not yet been made. In the evenings he would sense a cold breeze brush past his head even though there was not a draft in the house. Jim's dog Opie

would stare at some unseen object in the front room each evening. Jim had a non-human friendly domesticated wolf that would howl at mysterious objects in the nearby woods.

We started off by photographing the house in color and with our IR night vision cameras. One IR photo taken in what was left of the living room showed what appeared to be an entity in the process of manifesting. Next we used the PX Device, EVP Listener and Mel Meter. The PX Device is a device that monitors electromagnetic fields (EMF), and other environmental factors and uses the input to form words from an internal word list of over 2000 words. The device kept saying "FIFTEEN" and "SUFFER." We asked Jim if the words had any special meaning to him or the location. After a moment, Jim said "OH, MY GOD!!! My ex-wife died on January, 15th in a house fire. She was burned to death!"

Jim asked us if we would like to walk to her grave. We said yes, and he led us up the dirt road to his house. We went around to the back yard where we saw a lonely pine tree with an Indian arrow sticking out of the ground nearby. Jim told us that his ex-wife was buried under the pine tree. We were all silent for a few minutes. Jim asked if we would mind setting up our equipment on a small table over the grave. As soon as we did, the PX Device started talking again. It said "HUG ME, JIM" and "LOVING JIM."

Jim believes that his ex-wife was calling out to him from beyond the grave to let him know that she will always be near.

Wamble Mountain Ghost

By Tracey Todd Bragg
Rudement

Wamble Mountain, sometimes spelled Womble, lies in the range of the Shawnee foothills that stretch across several counties in Southern Illinois. It is positioned near the southwestern corner of Saline County in the edge of the Shawnee National Forest. Its elevation of 938 feet makes it just shy of the commonly accepted 1000 feet to classify it as a true mountain, although I wouldn't tell that to the locals if I were you.

Somewhere around 1815, a man by the name of Chism Estes settled his family in the area of Wamble Mountain, then a part of Gallatin County. Saline County was formed out of a part of Gallatin in 1847. Equality was the county seat at the time. All important business of the area was conducted there. Chism had many children, one in particular by the name of John. Once John entered adulthood, he married and settled near his family's farm. The story goes on that John traveled to Equality to sell some horses and cattle, and on his way back home, was murdered and robbed for the sum of money he had received.

The murder supposedly took place very near his childhood home and just across the ridge from where he lived. John was buried in an unmarked grave on that mountain. His murderers never received the justice they so rightly deserved. John left behind at least one son, James, who later fought and died in the Battle of Fort Donelson in Tennessee. My research did not reveal the location of James' interment, and you will soon see why I wonder where he rests.

Very late one night, somewhere around 2 a.m. about 4 or 5 years ago, a friend and I were taking a drive through the mountain road, mainly because I said I had never traveled on it. There was no other traffic, or so we thought. Reaching near the top of Wamble Mountain, we approached a man riding on horseback. Very unusual at 2 a.m., and he seemed to have come out of nowhere. We hadn't seen him in our headlights as we approached. It seemed we just suddenly came upon him. The horse was moving quite slowly, both the man and the horse kept their heads hung low.

Most riders, when approached from behind by a vehicle, will turn to look, but he never moved in that direction, just kept his head down. The man was oddly dressed; almost an 1800s style, with a light chambray shirt, very simple canvas pants, and a fedora style hat. His hat was not the flashy type, but it had a flat brim, as was common. He had something that appeared to be a shoulder bag of the kind used to carry black powder hung across his body and a rifle of some sort hung in the saddle of the horse.

It was a very cool night, somewhere in the 30s, but we had the truck windows partially down as the heater worked a little too well most of the time. Although the sides of the road were covered in dry leaves, there was absolutely no sound of the horse's hooves, no leaves crunching, and no clopping sound on the hard poorly-graveled road. Most horses will react to a vehicle, at least a flinch or side-step, as the car passes; but not this horse, it kept its steady slow pace straight ahead and his head down, just as his rider. And despite the air so cold you could see your breath; there was no steam from the nares of the horse.

Who did I see on Wamble Mountain? Some strange local who likes to ride in the middle of nowhere at 2 a.m.? Is John looking for his murderers or reliving the last moments of his life returning home? Or did James finally return home from Fort Donelson?

The Ghost On Haunted Hill

Eldorado

There is a hill opposite the old city reservoir in Eldorado that is considered haunted by the locals. Legend has it that in the mid-1800s a man was murdered on this hill and his ghost would often be seen by late night travelers.

One dark and lonely night, Old Judge Samuel Elder was returning home after conducting some business in Raleigh, which was the county seat at the time. He had remained in town a little longer than expected due to his habit of tarrying "over the cups." Knowing that he had better square himself with his wife and daughters, he had purchased some millinery cloth, which he tied to the saddle of his horse, Old Black Hawk.

The Judge was making good progress on his journey back home in Eldorado until he reached Haunted Hill. Old Black Hawk noticed something strange that made him snort and high tail it home at break-neck speed. The Judge held on to the reins like his life depended on it. Every now and then he would glance behind him. To his horror, he saw that a ghostly white object trailed along behind him and his horse. The faster the horse trotted, the faster the ghost chased them. Every turn was mirrored by the eerie apparition.

When the exhausted and terrified Judge and horse reached home, the entire family rushed outside to see the commotion. They found one end of domestic material tied to the saddle and the rest of it floating out toward Raleigh.

St. Clair County

UFO Sighting

St. Clair County

On the night of January 5, 2000, police in the St Clair County received numerous reports of a triangular shaped unidentified object in the sky. The UFO was reported to be two stories high and about the length of a football field. It was estimated that the UFO was flying at an altitude of about 1000 feet. The sightings were centered in an area that extended from Lebanon, Shiloh, Dupo and Millstadt.

The UFO sighting drew national attention and a week later a special team of investigators headed by a former FBI agent was brought in to determine if the UFO was an alien spacecraft. The team interviewed several credible witnesses including police officers. The descriptions of the UFO by witnesses were not what would be expected if the objects were conventional aircraft. The lighting on the UFO was not consistent with U.S. regulations for lighting of aircraft and the fight patterns far exceeded any known type of aircraft.

Officials at nearby Scott Air Force Base had no explanation for the UFO and said that the air traffic control towers at Scott Air Force Base and nearby Mid America Airport were both shut down at the time of the sightings.

Was the UFO some sort of Top Secret military aircraft from Scott Air Force Base or could it have been visitors from outer space? Your guess is as good as ours.

Union County

The Lost Treasure of Union County

Union County

In the mid-1800s, an old man by the name of Miller would go to town to purchase various items and always paid for them with silver dollars. After many months, it was discovered that the silver dollars he used were counterfeit. The old man was arrested and put on trial for counterfeiting. During the trial it was decided to weigh the silver dollars. It was then discovered that the counterfeit silver dollars weighed more than the legal tender silver dollars and the judge decided to turn the man loose. While everyone was still in the court room, the old man paid his attorney with a fist full of silver dollars.

No one knew where the old man got the silver for the counterfeit dollars and he never told his secret to anyone. Some believed that it was Indian silver the old man had used. Legend says that an Indian chief once said that the white man had no judgment and if he had, he would shoe his horses with gold horse shoes. It was believed that a cave near Alto Pass, Illinois was full of gold. When the white man came to Union County, the Indians sealed the cave and no one has been able to find it since then.

Many years ago a man was digging a well near the site that the cave is believed to be located at. While digging, the man heard strange sounds coming from the hole. The deeper he dug, the louder the sounds became. Some people thought that the wind was causing the moaning sounds. Others said that the area was cursed and that the moans he heard were from long dead Indians.

Hidden Indian Treasure

Alto Pass

An old story passed down through generations of Indians states that there is a hidden and now lost cave near Alto Pass that is filled with tons of gold. When the white men started coming to the area in great numbers, the Indians hid the precious gold in the cave for safe keeping. The place was kept such a secret that now, no one knows where it is located. Perhaps if the Great Spirit is willing, its location will be revealed someday to a worthy person.

King Neptune

Union County

A popular story of Southern Illinoisans is about King Neptune, the $19 million pig. If you ever have occasion to be driving near Anna, Illinois, drive about a mile east on Route 146 from the I-57 interstate, and look to your right. You will notice an old and worn tombstone of none other than a 700lb pig. Locals still love to stop and pay homage to this swine hero of WWII.

Raised as a 4-H project, Neptune was a Hereford swine, a red pig with a white face. When you add the blue blanket, crown, nail polish, and earrings, our hero made quite the dashing and patriotic figure, even if he was busting at the seams and on all fours.

A man from West Frankfort named Boner donated "Parker" Neptune to be served as a delicious main course at a fundraising pig roast. A local recruiter named Lingle in Marion, Illinois, came up with a different idea. Why not use Neptune as an auctioning gimmick? It worked.

In an effort to raise war bonds for the U.S.S. Illinois which was under construction, everything from his squeal (which went for $25 average) to his bristles (which would go for as high as $500) were auctioned off at rallies. King Neptune became immensely popular and demands for more appearances were staggering. The public adored him. Local Elks clubs (of which the pig became a lifelong member), sponsored more and more appearances throughout the state.

A bank paid for the upkeep for the pig, but requested Neptune's personal endorsement on the checks. They received a hoof print from our hero. Governor Green purchased the pig in 1943 for the state of Illinois to the tune of one million dollars. Before his traveling was said and done, King Neptune managed $19,000,000 by the mid 1940s, (equivalent to 200,000,000 in present day dollars).

At the young age of eight years old, King Neptune died of pneumonia. He received a full military burial. The faded inscription on his tombstone reads, "Buried here - King Neptune, famous Navy mascot pig auctioned for $19,000,000.00 in war bonds 1942-1946 to help make a free world." Because of local vandals a second and newer monument was placed for Neptune at the Trail of Tears Welcome Center on I-57 near the route 146 intersection.

— ● — ● — ● —

Anna State Hospital For The Insane

Anna

In 1869 the Illinois State Legislature authorized the building a new hospital in Anna, Illinois. It was known as the Southern Hospital for the Insane. Today the hospital is known as Choate Mental Health and Developmental Center.

Many of the buildings on the grounds of the hospital were built by residents as part of their rehabilitation. The first of several fires at the hospital occurred in 1881 and several upper floors of the hospital were damaged beyond repair and had to be removed.

Over the years, the hospital obtained a reputation of being haunted. Visitors would report seeing people running, and ghostly faces peering from windows. Cottages located on the campus are said to be haunted by nurses and prior insane patients who died many years ago.

Various underground tunnels connect some of the buildings. Basements of some of the buildings that were torn down after the fires remain underground and can be reached by some of the secret tunnels. The sealed up basements and tunnels seem to be a focal point for paranormal activity. Apparitions of people running have been reported in these areas.

One worker was in the tunnels late at night and felt a hand on his back. There was no one there. Other workers report a "devil dog" that attacks patients, leaving scratches all over their bodies.

The Medical and Surgical Building was where horrible lobotomies and electric shock treatments took place. Body parts were amputated in the lower level that contained the morgue and an incinerator to dispose of the body parts. Many people have reported strange noises like footsteps running in empty hallways and doors that slam shut where there are not any doors. Apparitions of people have been seen running. Other apparitions are of people standing in windows. One resident was attacked by a "devil dog." When the lights were turned on in the room it was noticed that the resident was the only one there and that he was covered with bloody scratches all over his body.

Many of the insane who died at the hospital are buried on the grounds. When the insane inmates of Anna State Hospital ceased living and became corpses, they were buried side by side in the order that they died. Anna State Hospital Cemetery is now a virtual week by week calendar of the dead.

Many staff members and visitors report the sounds of sobbing, screaming and other unworldly sounds coming from the graves.

Insane Sculpture

This is a close up of the very disturbing wooden sculpture made by a mental patient at Choate. Most of the hanged people are naked with the exception of at least two that are wearing dresses and appear to be female.

Choate Mental Health Center is located at 1000 N. Main St. in Anna.

The Man In Black Shrinking Ghost

Anna

Many years ago a young man was hanging out with some friends on Saturday night. About midnight they all decided to call it quits and go home. While walking home alone, one of the guys encountered a strange man dressed in a black suit and black hat with the brim flopped down. The man in black did not seem to be a real person. They feared that this man in black was a ghost or some kind of spirit that was going to cause him some harm.

The young man remembered that if you asked a question in the name of the Lord the ghost or spirit will answer you. The young man was really frightened and tried to ask, "Who in the name of the Lord are you?"

He was so scared that he was unable to make any sound. As if his thoughts were heard, the mysterious man in black started to tremble and shrink until he was about the height of a dog. The shrunken man in black, now transformed into a dog, flew away with his legs dangling and vanished over the railroad tracks.

Washington County

The First White Man To Die In Washington County

Lively Grove

A surveyor by the name of Asa Fletcher was the first white man to die in what is now Washington County. The untimely death of Asa Fletcher occurred on July 13, 1808, two years before the first white men came to settle the area.

Fletcher who was only 29 years old at the time was working with a U.S. government surveying crew on July 13, 1808 in the area that is now known as Lively Grove Township in Washington County. While in the performance of his official duties, Fletcher was bitten by a rattlesnake. Death was rapid and took place just two hours later. He was buried "on the first hill south of Mud Creek," which is probably over the Perry County line.

— ● — ● — ● —

Indian Massacre

Washington County

In 1810, the John Lively family settled in the area where government surveyor, Asa Fletcher was killed by a rattlesnake two years earlier. The Lively family had no way of knowing that this area would bring death to them as well.

John Lively had an old theory. He often said that one good white man could lick 20 Indians anytime anywhere. Just one year later his theory was put to the test with tragic results for the Lively family. The men folk of the family and a hired hand were working in the fields when they heard rifle fire and Indians making terrifying shrieks. It was obvious that the Indians were on the warpath and headed their way. The men quickly ran to the homestead only to find it already in flames.

The men knew they were no match for the marauding Indians and went for the nearest help which was located at Hill's Post, 15 miles away. A young boy that was with the group of men became exhausted and could go no further. They hid the boy under a log with the promise of returning as soon as help could be reached.

At long last, the rescue party arrived at the Lively homestead. The log cabin was only a smoldering pile of ashes. All of the Lively family that had taken refuge in the cabin were scalped and mutilated. The Indians had tossed the dead into the cow lot. A little boy was not among the dead and the rescue party went in search for him. A few miles away, they found the little boy dead and scalped. His shirt had been stuffed into a hole that was cut in his chest.

The young boy, who had joined the expedition to Hill's Post, hidden under the log was the only survivor.

Wayne County

Eerie Spirits of the Mt. Erie Area

By Michael Farmer
Mt. Erie

In an old cemetery (location not to be revealed), I encountered the entity of an old woman with flowing gray hair. I saw her only out of the corner of my eye and only for a couple of seconds. As I turned, she disappeared, but I felt something go through me with a blast of very cold air. I was completely disoriented for several minutes. A state of complete confusion had overtaken me.

The graveyard was surrounded by a fence and thick woods. The entrance was a small gate. I couldn't find it and started to walk into the woods. Esther had to guide me out. Not only was I confused and delirious, but also weak and exhausted. It was like my energy had been drained from me. Since that time, we have encountered strange fog or mist (visible to the eye) that would come and go on other occasions. This place is very spooky. It scares me not.

White County

The Man Whose Hobby Was Being A Hangman

White County

George Phillip Hanna was a Southern Illinois banker, farmer and volunteer hangman. He was born in Epworth, White County, Illinois on September 16, 1873 and became one of the wealthiest landowners in White County, Illinois. Hanna was a large bald man over 6 foot tall and weighing over 200 pounds. He witnessed his first hanging at age 22 in McLeansboro, Illinois in 1896. When the prison crew bungled the job. It was a cold day and witnesses could actually see the vapor from the man's breath as it took over half an hour for him to slowly strangle to death. Hanna said that it was "brutal, horrifying." Hanna decided to purchase his own rope and study hanging. The rope he used for hanging was handmade 4-ply long fiber hemp that he purchased for $65 in St Louis, Missouri.

Although Hanna officiated at over 70 hangings, he stated, "I haven't much nerve" and "I dread hangings. I'm upset for days before and afterwards. When I hanged Birger, a bad man, I hid the noose behind my back until the cap was adjusted." Hanna thought that he could perform hangings better if he used his own equipment. He built a portable scaffold that stood over 15 feet tall. This scaffold was used for the first time in Murphysboro, Illinois for the hanging of a black man. The hoods used to cover the head of the person to be hung were sewn by Hanna's wife. The prisoner was given their choice colors, black or white. Hanna would visit each prisoner before the execution and tell them "I am here to help you." He told them that he would try to spare them any misery and assured them that their death would be painless.

Most of the hangings went according to plan, some did not and some were even brutal. During one hanging in 1920, the condemned man fell to the ground and was severely injured when the rope broke. Hanna ran down the steps of the scaffold, picked up the condemned man and carried him to the floor of the scaffold. The man shouted out, "Hurry up, boys, and get me out of my misery."

After each execution, Hanna would refuse payment but would make one simple request...that he be given the weapon used to the commit the crime. Among the weapons once used by men he executed is the machine gun used by Charlie Birger in the Birger-Shelton gang feud, an axe, a rag-wrapped brick, a shotgun and numerous other murderous items. Hanna died September 6, 1948 in Evansville, Indiana.

Phil Hanna's Hangman Tools

Carmi

The L. Haas Store, built in 1896, is now home to the White County Historical Society. One of its most popular exhibits is the "Hanging Tools" of Phil Hanna including are various hangman ropes, hoods worn by the condemned and steel trap doors from the gallows. Hanna officiated at over 70 hangings during his career. He got into the business of public hangings when he was witness to a botched hanging as a young man. After that he studied various ways of hanging and devised a method that he considered more humane and would cause less suffering to the condemned.

Hanna would never pull the hangman's lever that operated the trap door to the gallows, he left that job to the county sheriff. The gallows scaffold was built by Hanna and he transported it from county to county and on occasion even out of state to various hangings. Prior to the hanging, Hanna would advise the condemned prisoner on how to conduct to minimize their suffering. Once on the scaffold, Hanna would adjust the knot of the hangman's noose around the prisoner's neck. Hanna never accepted cash for his services, just a souvenir of the crime.

White County Historical Society Vice President, Sue Ellen Smith holds up the black execution hood used by Phil Hanna.

The scaffold used by Phil Hanna was a wooden box frame made with four large posts and braced by wooden beam at the top and a wooden platform about half way up. Thirteen wooden steps led up to the platform. A metal trap door was positioned near the middle of the wooden platform. The double doors of the trap door were held shut by heavy metal latches that were connected to a black metal lever. When the leaver was pulled the latches would disengage allowing the double doors to swing downward causing the victim to drop at the end of a rope attached to the wooden crossbeam at the top of the scaffold.

The vice-president of the White County Historical Society granted the Little Egypt Ghost Society a private viewing of Phil Hanna's hanging tools. The display consisted of the metal trap door and hangman's lever that was part of Hanna's custom made gallows. The metal trap door was painted black and measured 34" X 34." It was actually made of two doors that opened in the middle. The hangman's lever was made of metal that was painted black. The lever measured 38" long and was connected to one corner of the trap door.

A glass case contained three black leather straps that were used to bind the condemned prisoner's arms and legs. Also in the glass case were two cloth hoods that covered the head and shoulders of the condemned prisoner. One hood was black and the other one was white. They were both hand made by Hanna's wife. Prior to an execution, Hanna would offer the condemned prisoner the choice of either the black or the white hood. Hanna did not like to use the white hood because the condemned prisoner's face could be seen through it. We were allowed to touch the hoods and we were amazed at how incredibly soft they felt.

The White County Historical Society is located at 203 N. Church Street in Carmi, Illinois.

The Legend of Black Annie

Carmi

Many years ago there was a tragic house fire on the north side of Carmi. Townspeople and firefighters rushed to the scene to battle the flames. After several hours all that was left of Annie's home was a smoldering heap of ash and burnt timbers. An anguished cry went up as Annie realized that none of her children made it out of the house. They had all been burned alive in the inferno.

For the rest of her life, Annie was in mourning and wore nothing but black. Many times late at night Annie would be seen walking along the gravel road. At other times she would be seen hiding in the shadows of the tree line along the roadside, waiting for a child to walk nearby. She would spring out, screeching "My children! My children!" while trying to grab the frightened child. Townspeople said that if Black Annie caught you, she would drag you off to a pile of rubble where her house once stood. There is a legend that in the nearby woods, Annie would skin the children she had captured and hang the skins from a large oak tree. She would keep some of the skins and make a dress out of them. For many years, parents would warn their children not to stay out late or Black Annie would catch them and skin them.

Mysterious Walking Statue With A Heartbeat

Carmi

Maple Ridge Cemetery, located near Burrell's Woods in Carmi, is the final resting place of William "Hoppy" Rebstock. According to his gravestone, he was born July 11, 1878 and died November 12, 1952. The stone is inscribed "Here lies a man who lived and died for his country, relatives and friends." A life sized statue of Hoppy stands on top of a marble pedestal at his grave. William Rebstock acquired the nickname Hoppy because he had a wooden leg.

Legend has it that once a year Hoppy comes down from his pedestal and walks around the cemetery. Several years ago, some visitors to the cemetery noticed that the statue of Hoppy was missing from the pedestal. After much searching, the missing statue was found in Burrell's Woods. Many people, including the police, concluded that it was probably a teenage prank. Remembering the legend of Hoppy's annual walkabout, some people were not so sure.

Some locals claim that the statue of Hoppy has a heartbeat. According to some sources, Hoppy was buried alive and if a person presses their ear to the chest of the statue, they will hear his heartbeat.

The cemetery's coordinates are N 38.092546 and W -88.187539.

The Big Prairie Ghost

By Rev. Keith Bradley
Carmi

East of Carmi is a vast track of land known as "Big Prairie." The floodwaters from the Big and Little Wabash rivers made this area ideal for farming and attracted earlier settlers to this lonely prairie. Toward the end of the 1800s Nelson Graves his wife Jane and daughters Margaret and Minnie struggled to make a life on this land.

One summer day Nelson traveled into town on business. Margaret and Minnie busied themselves with chores out of door while Jane worked inside. Suddenly the girl called to their mom, "Momma there is a woman out by the well come to visit. Come see, momma." Jane dried her hands from on a dishtowel while she walked to the door. Looking outside Jane saw the woman. As the blood drained from her face her hands began to shake. "Oh, girls, come away from her. "She is a 'haunt.' Come away girls and don't look at her. She will go away!" The girls did not understand but ran to their mother and buried their small faces into her apron. "Pray girls, pray and the haunt will go away."

When they looked up, the woman was gone just as suddenly as she appeared. "Oh girls, that was a sign," Jane cried. "Something has happened to your papa. That was a death omen let's go find him." The family took off in rush toward town, hoping and praying that nothing had happened. However, about a mile down the path to town that found Nelson Graves face down in the middle of the path. The mule he had lead was close by but Nelson appeared to have died of heart failure. The woman at the well had been a death omen for the Nelson family.

Big Prairie is still fertile farmland. Neighbors and towns are still a good distance from each other. The echoes of the pioneer can still be heard in the winds of prairie. Who can say if the woman at the well still visits the residence of this lonely expanse of land?

Williamson County

Grandma Cline Haunts the Library

Marion

Marion Carnegie Library located in Marion was opened to the public in 1916. The library stands on the site of the former "Grandma Cline" residence. The home was built in 1854 by Isaac Campbell. This property was acquired in 1914 for the sum of $5,003.17 from Serrelda Cline and her heirs. The Grandma Cline house was removed and the new library was constructed on the site. The library was constructed in 1915 with a grant of $18,000 from the Andrew Carnegie Foundation.

Librarians and patrons of the library have reported paranormal activity for many years. Dena, one of the librarians even thinks she knows who is haunting the library. The ghost is none other than my direct descendant, Grandma Cline (her real name was Serrelda Jane Cline, but was better known as Grandma Cline). Grandma Cline was born in February of 1826 and died in March of 1917. She is buried in Rose Hill Cemetery in Marion, IL.

Librarians and patrons at the Marion Carnegie Library have reported various paranormal activities in the old section of the library. These activities include cold spots, unexplained noises, books and chairs that move about on their own, the scent of lilac perfume and despite a strict no smoking policy, the smell of pipe smoke. Activities such as these are fairly normal at haunted locations. The one item that caught my immediate attention was the smell of pipe smoke.

According to my great, great grandma's obituary in the March 3, 1917 edition of the *Marion Daily Republican*, "Mrs. S. J. Cline, better known as Grandma Cline, died Saturday morning at 4:15. Grandma Cline was a unique personage and was loved by all who knew her. She was very fond of her pipe and during the time that she lived with her son, J.M. Cline, was often seen smoking."

It is our belief that the smell of pipe smoke is a ghostly residual of my great, great-grandma, Grandma Cline.

The Marion Carnegie Library is located at 206 S. Market Street in Marion, Illinois.

Buried Alive

Marion

During the 1960s, my grandpa was the sexton at the Marion City Cemeteries. I was in my pre-teens and would go to visit him at work during summer vacations. It was a real treat to "help" him mow the graveyard on the vintage yellow and white cub cadet tractors.

One hot summer day at Maplewood Cemetery left a lasting impression on me. My grandpa and some of his helpers were digging a grave in an older section of the cemetery. I watched with fascination as they dug deeper and deeper. One of the workers gave out an excited shout. They had accidentally dug into an old grave that was not plotted on the cemetery map. The coffin was a very old one and the lid was rotted through in several places. We could see the body of an ancient looking lady dressed in black. She looked like a skeleton with leather stretched over it.

What horrified us was the fact the body was twisted up in the coffin as if she had been in a struggle. Her empty eye sockets seemed to stare at us. Her mouth was wide open in a silent scream. The cloth lining of the coffin was ripped to shreds. It was obvious to everyone present that this poor soul had been buried alive. My grandpa and his workers filled in the grave and said a prayer over it. Who was buried in this mystery grave? To this day, no one knows for sure.

The cemetery is located along Route 37 north of Route 13 in Marion, Illinois.

Blackhawk Soldier Buried With His Horse

Marion

The Old Marion Cemetery established in 1849 contains 179 internments. The ravages of time and vandals have left only a few of the gravestones untouched. Five Civil War Confederate soldiers are buried here including Philip Thompson Corder, 7th Tennessee Cavalry, Confederate States Army. He was murdered on January 1, 1869 by Sam Cover in Marion, Illinois.

Another notable grave in this cemetery is that of Pvt. George H. Harrison, a veteran of the Black Hawk War fought in 1832 between the United States and Native Americans led by Chief Black Hawk and his "British Band" of Sauks, Meskwakis and Kickapoos. Many men from Illinois enlisted in the military to fight in this war including Harrison who enlisted as a private in Company J attached to the Fourth Regiment, Mounted Rangers, Illinois Volunteers. This state militia unit mustered out of service at the mouth of the Fox River on May 28, 1832. The former soldiers were allowed to keep their horses and take them home. According to local legend, when Private Harrison died he was buried with his beloved horse.

The cemetery is located along an alleyway just west of Court Street (Route 37) and south of the West Central Street and the railroad tracks. It contains many more burials than there are gravestones. Nearly all of the remaining stones date from the mid 1800s.

— ● — ● — ● —

Judge W.O. Potter Family Murders

807 N. Market St., Marion

The bodies of the family members were found at the Potters residence at 807 N Market St. Marion by Judge Potter's surviving son Maurice as he returned home from a business trip around the time of 2 a.m. on the date of October 24th, 1926. All members of the family were dressed in night clothes and were all believed to have been killed sometime around 1 a.m., the weapon is believed to have been a 20lb furnace shaker which was secured from within the basement of the house itself. Judge Potter himself was found in a cistern in the rear of the house where he had entered head first into 3 feet of water.

It is believed due to blood patterns and footprints found that Eloise (daughter) was killed first. The killer then surprised Lucille (daughter) in the bathroom and she was then killed by means of crushing her skull. Blood stains then lead across the hall to the room in which Lucille and the two young children were staying, Mrs. Potter is believed to have heard the children screaming, ran to help them and in doing so was also struck down by the killer. Eloise is thought to have not been killed immediately and was able to make her way to the bedroom where she died alongside her mother and the children. Bloody footprints were then followed down the back stairs.

In the hours before the murders there was nothing out of the ordinary about Judge Potter. His conduct was normal at the evening meal, and after dinner he read quietly while his granddaughters played around him. His son and daughter were dancing while a little granddaughter played a phonograph. As the surviving son was heading out for the night Judge Potter reportedly asked him to "come home early tonight." To those close to Judge Potter his deep depression was no secret, two of his brothers-in-law reported that he had relayed his despair unto them on the very morning that the family died. Judge Potter had met Judge D. T. Hartwell in the lobby of the First National

Bank and offered to help out, he spoke about how he had had a very bad night and that he had been about to harm his little girl, "wouldn't that be awful" Potter had said of the incident, and mentioned that he did in fact feel better.

Conversations Potter had had with friends at the time led them to believe that he judge was going through great financial troubles. In his last weeks of life Judge Potter was known to have lost close to 30lbs and he would frequently break down crying. The controversy is that Judge Potter was blamed for the murder of his family members and taking his own life by means of drowning before the evidence in the case was even examined and the autopsy on Judge Potter revealed no water in the lungs and deep lacerations in his head.

Former residents of this house reported hearing sound of a struggle in the rear of the house as well as feeling unexplained cold spots in various rooms. Several years ago the house was torn down and all that remains is an empty lot, a depression in the yard where the cistern was and the grisly memories of murder.

Gangsters Kill a Patrolman and His Pregnant Wife

Marion

Another brutal murder was that of an Illinois State Highway Patrolman of dubious repute, Lory Price, his wife Ethel, and their unborn child. Patrolman Price was tied in with certain Williamson County car thieves. The thieves would steal cars and then tell Price where to recover them. The thieves and Price would then split the reward money. At some point, Price and Charlie Birger had a falling out. On January 17, 1927, Price and his wife were abducted from their home and taken away in separate cars by gangsters.

Price's body was found two days later riddled by 18 gunshot wounds. His wife's body was found at the bottom of a mine shaft four months later. Trooper Price and his wife are buried in Odd Fellows Cemetery, Block A, Lot 1.

— ● — ● — ● —

The Hanging Of Rado Millich

By Tracey Todd Bragg
Marion

The name Charlie Birger can bring a mix of fear and admiration to folks in Southern Illinois. Despite being involved in organized crime, he was well known to be a protector of widows and the poor. Many cold evenings found coal being delivered free of charge to those in need in the Harrisburg area. School children received coins from the infamous desperado, just because he wanted to. He frequented the Orpheum Theater, near the square in Harrisburg, especially when the feature film starred Tom Mix.

Charlie was a mobster, and like any other mobster, Charlie had his band of followers. Men like Connie Ritter, Art Newman, Rado Millich, and Ray Hyland were at Charlie's beck and call, ready at all times to do his bidding. They lied, cheated, stole and killed, all in the name of Charlie Birger. And they also paid the price.

The Shady Rest was the headquarters for the Birger gang. Located in the woods off the road between Marion and Harrisburg, and just inside Williamson County, it was hidden well. Next to the road sat a barbecue stand, also run by Birger, a perfect façade for the criminal stronghold. Those who Birger allowed in enjoyed drinking, gambling, and cock-fighting at the Shady Rest. During Prohibition, such festivities were illegal.

Rado Millich often served as the caretaker of the Shady Rest. Millich was an immigrant coal miner. His roots were Montenegrin, a Slavic people that often migrated to Serbia, where it appears Millich was from. Rado had been injured in the mines, having his fingers cut off by a pit car in 1915 and never returned for work. Possibly this was the reason Millich became involved with the band of gangsters. An infamous picture of Birger and his men on a Model T Ford outside the Shady Rest shows Millich sitting on the running board; his right hand does appear deformed and possibly missing most of the fingers.

Ward "Casey" Jones was a bartender at the Shady Rest. During Birger's absence one day, an apparent argument broke out between Millich and Jones regarding who was actually in charge while Charlie was gone. Not a lot of detail is known about the fight other than it led to gunfire and ended with Jones dead. Millich and Eural Gowan, another of Birger's henchmen, placed the body outside the Shady Rest and left it there overnight. When Birger returned, he showed no grief for the dead man, but anger for the body being left beside the hideout. He ordered Millich and Gowan to dump the body into Saline Creek, where it was found near Equality, Illinois, on October 26, 1926.

Rado Millich and Gowan were eventually arrested for the murder. Millich always claimed it was self-defense. His recounting of the events was that he was walking from the barbecue stand to the cabin when Jones called his name. He turned and Jones opened fire on him with a machine gun. Apparently Jones was a terrible shot, as Millich came out untouched. Unluckily for Jones, Millich was a good shot. The pair was prosecuted by Arlie O. Boswell, a state's attorney of great renowned in Southern Illinois. In opening statements at the trial, Bowell pleaded to "put an end to the reign of terror created by Charlie Birger and his infamous band of murderers." Put an end to it they did. On July 7, 1927, Rado Millich was found guilty and sentenced to hang until dead.

A motion for a new trial was presented and overruled by Judge Hartwell and the date of execution was set for October 21, 1927, just shy of one year since the body of Casey Jones had been discovered. A second motion was filed under the instructions of the Serbian Consul in Chicago, was also turned down. The Consul even appealed to the

The hanging of Rado Millich, one of Charlie Birger's gangsters. The hanging took place at the Williamson County jail on January 21, 1927. Millich fainted just before the trap door on the gallows was sprung. The deputy sheriff (2nd from left) can be seen shoving Millich into the open trap door. *Photo courtesy of the Williamson County Historical Society*

governor for a stay of execution, which was referred to the State Board of Pardons and Paroles. There would be no stay.

On October 21, 1927, just before 10 a.m., Rado Millich was led to gallows borrowed from Jackson County and erected outside the jail in the alley, known as Paradise Alley. Millich began with a pre-written statement, maintaining his innocence by reason of self-defense. He then tore up the paper and continued in his broken English, his final words to the people of Williamson County. He went so far as to claim the gun had belonged to Arlie Boswell, and then implicated Birger in other crimes. He then looked to Sheriff Coleman and said "Thank you very much, go ahead." The trap was sprung and Rado Millich became the first of Birger's gang to be executed for murder, as well as the last man to be hanged in Williamson County. He is buried in the potter's field at Rose Hill Cemetery.

When told of Millich's last statement, Charlie Birger reportedly said "The last shot of a poor dumb fool at the man who sent him to die."

Chittyville Mystery Creature

Chittyville

On August 11, 1968, Tim Bullock and Barbara Smith were parked in their car near Chittyville just north of Herrin, Illinois. At about 8:30 P.M. what they described as a "ten foot tall giant figure "with a head as large as a steering wheel and a round, hairy face" suddenly came out of the bushes. The creature picked up some dirt and threw it at the couple through the open car window. The couple were badly frightened and sped out of the area in a hurry. The next day Bullock returned to the area to check it out. He found several deep depressions in the grass where the creature had been standing. There were several reports over a two week period that dogs had been "carrying on." The editor of the

Herrin Spokesman thought that it was all the work of practical jokers and did not print the story in the newspaper.

— ● — ● — ● —

Marion V.A. Hospital UFO Flap

Marion

In June of 1967 the area around the Marion Veterans Administration Hospital was visited by a huge UFO that hovered above. This UFO was described as a "mother" ship surrounded by 5 smaller craft. Time seemed to stand still in a 1 ½ mile perimeter around the hospital. It was as if this area had been "domed off" and a buffer zone caused immediate temporary paralysis if anyone attempted to enter the event zone.

Many people experienced a hazy consciousness as they witnessed the ordeal. Was it a case of mass hypnosis that allowed some observers to witness the event? Perhaps it was some sort of power play by aliens to demonstrate their power. Several people became alarmed as a large airborne craft of unknown origin hovered over the V.A. Hospital and a portion of Interstate 57 to the west.

As people gazed at the UFO they were entered a state of dazed consciousness and were beckoned to the V.A. Hospital grounds. Just to the east of the hospital grounds alien creatures emerged from the yards on 4th Street while another group of aliens were seen briskly walking along West Cherry Street. Many people were seen emerging from the V.A. Hospital being escorted and nudged by the aliens. The aliens appeared to be slightly less than 5 foot tall and seemed to be wearing some sort of helmets. A bunch of children were herded into a smaller UFO that had two misty tubes extending down to the ground. The children were sucked up into the tubes two at a time. Once aboard the craft they were positioned behind a screen that projected a color image of the insides of their bodies.

A smaller UFO was observed transporting people from further eastward of the hospital into the "domed off" area surrounding the hospital. All traffic, both north and southbound on I-57 was at a standstill over an approximate 1 ½ mile stretch.

The UFOs did not produce any sounds. The aliens aboard worked in short shifts ushering people around to various small crafts that were hovering nearby. These small craft come from a larger "mother" ship. The aliens seemed to tire easily and some would be seen falling to the ground from the crafts. After falling to earth, they were levitated into a smaller craft and quickly taken away. Some sort of medical experiment were performed on the people taken aboard. After about 2 ½ hours everyone taken aboard the craft were returned to their original locations.

What actually happened on that summer day in June of 1967 remains a closely guarded secret and is the subject of debate to this day.

Jailhouse Ghost

Marion

County jails are known for intrigue, tragedy, and terror. Going to jail can be a scary experience, especially if your bunkmate is a dead man.

In the spring of 1986, Calvin was arrested for conspiracy to commit murder. He allegedly offered an undercover law enforcement officer $500 to kill his wife. This act landed Calvin in the Williamson County Jail in Marion, Illinois. He was assigned to one of the top bunks in "E" Block. During the early morning hours of the midnight shift, the correctional officers were alerted to yells and screams coming from the inmates of "E" Block. One of the inmates who shared a cell with Calvin was hysterical. He had awakened from a fitful sleep by a warm, sticky, wet dripping sensation from the bunk above his. There was a towel draped over the side of the bunk that appeared to be wet and dark. On closer observation it was evident that it was fresh BLOOD... and lots of it too.

Calvin had taken his eye glasses and broken the lenses out of them. He used the broken lenses to slash the veins and arteries inside both elbows. He bled to death in about 20 minutes. Correctional staff and ambulance personnel removed Calvin's body from the cell and the inmates were given mops and buckets to clean up the bloody mess.

Former correctional officers reported that a few nights later strange things began to happen in the jail on the midnight shift. The electronic doors in the cellblocks that were operated by an officer in Central Control would mysteriously open and close all by themselves. Security gates in one of the hallways would malfunction and open and close also. Many of the superstitious inmates were of the opinion that the ghost of Calvin was causing the electrical disturbances. No logical explanation for the doors and gates opening and closing was ever found.

— • — • — • —

Where are the Herrin Massacre victims buried?

Herrin

On June 22, 1922, forty-eight non-union coal miners were lined up in front of a barbed wire fence near the power house that provides electricity for the Coal Belt Electric Railroad not far from Crenshaw Crossing between Marion and Herrin. Hugh Willis, president of the miner's union, ordered some of his fellow union members to take the non-union miners into the woods and kill all that they could. Facing them were over one hundred union coal miners armed with pistols, rifles, and shotguns. The non-union miners were given the order to "RUN!"

The union miners opened fire with every weapon they had. After the first volleys of fire, twenty men lay dead or wounded on the ground. One of the men who had been shot multiple times was still on his feet clinging to a tree for support. One of the union miners, by the name of Peter Hiller, reportedly walked up to the mortally wounded man and said "You big son of a bitch, can't we kill you?" Hiller placed his pistol against the side of the dying man and shot him dead. Another non-union miner was discovered lying wounded on the ground. When it was noticed that he was still breathing, a union miner shot his lower jaw off and then put another bullet in his head, killing him instantly. One man had been shot in the chest by a shotgun and the hole was so big that his heart could be seen.

Three of the non-union miners got away and were about a half mile north east of the massacre site when they were spotted by Bert Grace and other union miners. Two of them were shot dead and the other one was lynched from a low hanging tree limb and then riddled with bullets. Two other non-union miners had made it to the safety of a nearby barn when they were discovered by union miners. One was shot dead and the other one wounded.

Six surviving non-union miners were quickly captured and taken to Herrin. It was decided that these pitiful, wounded, and scared men would be forced to march to the Herrin City Cemetery. Leva Mann, a Herrin union miner, took charge of the prisoners for the death march to the cemetery. All along the two mile march to the cemetery the men were beaten, insulted, and jeered. At one point they were forced to crawl on their hands and knees. Near the entrance to the cemetery, the men had a rope tied around their necks. A bystander shot one of them in the foot causing him to fall and bring down his fellow captives. As the six men struggled on the ground, a group of ten union miners shot them. Three of the men were killed and the other three still showed signs of life.

Mob Victims Go to Potter's Field

One of the wounded men begged for water. Bert Grace kicked the thirsty man and said, "You'll get no water here goddamn you!" Joe Carnaghi then shot the thirsty miner in the shoulder and blood shot up a foot in the air. Another union miner stepped forward and emptied his pistol into the six men on the ground. Peter Hiller got out his pocket knife and cut each of the victim's throats. Reportedly, a woman with a baby came forward and stepped on one of the dead men's wounds until blood gushed out.

Sixteen of the dead were taken to a temporary morgue set up in the Dillard Building in Herrin. The Albert Storme Funeral Home was put in charge of preparing the dead miners for burial. The bodies were embalmed with Esco Ro-Co embalming fluid, dressed, and then placed in $80 oval top, octagon caskets from the Belleville Casket Company. These sixteen men were buried in unmarked graves in the "Potters Field" section of the Herrin City Cemetery. The Herrin City Cemetery was now home to more men killed in gunfights than Boothill Cemetery in Tombstone, Arizona. The dead men were:

Antonio Molkovich: Erie, Pennsylvania. World War I veteran.
Robert Marsh: Chicago, Illinois. World War I veteran.
Robert Anderson: Kent County, Michigan. World War I veteran.
Raymond Jacobs: Allentown, Pennsylvania.

John Emil: Chicago, Illinois.

Fred Lang: Chicago, Illinois

James Sayghizo: Chicago, Illinois. U.S. Army Veteran.

Horatio Gosman: New York City, New York.

Arthur Miller: New York City, New York.

John C. Smith: Chicago, Illinois. U.S. Army Veteran.

Edward Miller: Chicago, Illinois.

William Davis: Chicago, Illinois.

John Casper: Chicago, Illinois.

Allen C. Norine: Chicago, Illinois.

G. Ward: Chicago, Illinois. World War I veteran.

Unknown.

Five of the murdered miners were exhumed and claimed by grieving family members. Robert Anderson was claimed by his brother. Robert Marsh was taken back to Chicago for burial. Horatio Gosman was taken back to New York by his friends. Arthur Miller was claimed by his father. All of the bodies had been buried under a numbering system. Some of the locals wanted to keep the dead men nameless. The numbering sequence was not very accurate and Arthur Miller's father discovered that the grave that was supposed to contain his son actually held the body of another man. Eleven graves had to be opened before the body of Arthur Miller was found.

The only grave of the Herrin Massacre victims that was ever properly marked was that of Antonio Molkovich. In 1922, the Herrin post of the American Legion erected a white wooden cross that stated his name, his World War veteran status and listed his wartime service. The cross on Molkovich's grave survived until at least 1932. By 1951 the cross was missing from the grave. The location of the graves of the massacre victims was erased from the memory of many people.

Flash forward to the winter of 2009. Anna, Illinois native and radio personality Scott Doody went on a simple road trip. After reading Paul

Angle's book, *Bloody Williamson*, and learning about the Herrin Massacre, Scott wanted to see for himself where the bloody stories took place. In particular he wanted to visit the grave of the World War One hero Antonio Molkovich and take a photograph of the cross marking his grave. Scott went to the Herrin City Cemetery and spent several hours searching in vain for the white cross, or any indication of where the massacre victims were buried. Instead, he was approached by a man in the cemetery who said, "If you're looking for them scabs, you ain't gonna find em...nobody knows where they are." How do you lose track of 16 murder victims all buried at the same time in a small cemetery? Scott was determined to find out.

Scott wanted to replace the marker on Molkovich's grave. To do so, he would need the cooperation of the Herrin city officials. Scott contacted Herrin mayor Vic Ritter to set up a meeting to discuss his plans. On the appointed day, Scott met with the mayor and explained that he wanted to replace the grave marker of Molkovich the war hero. Mayor Vic Ritter wanted to know who he was and what happed to his grave marker. According to Scott, when he explained to the mayor that Molkovich was one of the Herrin Massacre victims and was buried with fifteen other non-union miners who had been murdered, the tone of the meeting immediately changed.

Mayor Ritter paused for a moment and said, "Let me see if I've got this straight. You're from Union County (Anna) and you want to come up here and piss in my backyard?" Scott looked up at the Herrin City seal on the wall. It featured a World War I doughboy. He pointed that out and said that the town must be proud of its veterans since they had a doughboy on their city seal. He argued that if there was a doughboy in the city cemetery, he deserved to have his grave properly marked.

Finally, the mayor responded, "I don't run the cemetery. You need to go out and see "Jumbo" Cravens. He is the cemetery sexton and you'll have to work with him on this." Mayor Ritter then told Scott that he did not think he should replace the grave marker since the massacre was not something that folk liked to talk about in Herrin.

The next morning, Scott met with Jumbo Cravens at the Herrin City Cemetery. Cravens said that the mayor had called him and told him what Scott was up to. Jumbo said, "I don't know nothing about where that guy is. Been a lot of people out here over the years looking for them scabs, but nobody knows where they are." After much debate, Scott was granted access to the cemetery to search for the graves.

Scott located the records of the Storme Funeral Home then temporarily on loan to the Williamson County Historical Society in Marion. One volume covering June 1922 contained the records of the funerals of the massacre victims. The records stated that all of the murdered men were buried in Herrin Potter Field. Photographs taken of the cross on Molkovich's grave show that he was buried in the third row of the four rows massacre victim graves.

Scott was granted access to the records room vault at Herrin City Hall. A woman who worked in the records room told Scott that they didn't have any records for the cemetery and that she should know because she had worked there for thirty years. Scott looked down at a bottom shelf and saw a large box with the words "CEMETERY RECORDS" written across the front. Scott grabbed the box and said "Well Ma'am...I guess you must have overlooked this box that says cemetery records on it." Later, while searching through the contents of the box, Scott discovered that each block in the cemetery had multiple sales of lots except for one. Block fifteen had no plots sold. He had found the Potter's Field. The only problem was that there was not an east west two-lot array that would hold 16 graves of the massacre victims. Block fifteen was filled with modern graves.

A 97-year-old lady who lived all her life next to the cemetery contacted Scott. She had been 9-years-old at the time of the massacre. She wanted him to meet her at the cemetery so she could show him where the massacre victims were buried. When they arrived at the cemetery, the lady said, "That soldier you're looking for is buried (pointing with her finger) right up there." She pointed to the dead center of block fifteen. She then went on to state that the area was the "paupers field" and that she told the man who runs the place that he was burying people on top of them.

Scott decided it was time to talk to the cemetery officials about Block 15 actually being the old Potter's Field. He said that a person in their 90s was good enough to show him where the potter's field was located and that the massacre victims were buried there as well. According to Scott, the official became angry, "That f***king school teacher and her goddamn nosy nephew!" He knew he was defeated. He leaned back on his mower and said, "Well, she should know." The victims of the 1922 Herrin Massacre are buried in block fifteen of the Herrin City Cemetery *under* the graves of modern burials.

The cemetery is located at the intersection of Stotlar and Bandyville Roads east of Herrin.

— ● — ● — ● —

The Grave of S. Glenn Young

Herrin

In the 1920s, the Ku Klux Klan in Williamson County was essentially a prohibition party. Prohibition law enforcement was the fundamental issue; race and religion had little to do with it. In 1923, the Klan began organizing in Williamson County, holding meetings attended by more than 5,000 citizens. The Klan in Williamson County drew large community support.

The Klan found a charismatic leader; S. Glenn Young, a former federal law enforcement officer. Federal authorities deputized the Klan to help enforce prohibition laws. Many public officials of Williamson County were allied with the bootleggers and were driven from office. They were replaced by Klan members. On January 24, 1925, Williamson County deputy sheriff (and bootlegger) Ora Thomas and S. Glenn Young shot and killed each other in a cigar store in downtown Herrin, Illinois.

The coroner's report of O.A. Jenkins, Undertaker, stated that one bullet entered the right breast of S. Glenn Young about two and a half or three inches below armpit. It ranged down and logged under the skin on left side four inches below left lower shoulder blade. Jenkins stated that he cut that bullet out. It was a .45 cal. steel jacket bullet. The second bullet entered 2.5 inches below the other. It took a straight course coming out the left side. Both bullets went through the heart. The two wounds were sufficient to kill. A third bullet grazed the little finger of the right hand. It was about one inch long.

The funeral of S. Glenn Young was attended by over 15,000 people.

S. Glenn Young was buried in full Klan regalia in this concrete vault built by William Lough and Sons. The casket was covered with between 18 to 20 inches of concrete and steel reinforcing on the top, bottom and sides.

The Herrin City Cemetery is located at the intersection of East Stotlar Street and Bandyville Road east of Herrin, Illinois.

Evil Darkness

Herrin

From time to time, the Little Egypt Ghost Society receives calls from individuals and businesses requesting our help with supernatural happenings. A Herrin business owner (name and location on file with the Little Egypt Ghost Society) contacted us about some strange happenings at their place of business. After being told what was happening at the location and researching the history of the building it was located in, we became very interested in checking out this building. The building was located in one of older buildings in Herrin and was actually used by gangsters in the prohibition era.

We set up an initial interview with the business owner to be conducted after normal business hours. Our client was so upset about the strange occurrences at the place of business that we conducted the interview in the parking lot when no one else was around. The client informed us that she had sought help with another group involved with the paranormal with limited success.

The client told us about spontaneous fires, electrical disturbances, fleeting shadows and movements that would occur as well as feelings of an evil presence and dread. Before entering the building we conducted a walk around of the premises and looked into the windows. In the front lobby area we noticed that a curtain what was hanging floor to ceiling was moving as if someone or something was moving behind it.

We entered the lobby, the curtain was one of the first things we checked out. There were not any vents, fans or anything else that would have caused the curtain to move. We used our Kestrel anemometers to check for drafts and found none. Next we used our Mel-8704, KII and Ghost Meters establish a baseline of the EMF that is normally present in the office. We then photographed the various rooms with our digital and IR cameras.

Several days later we returned to the office building for a late night investigation. Upon entering the building we noted that there was a darkness not only of the night but another force in the room which at times seemed to follow us around. After we brought in our ghost hunting equipment, we asked our client to lock all doors on the outside of the building so that we would not be disturbed and no unauthorized people could enter without our knowledge.

Once we were all locked inside, we began the investigation. We conducted an EMF sweep with our meters and discovered some readings in the 2-7 milligauss range that were not noted previously. About that time one of the lamps in the office began to flicker. A dark shadow darted across the lobby. It was not a shadow on the wall, it was a shadow seemingly projected in the center of the room. Just then, we heard a commotion upstairs that sounded like furniture was being moved and large heavy objects being thrown.

There were harsh voices and sounds of stomping footsteps as well. Knowing that all the doors were locked from the inside and there was no one in the building except for our 4 team members and the client, we became concerned and curious. Rick and I ran upstairs to see who was there. After a few minutes they came downstairs scratching their heads. They said there was no one up there and everything was in perfect order.

Rick, our Reiki Master, then decided to do a cleansing thinking that it was something possibly following our client (our client had a lot of turmoil going on in their life at this time). Rick and his assistant had our client lie down on a table with instructions to relax. Soothing meditation music was playing on the mp3 while we all stood around in silence. After about 45 minutes of starting the reiki session, everything seemed peaceful in the building. It was as if we all were enveloped in a soothing white light.

Within a week, the client called and requested that we return to the office building during business hours to observe the normal routine of the business activities. Upon arrival, we noticed a "darkness" to the building which was darker than in the night hours. We noted that small children were afraid of certain rooms or areas of the building also. At the end of the business day, the client and I decided to conduct another cleansing of the area.

I brought in white sage, lavender oil and camphor to help drive evil influences out of the building. We recited prayers of protection and demanded that the darkness leave. We told the evil forces that they were not welcome. Then, right before our eyes we saw a dark figure that looked like a giant salamander shadow figure crawl from under a table, right up the wall and up into the ceiling.

The business owner has relocated to another location out of the area. To this day whatever is in the building will probably reside in the building and continue there as long as the building also is there.

Here is what happened in our client's own words.

"My business was languishing. I called a local psychic to help and she and her friend confirmed as they worked independently. They found the same spots I had suspected. They said it was indeed haunted with two very strong negative energies, and one was directed straight at the place where I sat. (I had fallen out of chairs twice out of the blue and both chairs had just crumbled under me for no good reason. There were many other incidents.

"Anyway, the psychic and her friend worked for 4-5 hrs to get rid of the negative energies, mostly through calling on Archangel Michael). Also, once I had validation and confirmation of my suspicions I started strong prayers. The power of righteous anger and strong intent in taking control of a place with my positive energy and prayer made a huge difference and my business picked up 10 times. Also the overall darkness lifted and areas where it would be freezing cold no matter what the weather disappeared.

"All was fine for 6 months or so. The prayers and images of gods and angels and my positive intentions were working and the ghosts had stepped back to let me do my work. I could still see a few places where they was darkness but it was okay as they were not interfering with my business and we all stayed out of each other's way. "I called the Little Egypt Ghost Society because a series of unexplained events began to happen. Things falling suddenly, glass shattering spontaneously, fires etc. It got progressively worse and I suddenly began to sense an uninvited new presence in the office. I placed a floor lamp there, no avail, some people would get all hyperactive when they were in that spot others complained they felt claustrophobic etc. I took my dog to work and he went and sat in that spot. I even stood there and said whoever was there needed to leave. A significant increase in the number of crises occurring in my business now started to show up.

"I wrote to you then and you called it a level 4-5 poltergeist attack. I requested your help. When you came to my office you noticed the curtains moving, and when we stood in front of it the curtain bulged out completely as if a large tall big built person was behind it and wanted us to see them. All three of us were shocked to see how blatantly it bulged out. You intuitively sensed a female presence. I however said I had been seeing, for at least a week, a dark figure of small build standing in the corner next to the bulging curtain.

"You advised me to place the ox picture there. As soon as I did, I sensed the darkness clear from that area. One entered the room where you set up your equipment that night you came and another came and stood behind me as I could feel the hair on the back of my neck standing up and chills running up and down. That presence wanted to kill me as the darkness would not budge from there no matter which god or angel pictures I hanged or how many live plants and lights I placed or lavender I sprinkled. I could see the arm of a person behind me and realized this was the female presence that you had felt.

"I happened to mention to a client/friend all that was happening and said there was a dark person whose name seemed to be Michael. She gave a start and said Michael was her late father.

"I called you for a second consultation and told you where I knew Michael would be located - he had entered the room and lights kept blinking nonstop as he tried to get our attention. Rick, the Reiki expert functioned as a medium and talked to the spirit who was in the room using the pendulum. He said he was Michael alright and he had come there, to protect from the negativity, his family as they were my clients. Also he did not know he had been dead for 10 yrs (he had a sudden and unexpected death). Rick had him cross over.

"I was told then there was no negativity and if there was it was gone. Over the next few days I questioned this. Many of my clients started to react by being unsettled and one went so far as to say he could see a monster up in the ceiling. In that same room new batteries would die and one client even said he could see a monster."

Stalked by a Finger

Herrin

For a short time just prior to World War I, the city of Herrin was stalked by a severed finger. The severed finger was the terror of the town causing many people to jump in horror when poked in the ribs or on their back by an unseen digit. Who did the finger belong to? Where did the finger come from? Where did the finger go? The answers to these questions remain a mystery to this day.

— ● — ● — ● —

Mysterious Happenings at Ordill

Crab Orchard National Wildlife Refuge

Since the mid-1960s, there have been many reports of strange and unusual activity at the Explosives/Munitions Manufacturing Area (EMMA) Operable Unit (OU) in the former Illinois Ordinance Plant (Ordill Area), particularly in the Crab Orchard Cemetery Area (COC) of the Crab Orchard National Refuge between Marion and Carbondale, Illinois. The Crab Orchard Cemetery Area is named due to the proximity of Hampton Cemetery which is located in an area of the Refuge that is closed to the public.

COC site #1 is approximately 100 x 200 feet. It contains a small circular depression near the center. An east/west oriented berm extends along the north end of the site. This site is suspected of formerly being a burial and detonation disposal area.

COC site #2 is approximately 250 x 350 feet and encompasses an old burn furnace and two depressions.

COC site #3 is a large area subdivided into two smaller areas. This site exhibits indications of explosives/munitions activity. A number of suspect berms and mounds with several detected magnetic anomalies

are located within this site. The south side of this site is fenced and heavily wooded. Various sized pieces of TNT, metal debris and transite tile (contains asbestos) are scattered across the northern half of the site.

COC site #4 is located across the road and slightly north of COC site #3. It is rectangular and measures approximately 250 x 600 feet. This area is heavily wooded with a number of shallow depressions scattered throughout.

COC site #5 is a fenced, heavily vegetated area approximately 210 x 280 feet. A shallow depression is located in the southwestern corner of the site. TNT concentrations have been detected in the soil of this site.

COC site #6 is approximately 6 acres and is triangular in shape. This area is fenced and contains several depressions in the central and northern portions of the site. These depressions are the result of detonation disposal of TNT. There are many small metal fragments scattered around these depressions.

COC site #7 consists of approximately 2 acres of open area within a large field. An intact land mine was found at this site. The mine was destroyed by an exploded ordnance demolition (EOD) team.

COC site #8 is located in an open area within a field that is currently farmed. Magnetic anomalies have been found in this area.

COC site #9 is an irregularly shaped area approximately four acres in size. The area is heavily vegetated with fencing around the northern portion of the site. There are several man made depressions at this site. Two located near the southern end and the others located near the center and northern portions of the site.

COC site #10 is approximately 120 feet square and consists of a fenced area on the northern edge of a corn field. There are 85 bunkers in Area 13 that were built for the storage of 500-pound bombs. Many of the bunkers are currently used by Olin Corporation and U.S. Powder to store explosives.

Oliver, a former security guard for one of the government contractors in the Ordill area, reported that on several occasions he observed and was stalked by what he described at a seven foot tall humanoid creature covered with light brown matted hair covered in mud. This creature closely matched the description of the Big Muddy Monster (actually a hoax – details on file with Little Egypt Ghost Society) that had been reported in the Murphysboro, Illinois area in the mid '70s.

Farmers and hunters in the area have reported sightings of a half man half bat-like creature with glowing red eyes. It has been seen flying out of a wooded area, landing near a pond where it appeared to take a drink and then would circle the field before returning to the wooded area.

Ghost lights have also been seen hovering and bouncing around the depressions found in the various COC areas of the refuge. They are described as orange in hue and vary in size from that of a baseball to larger than a beach ball.

There have been various reports of UFO activity over the refuge. A young couple was parked near one of the access roads and reported seeing a large triangular shaped object fly overhead in a northwest to southeast direction. It appeared just above treetop level and made no sound as it traveled at great speed. A man was riding his motorcycle in the refuge when he decided to pull to the side of the road to relieve himself in the ditch. He said as soon as he zipped up his pants, he was "buzzed by three glowing balls of light." They emitted a humming and sound and he felt like he was vibrating as if he was having an MRI exam. These stories are only the tip of the iceberg when it comes to high strangeness at the Crab Orchard Wildlife Refuge. Since most of the area is closed to the public, we will probably never know what lurks within its boundaries.

The Crab Orchard Refuge is located south of Route 13 and west of Route 148 in Williamson County, Illinois.

Creepy New Developments at the Old Munitions Area

By Lisa Cline
Crab Orchard National Wildlife Area

Bruce asked me to go photograph different areas for our book. So my son Christopher and I decided late one afternoon to go to the old munitions area and have a look around. We drove out to the Crab Orchard Munitions Area and when we arrived there the air seemed to have a really tense feeling to it. The air was stifling and made us feel restless.

We decided to get out of the car and start taking photos regardless of how tense we were feeling. I began taking photos of the area and noticed that there was a dark hand-like object on the images. Thinking I must have somehow got my hand in the way, I retook the photos and noticed that the dark object was still in some of the images. Then, my camera stopped working even though it had fresh batteries and a new memory card in it. No matter what I tried, my camera would not work.

I got out my other camera and started taking photos of the old munitions bunkers and noticed that the same dark hand like object was on these images as well. As I continued to photograph the area, the second camera I was using malfunctioned and would not turn on again. Finally, after resting with it for a few minutes, I was able to resume photographing the area, but noticed that some images would not turn out.

As I was photographing, my son said, "Mom, did you hear that?" and we both looked at one another and thought someone was near us shooting an old gun. We heard a sound like, "Pow, pow, pow, pow" and for a few seconds there was quietness. Then we heard it again, "Pow, pow, pow, pow." We decided we had better get back in the car. Knowing the area had armed guards, we decided maybe we should leave.

The air began to feel even tenser. As we got back into the car, my son looks in the mirror and said, "Um, mom, look." As I looked up, I saw a black shadow object that looked like a WWII soldier behind our car. I asked my son what he saw and he said, "Mom, it was a soldier bent down like he was fight." As we left we were discussing the things that had happened. We check the cameras and noticed that they were once more in perfect working order.

Crab Orchard Lake

Crab Orchard National Wildlife Area

In 1936, work was started on the Crab Orchard Creek Project. The purpose of this project was to construct three lakes for recreational use and as an industrial water supply. To make way for the proposed lake, a portion of Illinois Route 13 between Marion and Carbondale had to be relocated about a half mile to the north. Crab Orchard Lake was completed in 1939 by the Works Progress Administration (WPA).

There are portions of Old Route 13 that still lie beneath the waters of Crab Orchard Lake. During times of extreme drought, boaters can catch a glimpse of the old road. Several night-time boaters have reported sightings of ghostly lights under the water in the vicinity of where the old road lies. Could these lights that are seen be the phantom cars of the 1920s and '30s that used to travel the old route?

George W. Sisney and the Bloody Vendetta

Carterville

Those of you familiar with the "Bloody Vendetta" of the late 1800s in Southern Illinois will be interested in my latest discovery. I have located the grave of one of the principal characters, Capt. George W. Sisney. He was a captain in the 81st Illinois Volunteer Infantry, Co. G during the Civil War and elected sheriff in 1866.

The Bloody Vendetta started in 1862 with a disagreement between John Sisney and Marshall Crain. In 1869, there was a fight between Samuel Brethers, George W. Sisney and David Bulliner over a bunch of oats. In 1872 there was further trouble when Thomas Russell and John Bulliner started dating the same woman, Sarah Stocks. On Christmas

Day in 1872, there was a riot in Carterville that involved the Sisneys and Crains.

On March 27, 1874, George and David Bulliner were killed in a shooting at church. On May 15, 1874, the Bulliners were involved in killing James Henderson. On July 28, 1875, George W. Sisney was shot and killed in his home by Marshall Crain.

George W. Sisney's home was located on the northeast corner of the square in Carbondale. The house extended eastward and faced south. On the night of July 28, 1875, George W. Sisney was sitting near a window on the south side of the house playing dominoes with one of his friends. An assassin was lurking on the porch in his sock feet and shot through the window. Sisney was struck by the shot under his left nipple leaving a hole about 2 inches in diameter. As he was shot, Sisney cried out "Oh, Lord, I am shot! Lord, have mercy on me!" Sisney remained seated upright in his chair for one and a half hours after he was shot dead. He was buried with full Masonic honors.

My wife and I located Capt. George W. Sisney's grave in a small unnamed cemetery on the south side of Old Route 13 about .2 miles from Division Street in the Crab Orchard Refuge. While walking through the cemetery just south of Sisney's grave, we both smelled the strong scent of lilacs and hyacinths. We looked everywhere, but could not find any flowers in the entire graveyard. The cemetery is very quiet and peaceful. We will be returning soon to conduct some EVP experiments and to take EMF and other readings. George W. Sisney was a captain in the Civil War and a Mason; perhaps I can give his spirit a direct order to respond to our experiments since I am a lieutenant colonel in the Army Reserve and a 32nd degree Mason?

— ● — ● — ● —

Eyewitness Events in the Bloody Vendetta

Williamson County

The years of 1875-76 were rough for Williamson County with the murders and resulting trials of a number of county citizens related to the culmination of the "Bloody Vendetta" era. The following are notes from the papers of that date:

January 14, 1875 – I hear Mr. Sisney has already moved away on account of further expected danger.

February 4, 1875 – George W. Sisney called on us Tuesday last. He has very bad wound and thinks his arm will likely be a cripple for life… has moved to Carbondale.

July 1, 1875 – Last Monday night some beastly human fired a heavy charge of buckshot into the dwelling of Marshall Crain at Crainville. Some of the shot struck the bed on which Mr. Crain usually sleeps. None of the family was home.

July 30, 1875 – Capt. George W. Sisney was murdered at home in Carbondale Wednesday at 9:30 p.m. He had gone to bed, but was called up at that hour by Overton Stanley of Johnson County for purpose of getting him to put his security on a note and also to settle some private little demand that Sisney held against him. They were sitting on first floor, completed business and Sisney said it was about time to retire, almost instantly a shot was fired through the window, and struck him in the breast near the right nipple. The window was protected only by a wire mosquito bar. He only spoke words, "Oh, Lord, I am killed." This was third or fourth time open and bold attempt was made on his life. He was. buried in the Stancil graveyard near his farm in Williamson County and was Mason 12 or 15 years. He leaves a wife and eight children. He was a captain in Company G, 81st Regiment, Illinois Volunteers, and was severely wounded at Vicksburg in May 1863. He resigned August 3, 1863.

August 19, 1875 – Col. D. H. Brush has offered a $500 reward for parties who murdered Captain G. W. Sisney.

September 16, 1875 – Friday morning B. F. Lowe arrived here from Cairo with a man named Samuel Music charged with killing Mr. Spence at Crainville on July 11th. He confessed and said the killing was done by an organized clan and that Noah W Crain., William Crain, Jasper Crain, Samuel B. Crain, Marshall Crain, Allen Baker and John Bulliner were in the organization All were arrested except Marshall Crain who has fled the country.

September 23, 1875 – Samuel Music says Marshall Crain, brother of "Yaller" Bill and "Jep" did the shooting of both Sisney and Spence. Said Wes Crain is Marshall's brother, "Jep" and "Yaller Bill" are brothers and Marshall is a brother of theirs.

September 24, 1875 – Samuel Music confessed to murder and as a result Samuel R. Crain, "Big Jep" Crain, "Yaller" Bill Crain, "Black Bill" Crain, John Bulliner and Allen Baker were arrested. All were charged with being connected with murders of Sisney at Carbondale and Spence at Crainville. Only Marshall Crain remains at large.

September 30, 1875 – Last Sunday B. P. Lowe arrived from Arkansas with Marshall Crain, captured at Pocahontas. Crain was armed with a shotgun, rifle and pistol (the one Spence was shot with), but Frank caught him napping. He was taken to Murphysboro and placed under guard, the jail being so crowded, there was no room for him.

October 13, 1875 – Marshall Crain attempted an escape from the Murphysboro Jail Sunday. Just after midnight he told guards he needed to step outside and answer a call of nature. He threw handful of lime in the guard's face, but was captured before he got out of town.

October 14, 1875 – Allen Baker and John Bulliner were sentenced to 25 years for murder of George W. Sisney in Jackson County.

October 1875 – Marshall Crain plead not guilty on Tuesday to murder of William Spence. He pled guilty on Wednesday.

October 28, 1875 – Marshall Crain was sentenced to hang for the murder of William Spence. His wife wept bitterly. He sent for Wash Sisney to visit him and confessed to killing his father and pled with him to forgive him.

December 1, 1875 – Marshall Crain, sentenced to be hung for the murder of William Spence, was baptized in Mann and Edwards mill pond last Sunday afternoon by Elder W. H. Boles. He was dressed in a long white robe and desired to wear that when he goes to the gallows. He was under the guard of 10 militia men, commanded by Lt. Hendrickson. There was a large crowd considering the bad weather.

December 9, 1875 – An order was drawn up for $1,000 in favor of B. P. Lowe, the reward for the conviction of Marshall Crain.

December 23, 1875 – Marshall Crain attempted a Jail break Tuesday night. He sawed through a ceiling which is a nine inch timber and made it to the roof. He tore a blanket and made a rope, but was captured.

January 20, 1876 – The paper is late this week because of the hanging of Marshall Crain which took place at 10 o'clock Friday. He went to the gallows, built by Samuel Ireland, in the white robe he was baptized in. The jury that convicted him included Henry Gray, M. V. Felts, Isham Harris, Scott Tippy, George Brock, W. W. Young, John H. Manier, J. W. Everett, Henry Wise, George Ward, William Aikman and William S. Washburn. All were present at hanging. He read a 24 verse poem, two verses of "There is a Fountain filled With Blood" were sung and Rev. W. Sandford Gee of Mount Vernon made appropriate remarks.

Brice Holland cut the rope with a hand axe that caused him to fall. The body was placed in a coffin and placed in the street for the crowd to see.

The only family of his at the hanging was his brother Warren and a distant cousin, L. D. Crain. They were up in the hall but did not look at him on the gallows. He was the son of William Crain who owned a horse mill on Phelps Prairie, five miles west of here, who has been dead some time. Marshall was about 27 years old, married with no children. Two of his brothers, William J. and Noah W. were indicted as accessories in the killing of Spence. Marshall had attempted to kill Sisney two times before. The third time he killed him by shooting him in the breast thru a screen of the window with a double barreled shotgun in Carbondale on July 28, 1875. He seriously wounded Sisney and a young man named Hindman on December 12, 1874 in Sisney's house, nine miles west of Marion. John Bulliner hired him and had Allen Baker as accomplice.

February 1876 – An interview at the jail Thursday with Marshall Crain was published in the *Globe-Democrat*. He said his name was Marshall Thomas Crain, born December 6, 1848, married Rhoda Rich 4 Mar 1874 at Mount Carbon, Illinois. His parents have been dead about nine years. He first became connected with the vendetta in the spring of 1874 between the death of Dave Bulliner and James Henderson. He withdrew, but then heard John Bulliner had hired someone to fire into my house or had done it himself. After that he rejoined.

In October 1874, he said nobody was with him when he killed Sisney. Samuel Music was with him when he killed Spence. Music knew $5,000 was to pass through the hands of Spence that day, to be paid to John Landrum. He wanted to get it and leave the country Spence was shot twice with a shotgun and once with a pistol. We were in the store about five minutes after the shooting I shot both of them because of prejudice, but the Bulliner boys agreed to pay me $200, I have received it all except $5. I swore falsely against Allen Baker in Murphysboro. Baker said his father fired into his (Baker's) room as a blind. Bulliner gave Mart Dial and Jonas J. Elliott $300 to kill Henderson. I only told one-fifth of what I know of Bulliner. I left the county two weeks after the death of Spence. I wish my body to be given to my relatives who will bury me in Hampton Cemetery. I want to be buried in a white linen shroud with the robe I was baptized in over the shroud.

Feb 3, 1876 – Witnesses for the People in the Crain trial in Cairo: Samuel Music, John Ditmore, H. V. Ferrell, J. W. Landrum, Mary C. Tippy, William Hendrickson, Martin Davis, Leonard Fuller, Narcissa Waggoner, Newman Grimes, H. W. Johnson, Monroe Rollan, Ann Impson, John Craig, William Rollan, Thomas Duncan and James Hampton alias Joseph Hostetter. W. W. Clemens was the attorney for the defendants. Samuel Music said Jep Crain is a brother to Marshall and "Black Bill" Crain is his cousin. Other witnesses: Worth Tippy, I. C. Fuller, Henry Bowles, James Samuels, Wesley Crain brother to "Big Jep", D. B. Ward, James Hampton, N. J. Crain, James Craig, Mary A. Crain, Mrs. Anna Crain, stepmother to Black Bill, Sarah Hampton, daughter of Louisa, Phillip T. Smith, John Smith, Philip D. Smith, Samuel Crain, N. E. Morris, Charles H. Denison, Calvin Craig, Robert Craig, William J. Mackadoo of Jefferson County and David Crawford an old man in soldier's clothes from Jefferson County. "Black Bill" Crain and "Big Jep" Crain were sentenced to 20 years.

April 13, 1876 – James Kelly, residing on the farm of John Goodall one-half mile north of here, was kicked by a mule and almost instantly killed Wednesday morning, last He was a juror in the case of the people vs Aaron Neal for manslaughter. He is the same Kelly who acted as executioner at the hanging of Marshall Crain.

Ma Hatchett

Colp

During the 1920s, Colp, Illinois was a rip snortin', wide open town with a wild reputation. The town boasted several coal mines nearby and even more taverns. Such was the renown of Colp that Ike and Tina

Turner once performed there. The entertainment offered in Colp was second to none, and the most sought after entertainment was offered at a place known as "Ma" Hatchet's. She purchased the tavern, restaurant, brothel in 1923. It consisted of her house with a six bedroom addition attached by passageways. Men would come from all the surrounding communities to partake of some very special entertainment that Ma Hatchet offered. You see, Ma Hatchet's place was a brothel.

Ma Hatchet would only hire black girls and would only let them service white men. If any of her girls were caught with a black man, they would be sent packing. All the women were clean, well dressed and poised. They all had regular checkups with a local doctor. The going rate for Ma Hatchet's ladies was $5 to $50 depending on their specialty. One man sent a letter to a local newspaper stating that he had been to Ma Hatchett's place many times and considered it to be the best and cleanest brothel in 37 states and five foreign countries. He went on to say that he had personally seen several respected members of the community there such as doctors, ministers, lawyers, and businessmen.

Ma Hatchett became very wealthy with her business venture. She was very civic minded and gave freely to local charities and those in need. In 1957, the Illinois State Police raided Ma Hatchett's, shutting it down after more than 30 years of service to the public. Even after Ma Hatchett's was shut down, many of her girls continued their profession with their favorite customers.

Witches of Williamson County

Williamson County

Milo Erwin wrote in the *History of Williamson County, Illinois*:

> *From 1818 to 1835, there were a great many witches in this county. The most noted one was an old lady by the name of Eva*

Locker, who lived on Davis' Prairie. She could do wonders, and inflict horrible spells on the young, such as fits, twitches, jerks and such like; and many an old lady took the rickets at the mere sound of her name. When she inflicted a dangerous spell, the parties had to send to Hamilton County for Charley Lee, the great witch-master to cure them. This he did by shooting her picture with a silver ball and some other foolery. It was a nice sight to see this old fool set up his board and then measure, point and cipher around like an artillery man planting his battery, while the whole family was standing around veiled and with the solemnity and anxiety of a funeral. None of the wizards of this county could do anything with Eva. They had to pale their intellectual fires and sink into insignificance before the great wizard of Hamilton County.

When a man concluded that his neighbor was killing too many deer around his field, he would spell his gun, which he did by going out early in the morning, and, on hearing the crack of his rifle he walked backward to a hickory wythe, which he tied in a knot in the name of the devil. This rendered the gun worthless until the knot was untied, or it might be taken off by putting nine new pins in the gun and fining it with a peculiar kind of lye, corking it up and setting it away for nine days. One old man told me he tried this, and it broke the spell. He had drawn right down on a deer just before that, not over twenty steps distant, and never cut a hair. Cows, when bewitched, would go into mud holes and no man could drive them out; but the wizard, by laying the open Bible on their backs, could bring them out; or cut the curls out of their forehead and their tails off, and put nine pins in their tail and burn the curls with a poker. This would bring the witch to the spot, and then the matter was settled in the way our fathers settled their business.

Witches were said to milk the cows of the neighbors by means of a towel hung up over the door, when the milk was extracted from the fringe. If such deviltry was practiced now-a-days, the parties would be arrested for stealing. In place of having a herd of bobtailed cows, we have laws against cruelty to animals.

There was an idea that if you read certain books used by the Hard-shell Baptists, that the devil would appear. Happily for the honor of human nature, the belief in those foolish and absurd pretensions has been discontinued, for forty years by an enlightened public. Medical science has revealed remedies for those strange diseases whose symptoms were so little understood. The spell has been broken from the gun forever by untying the knot of ignorance, and letting the light of reason flood the mind.

— ● — ● — ● —

Murder at Number Seven Row

Williamson County

In 1902, No. 7 Row was a coal mine town built by the Big Muddy Coal and Iron Company in Williamson County. It was a. Certain men in town were known for getting drunk and causing a big fuss. One night, three of the men got in a big fight. One of them was struck on the head with a hammer, killing him instantly. The other two men found a cheese knife nearby and hacked the dead man's head off with it. The dead man was carried a short distance away and thrown onto the middle of the Missouri Pacific Railroad tracks. His severed head was placed to the outside of the tracks.

The engineer of an oncoming steam locomotive pulling empty coal cars stopped the train just short of the dead man. No other trains had passed by since the day before and the body was still warm. The murderers were caught about an hour later. We have no idea what happened to the murderers. It is very likely that they were hung by an angry mob. Are these railroad tracks haunted today by the horror that took place there over 100 years ago? Go just east of Herrin to the southwest quarter of the southeast quarter of Section 20 of Herrin Township and find out for yourself.

— ● — ● — ● —

Haunted Hook Mausoleum

Johnston City

Many cemeteries have stories about a haunted grave that gives off the scent of roses or some other flower. Lakeview Cemetery in Johnston City is the location of such a grave. But this haunting is somewhat unique. If you visit this cemetery late at night, you had better be wearing your running shoes.

Lakeview Cemetery overlooks Arrowhead Lake. Just as you enter the front gate of the cemetery, you will notice a stone mausoleum. This is the Hook family tomb. According to legend, if you knock on the door to the tomb you will smell roses. While this is not so unusual what happens next is. After knocking on the door, brave (or foolish) visitors should walk around the mausoleum three times while calling out Mr. Hook's name. What happens next is really creepy. If the conditions are right, you will hear a loud groan and the sound of a wooden coffin lip being slammed. The ghost of Mr. Hook will come out of the mausoleum and chase you away from his tomb.

For several years the door to the mausoleum is bricked shut. Is it to keep the curious out of the tomb or to keep Mr. Hook inside the tomb?

A Pioneer Cemetery

Williamson County

A lonely cemetery is located in Williamson County on Rocky Comfort Road between Little Grassy Lake and Devil's Kitchen Lake. During the early 1800s, a pioneer family was traveling west through Southern Illinois to what they hoped would be their new homestead. At some point during their journey, the entire family contracted the highly contagious disease of the "Pox."

The settlers of the Lick Creek were very concerned about the possibility of being infected with the pox from these strangers. They quickly decided that the only safe thing for them to do was to corral the infected pioneers in a certain area and to place guards nearby so that they would not escape and possibly infect others. The orders given to the guards were "shoot to kill" if any tried to leave the quarantine area.

This vigil was kept over the pioneers until every one of them had died. It was decided to wait until the bodies had been picked clean by scavengers before burial. Only when the bodies were picked clean down to the bone, were the unfortunates buried.

Southern Illinois

Photo of President Lincoln

Ken Gray Congressional Museum

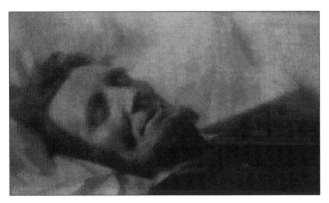

This photo of Abraham Lincoln is the only one like it in existence. It is from the collection of former U.S. Rep. Ken Grey. The West Frankfort lawmaker said that the picture was taken at the White House by a man and his camera was taken away by Secretary of War Edwin Stanton. The photo actually contains the name of the man who took the photo on the back of it. Congressman Gray stated that when Stanton passed they went through his things and he took the photo. He has had it for over 50 years. The Library of Congress requested the original photo and he told them not until after he is dead. It is thought that this is the only picture in the world of his corpse and not even the National Archives in Washington or Library of Congress has a picture truly makes this amazing. I thanked the Congressman for allowing us to share in his national treasure.

Ken Grey represented Southern Illinois in Congress and earned the nickname the "Prince of Pork" for bringing $7 billion in projects to his district. He died Saturday, July 12, 2014, at the age of 89.

What in the Devil?

It seems that the Devil has staked a claim in Southern Illinois. Many sites and areas in Little Egypt are named in honor of the diabolical one.

Grand Tower is the home of several landmarks named for the Prince of Darkness. The rocky hills by the Mississippi River are known as the Devil's Backbone. Just to the north is a hill known as the Devil's Bake Oven where iron was produced in brick lined ovens, the remains of which can still be seen today. On the far side of the river is an island known as Tower Rock and just downstream is an area known as the Devil's Whirlpool. Many boats and lives have been lost here.

• In Giant City State Park there is a rock formation that resembles a table that is known as the Devil's Stand Table.

• A few miles to the east is Devil's Kitchen Lake created when a rocky creek bed had a dam built across it. The creek bed contained a deep pool that was known as Devil's Well.

• Bell Smith Springs is the home of a natural stone bridge known as Satan's Backbone.

• A few miles south of Steeleville one can find Rock Castle Creek. The creek has two deep holes known as Little Devil's Hole and Big Devil's Hole.

• There is a valley in Union County known as You Be Damned Hollow. Hell's Half Acre can be found in Lawrence County. If you speak of the Devil and want to go to Hell and back, you need look no further than Little Egypt.

Named by Death

Death leaves its mark wherever it goes. Several Southern Illinois towns and landmarks received their names from some connection with death, or death is all that remains of them.

• In 1839, Bainbridge was the first seat of Williamson County. Today, Bainbridge exists as a very small cemetery on Bainbridge Trail Road and is now part of Marion.

• Dog Hollow is a valley in Pope County. It is located 12 miles south of Harrisburg. A local legend told by John W. Allen is that "Two young men had seen their girls safely home from a church service. They were returning at a late hour through the hollow. By their story they were pursued by a headless dog. Thus the hollow received its name and has ever since been called Dog Hollow."

• Ellis Mound in Hamilton County received its name from the Ellis family who buried one of their children near the trail as they passed through the area in the 1880's.

• Lively Grove in Washington County received its name when the John Lively family was killed by Indians in 1813.

• Rector Township in Saline County received its name from John Rector who was killed by Shawnee Indians near Rector Creek in 1805.

• Rosiclare in Hardin County received its name from the daughters of an early settler who were drowned in a boating accident. Their names were Rose and Clare.

• Schoharie Prairie in Williamson County received its name when a band of vigilantes were whipping a hog thief. One of the vigilantes yelled out, "Score him, Harry!" The site has been known as Scoreharry and then Schoharrie ever since.

• Vancil Bend, a loop in the Big Muddy River in Williamson County received its name after Isaac Vancil, an early settler, was hanged by vigilantes when he refused to leave the area.

• Wartrace in Johnson County received its name when a veteran returned home from the Civil War and stole a horse after killing the owner. The man was captured, given a quick trial, and then hanged. Citizens of the community decided to rename it Wartrace hoping that the incident would be the last trace of the Civil War.

Book Possessed by Evil Spirits

Several years ago I attended a book signing in for a book entitled *"Agatha's Journey: 1828 - 1998"* by S. E. Penrose. The book tells the story of how the author's family moved to Naperville in 1980 and moved into a house that was filled with terrifying and evil spirits. One of the spirits, Agatha Wilson, chose to stay and tell her story, waiting more than 160 years for the opportunity.

The author read some passages from her book and told us about the horrifying experiences she and her family had with the spirits. At the close of the program I purchased a copy of the book and had the author autograph it for me.

Once I got back home, I spent several nights reading the book. I often thought of how exciting it must have been to live in a haunted house like the one in the book.

One night after I had finished reading the book, I laid it on the floor next to my bed and went to sleep. At some point during the night, I felt a chill and noticed that my bed covers were lying in the floor next to my bed. I got up and returned the covers to the bed and went back to sleep. A short time later I was aware of some movement and a cold chill again.

My bed covers were moving off the side of the bed and onto the floor. I grabbed the covers and pulled them back over me.

Much to my horror, the covers were tugged once more over the side of the bed and then drug underneath the bed. Someone or something was under the bed pulling my covers. I pulled hard and the covers snapped loose and flew across the room. I checked under the bed and the only thing I saw was the book.

I found out later that the book was self published by the author and that she stored copies of the book in the basement of her house. The basement was where most of the evil and terrifying things took place. Were the books possessed by some evil attachment and did anyone else have similar experiences? I do not know for sure. All I do know is that the copy I owned was definitely haunted.

Pig Island

Ohio River

In the early 1800s, the Underground Railroad helped slaves in their escape from Southern Illinois. Many slaves seeking freedom were hidden on an island on the Ohio River between Illinois and Kentucky.

John Crenshaw of the Old Slave House and "Reverse Underground Railroad" fame found out that some slaves were hidden on the island. Being the enterprising businessman that he was, Crenshaw decided that he would capture these escaped slaves and sell them at a large profit. Slave hunters went searching for the slaves on the island. The slaves were very well hidden and evaded capture. Crenshaw became very angry and frustrated that the slaves had eluded him. A new plan was hatched. Crenshaw sent the slave hunters back to the island with a boat loaded with vicious, very hungry wild hogs. The hunters used bullhorns to loudly announce to the slaves that they had one hour to surrender or the wild hogs would be released.

The slaves, being afraid of being captured and being sent back into slavery, stayed in their hiding places. After the allotted amount of time, the hungry hogs were released. The hogs accomplished what the hunters had failed, they located and savagely devoured each and every one of the slaves.

For many years afterward, boatmen and other river traveler heard the most pitiful and terrifying screams coming from the island. They soon named it Pig Island. Today, it is uncertain if Pig Island still exists. Some likely locations for Pig Island are listed in the 1818 edition of *The Navigator* published by Cramer & Spear.

The possible locations are Stevenson's Island at Ohio River mile 1006, Island No. 85 at mile 1009, Battery Rock Bar at mile 1013, Trade Water Island at mile 1015 or Cave-in-Rock Island at mile 1022.

Revenge by Indian Spirits

Some old timers in Southern Illinois were telling a story about a man who was mysteriously killed by Indian spirits. There was a Southern Illinois man who made a hobby/business out of digging up Indian burial mounds and selling the relics that he found. He would travel all over Southern Illinois in search of ancient Indian burial sites. The man would pay farmers large sums of money for the opportunity to dig on their property. Once he located the burial mound he would dig and remove all the relics and artifacts that were of any great value. He would dump all the bones that he dug up in a pile on top of the mounds. The relics were sold for high prices to various collectors.

One night before a big relic digging trip the man went to bed early telling his wife that he did not feel well. During the night his wife heard blood curdling screams coming from the bedroom. When she opened the door, she discovered her husband covered in blood. The body was taken to the morgue for an autopsy where the doctor discovered twelve flint arrow heads embedded in the dead body. The spirits of the dead Indians must have paid the man a midnight visit for revenge.

Root Beer and Embalming Fluid

While I was a student in the SIU Mortuary Science and Funeral Service program in the mid '70s, we studied the history of embalming.

Prior to the Civil War, embalming was very uncommon, unless of course, you were an Egyptian mummy. During the Civil War, Dr. Thomas Holmes discovered that there was a market for sending dead soldiers back home for burial. To ensure that the dead were presentable for viewing and burial, he developed an arsenic based embalming fluid. While arsenic was great for preserving dead bodies, it was deadly to the living (great for business though).

After the Civil War, Dr. Holmes opened a drug store in Brooklyn. Business was great and Dr. Holmes soon started experiments on other formulas. He came up with a very tasty formula for homemade root beer. Both his embalming fluid and root beer were in great demand.

In order to attract even more customers to stop by the drugstore for a frosty mug of root beer, he displayed the head of a very attractive and very dead young female that he had embalmed with his own arsenic embalming fluid. The embalmed head was displayed in his storefront window for many years.

Although, Dr. Thomas Holmes is the "Father of Embalming", he requested not to be embalmed after he died. Dr. Holmes died in 1900. During renovations on his drugstore, 20 embalmed corpses were found buried in the basement. This brings to mind Dr. H. H. Holmes of Chicago Columbian Exposition fame. Dr. H. H. Holmes was the first documented serial killer. He built a hotel later to be known as the "Murder Castle" which was specifically designed with murder in mind. As many as 200 females were tortured, murdered and dissected in the basement of the "Murder Castle."

Is there any relationship? You tell me.

— ● — ● — ● —

Creepy Moments from the Past

It was one of those "dark and stormy" nights (for real) when I was a young embalmer on the midnight shift. I had been called out in the middle of the night to make a removal at a local hospital. A torrential spring storm began to rage outside as I was embalming the fresh corpse in the basement 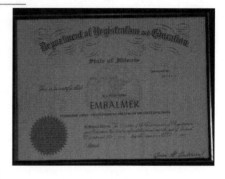 prep room of the funeral home where I worked. Lighting would flash soon to be followed by the loud crash of thunder. The corpse was not co-operating and I had to perform a 6-point injection.

Needless to say, this made matters very messy. I had blood splattered all over the embalming table, the floor and even some on the walls. I needed to go to the back room of the basement to get the mop and bucket to clean up the mess. Unknown to me at the time, the sewer in the back room had backed up with all the water from the storm outside. As I opened the door, I noticed that the lights were off in the back room and I had to take about 10 steps to where the light cord was located. I noticed that the floor was very wet.

Just as I flicked on the lights, I got the shock of my life. The entire floor was flooded with blood! All the blood from the dead body had backed up through the sewer and was now surrounding my feet! Oh, the horrors.

— ● — ● — ● —

The Jiffy Cat

Shawnee National Forest

Lurking somewhere in the dark, lush woods of the Shawnee National Forest in southeastern Illinois is a mysterious creature known as the Jiffy Cat. Many campers, hunters, and late evening hikers have reported the high pitched scream of this feline crypto creature.

The Jiffy Cat has been described as half big cat and half monster. A targeted human will hear strange unidentified growling and screaming sounds before being violently attacked. The victim is usually paralyzed with fear and unable to escape.

So what exactly is a Jiffy Cat? Some people theorize that the Jiffy Cat is actually a cougar.

There have been rumors that the Illinois Department of Natural Resources released some cougars in the Shawnee National Forest to be used for deer population control. However, a state wildlife biologist stated that "As an agency we don't have any interest in using cougars for deer control."

A young couple was camped at One Horse Gap near Herod in Pope County when they heard the scream of a big cat. Remembering stories about the Jiffy Cat, they were petrified from fear. They ran for the safety of their truck only to discover that the doors were locked and the keys were in the ignition. They ran back to their camp and threw some logs on the campfire until it was blazing about five feet in the air. The Jiffy Cat did not show itself and the campers were thankful for that.

While officially the state denies the existence of cougars and Jiffy Cats in Southern Illinois, conservation officers do say that people shouldn't make rapid or aggressive movements if confronted by one of the big cats.

Mysterious Blue-Gray Tombstones

Southern Illinois

A typical white bronze marker.

You are walking through a cemetery on a dark and lonely night. Up ahead you notice a bluish-grey glow among the gravestones.

You approach cautiously, not for sure knowing what it is. When you are few feet away you notice that it is a tombstone. Out of curiosity you tap on it with your hand. To your amazement you hear a hollow echo. What is it? You have encountered a somewhat rare "white bronze" grave maker.

While not actually bronze, they are made of zinc. The fancy name "white bronze" was just a marketing scheme to make the zinc grave markers sound more appealing. So where did these zinc grave markers come from? They were made by the Monumental Bronze Company in Bridgeport, Connecticut from

1874 until 1914. These grave markers stand out in cemeteries due to their characteristic blue grey color. The zinc gravestones range from two feet high to about 14 feet high and are usually in the shape of an obelisk. The zinc metal used in these grave markers is nearly 100 percent pure.

In 1873, two men, M. A. Richardson and C. J. Willard, perfected the process of casting zinc as grave markers. Since they did not have enough money to set up a factory, they contracted with W. W. Evans who sold the zinc casting rights to Wilson, Parsons and Company in Bridgeport, Connecticut. Plaster casts were made from wax molds in the factory by an artist. The finished pieces were fused together using hot zinc. After the grave marker sections were cast and assembled, they were sandblasted and then treated with a coating of linseed oil and then blasted with steam under a minimum pressure of 50 p.s.i.

The zinc weathers very well and many of the grave markers look as good today as they did the day they were first installed. These grave markers age better than marble. The only disadvantage of these grave markers is that zinc is brittle and the markers can be broken.

The zinc grave markers are hollow with vertical seams at the corners. Most of the zinc grave markers had removable panels that could be removed and replaced with a special tool that looked like a screwdriver with a negative rosette bolt head. There are local legends that cemetery workers would hide their tools inside the tall monuments. Other stories tell how certain criminals would hide their loot inside them. During Prohibition it was said that bootleggers would remove a panel from the grave markers and place liquor inside to be retrieved later by customers.

If you are lucky enough to locate a white bronze grave marker in one of older cemeteries in Southern Illinois you may wonder what secrets it may contain. Could there been long forgotten stolen loot, a stash of liquor, or just some old gravedigger tools?

The Headless Black Shadow

Southern Illinois has had its share of witches. Some witches were good, some were bad, and others were just plain scary. In the early 1800s, a young man was courting the daughter of a witch. The witch was not very fond of the young man or his intentions for her daughter. One evening as the young man went to fetch his date for the barn dance, he heard what sounded like a wild goose holler and the wind kicked up and blew off his hat. The man picked up his hat and saddled up his horse for the trip to pick up his date for the evening.

Later that night, as the young man took his date home, the lady invited him to stay the night or the devil might catch him on his ride back home. The young man said that he would take his chances with the devil. The lady asked him if he had heard a wild goose as he came to her house that evening. When he replied that he had indeed heard a wild goose, the lady said that "right there is where he will get you as you go back."

On his way back home, the young man soon forgot about what his lady friend had told him. When he got near the spot where he heard the wild goose earlier, his horse stopped in the middle of the trail. The horse refused to go any further. The man looked toward a fence corner and noticed a headless black shadow that was tapping out a tune with its feet. This startled the horse who took off at a full gallop. The headless black shadow darted alongside of the horse and rider.

All of a sudden, the black shadow seemed to grow a mouth that was large enough to swallow the man. The black shadow chased the horse and rider all the way back to the young man's barn-lot. The frightened young man put his horse in the stable. He ran all the way to his house and told his family about what had happened. Everyone decided that they had better stay in the house for the rest of the night because they might see it too.

The Mutant Coon

Undisclosed Location – Southern Illinois

███████ has been stalked by a strange creature known locally as the "Mutant Coon."

Now this raccoon is no ordinary coon. It lived in the vicinity of ████████. One dark night the coon was scavenging for food and discovered a storage container located near the ██████ that contained ████████ from the ██████. The clever coon soon was able to open the container and investigate the contents. The container was full of ██████.

Since the coon was very hungry it decided to try out this new and unusual delicacy. Night after night the coon raided the container. The diet of this new and unusual "food" soon transformed the coon. After many days and weeks of feasting on ██████ the coon grew to ginormous size.

The coon had a taste for ██████ and became the terror of ██████. Night after night when people ventured near the area, they were confronted by this mutant coon that had a taste for ██████. Anyone in the area late at night was accosted by the mutant coon as it would try to attack them.

One evening, the mutant coon's lair was discovered. It lived in a storm drain. The coon would stick out his paw which was the size of a catcher's mitt from the storm drain. Some brave individuals decided to bait the coon with a can of Hormel chili.

The opened can was placed near the storm drain and soon a huge coon paw darted out and grabbed the can. It is believed he ate the chili, can and all! It has been several years since the mutant coon has been spotted. Who knows, but there may be some mutant offspring of this terrifying coon that also have the taste for ██████.

— ● — ● — ● —

Mystery Beast Spotted

Northern Boundary of Area 618

On the way to work one morning, Kathy Readnour had the strangest thing happen. She was driving on a dark and lonely road when she saw the blur of an animal come running like the Devil himself was chasing it. It crossed in front of her within inches of her car as well as a truck coming in the other lane. Kathy had no clue how she avoided it. It was about the size of an average sized adult deer but it had short shaggy grey mottled fur. Its head was down like a horse running in a race, its ears were plastered down like a scared dog, and its tail was tucked between its legs. It ran at a gallop with incredible speed. It did have hooves like a deer; cloven hooves. Kathy has been married to a deer hunter for 37 years and has seen her fair share of deer, and this wasn't a deer. A co-worker heard reports of people seeing an alpaca-type animal loose in that area.

Angel P. saw a similar creature near Effingham. "I didn't see its feet so I don't know about the hooves, but it was huge, way bigger than most any dog, but had a dog like feel. It was a dark grey and ran right in front of us as we drove through Oak Lawn Cemetery. I yelled out what the f*** was that! My husband decided he was just going to pretend he saw nothing. It scared me to death."

Mystery "Booms" Of Southern Illinois

In March 2013, many residents of southeastern Illinois started reporting strange "booms," shock waves, rumbling, and rattling. This mysterious phenomenon had many residents on edge with officials offering no explanation of the activity.

The loud booms made many think of the New Madrid Fault. This seismic zone is a prolific source of intra-plate earthquakes in the

Midwest stretching to the southwest of New Madrid, Missouri. Angela Howser of *Disclosure* contacted the U.S. Geological Survey and they ruled out seismic activity. The Federal Aviation Administration ruled out a "sonic boom." When she contacted the state mining regulators they ruled out any mining blasting activity.

Some Saline County residents suggested that meteorites caused the booms. Several in Carrier Mills reported a flash of light on the clear sunny afternoon. No one was certain of the point of origin of the flash. About 10:30 p.m. March 16, 2013, several people in Harrisburg heard a boom and saw a flash of light. One theory suggests some sort of electrical charge is discharging in the atmosphere. No one knows if this charge is caused by something in the atmosphere, something in the ground, or something in between.

The mystery booms could be connected with the "extinct" volcano, Hicks Dome, in Hardin County. Angela Howser stated that the majority of the booms reports come from the Hicks Dome area. Thermal maps of Hardin and surrounding counties show the dispersion of fluorspar (essential in enriching uranium, such as is done at the Honeywell plant in Metropolis), silver and gemstones such as sapphire and ruby.

The thermal maps also showed that a large amount of thorium was located underground. As any high school chemistry student knows, Thorium-232 becomes Thorium-233 when bombarded with neutrons, which decays into Uranium-233 and is used as nuclear fuel. Experts say that the Hicks volcano last erupted millions of years ago, but what if it erupted only a few hundred years ago, before there were people keeping records? Could static from an underground lava/magma flow be the disruptive force causing the mystery booms? Southern Illinois sits on top of two seismic zones, New Madrid and the Wabash Valley Seismic Zone. These zones create enormous earthquake potential. Be it either volcanic or earthquake activity, we had better prepare now for a disaster of biblical proportions.

Sources and Suggested Reading

Allen, John W. *It Happened in Southern Illinois*. Carbondale: SIU Press. 1968.

Allen, John W. *Legends and Lore of Southern Illinois*. Carbondale: SIU Press. 1963.

Callary, Edward. *Place Names of Illinois*. University of Illinois Press. 2009.

Cline, Bruce and Lisa Cline. *History, Mystery and Hauntings of Southern Illinois*. Black Oak Media, Inc. 2011

Cline, Bruce. *More History, Mystery and Hauntings of Southern Illinois*. Black Oak Media, Inc. 2012.

Cline, Bruce and Tracey Todd Bragg. *Even More History, Mystery and Hauntings of Southern Illinois*. Black Oak Media, Inc. 2013.

Doody, Scott. *Herrin Massacre*. Lulu.com. 2013.

Erwin, Milo. *The History of Williamson County Illinois*. Williamson County Historical Society. 1976.

Erwin, Milo and Jon Musgrave. *The Bloody Vendetta of Southern Illinois*. IllinoisHistory.com. 2006.

The Historic Town Square Carbondale, Illinois. City of Carbondale Development Services Department. 1997.

Hale, Stan J. *Williamson County Illinois Sesquicentennial History*. Turner Pub. Co. 1993.

Hall, Ruby Franklin. *Stories of the Lamb Community Hardin County, Illinois*. 1970.

Iseminger, William R. *Cahokia Mounds: America's First City*. The History Press. 2010.

Jung, Jim. *Weird Egypt*. Wooley Worm Press. 2006.

Kleen, Michael. *Haunting Illinois: A Tourist Guide to the Weird and Wild Places of the Prairie State*. Thunder Bay Press; 3rd edition. 2014.

Kleen, Michael. *Paranormal Illinois*. Schiffer Publishing, Ltd. 2010.

Lansden, John M. *A History of the City of Cairo, Illinois*. SIU Press. 1910.

Magee, Judy. *Cavern of Crime*. Riverfolk Publishing Co. 1973.

Mason, Angela. *Death Rides the Sky: The Story of the 1925 Tri-State Tornado*. Black Oak Media, Inc. 2012.

Meggs, Kale. *99 Nooses: Illinois Justice at the End of a Rope, 1779-1896*. Black Oak Media, Inc. 2012.

Moore, Mary Jo. *The Potter Family Tragedy*. Marion Living Magazine. May 2007.

Musgrave, Jon. *Slaves, Salt, Sex & Mr. Crenshaw: The Real Story of the Old Slave House and America's Reverse Underground Railroad*. IllinoisHistory.com. 2005.

Paisley, Oldham. *Oldham Paisley's Scrapbooks*. Williamson County Historical Society.

The History of Saline County. Saline County Genealogical Society. 1997.

Legacies of Little Egypt. Southern Illinoisan. D-Books Publishing, Inc. 1997.

About the Author

Bruce Cline is a paranormal investigator and ghost historian. He was born and raised in Southern Illinois and currently lives in Carbondale, Illinois. He received B.S. and B.A. Degrees from Southern Illinois University in Carbondale, Illinois. He is a former law enforcement officer and currently works as a Radiologic Technologist specializing in CT/MRI and is a retired U.S. Army Corps of Engineers Lieutenant Colonel. He is also an Illinois licensed Funeral Director and Embalmer.

Bruce has had a long time fascination with history, folklore, and ghost stories. In 1967 he started the GASLIGHT GHOST CLUB which would meet in his backyard tree house to tell ghost stories.

In 2007, Bruce and Lisa Cline formed the Little Egypt Ghost Society. Since that time, the Little Egypt Ghost Society has traveled extensively throughout the Midwest in search of the history, mystery, and hauntings of interesting people, places, and things.

Bruce Cline and the Little Egypt Ghost Society have been featured in the *Southern Illinoisan*, *Harrisburg Daily Register*, *Disclosure*, *The Carbondale Times* and the *Daily Egyptian* newspapers. They have also been featured on WOOZ, WDBX, WRUL and WROY radio as well as WSIL and WSIU TV.

The LITTLE EGYPT GHOST SOCIETY is a non-profit research group based in Carbondale, Illinois. We are dedicated to the investigation of paranormal activity. Our goal is to explore the history, mystery and hauntings of Southern Illinois and ultimately strive for clearer knowledge of the supernatural.

Little Egypt Ghost Society

Southern Illinois

Our approach to investigating paranormal activity is scientific. We attempt to document claims of paranormal activity using a variety of state of the art, multi-media equipment. All findings are carefully reviewed by our team of paranormal experts with an open yet skeptical mind to rule out any possible natural causes.

The LITTLE EGYPT GHOST SOCIETY does not claim to have all the answers but our experience and knowledge of the field has allowed us to provide accurate results.

Index